With Kind Regards.

David Alton.

What Kind of Country?

Dedicated to the memory of David Penhaligon M.P.

> *When he shall die,*
> *Take him and cut him out in little stars,*
> *And he will make the face of Heaven so fine,*
> *That all the world will be in love with night,*
> *And pay no worship to the garish sun.*

– Romeo and Juliet

Acknowledgements and Thanks:

To friends, colleagues and staff for help and advice. I am especially indebted to John Fothergill. Others who lent a hand include David Campanale, Chris Davies, Chris Graffius, Stephen Grey, Alison Holmes, Matt Lambert, Evan Cameron and Catrine Stothers. Thanks also to my constituency Chairman, John Hemingway MBE, my secretary, Jackie Winter, and Sir Trevor Jones, friend and mentor over many years; to the Rev. Alan Godson his wife Lesley and friends at St. Mary's, Edge Hill, for their support; to the community at Prinknash Abbey where some of the text was written; and to Lizzie Bell for her encouragement.

What Kind of Country?

David Alton

Marshall Pickering

Marshall Morgan and Scott
Marshall Pickering
3 Beggarwood Lane, Basingstoke, Hants RG23 7LP, UK

Copyright © 1988 David Alton
First published in 1988 by Marshall Morgan and Scott Publications Ltd
Part of the Marshall Pickering Holdings Group
A subsidiary of the Zondervan Corporation

British Library CIP Data
Alton, David
    What kind of country.
    1. Christianity
    I. Title
    200 BR121.2
    ISBN 0–551–01612–4

Printed in Great Britain by Richard Clay Ltd, Bungay, Suffolk.

CONTENTS

FOREWORD

Immediately after the 1987 General Election Marshall Pickering asked me to write a book 'about politics'. The essays which follow are the product of work and speeches, travel and time spent in Westminster and at the grass-roots during almost sixteen years as a representative – nine of them spent in parliament. Before that, my attitudes were formed in Britain's most turbulent council chamber: Liverpool. Building on things with which I am familiar, this book seeks to challenge the accepted orthodoxy on a number of contemporary issues; but it also tries to show why politics matters – and what has been, and might be, achieved through the political process. It does not attempt to set out some grand game plan or to outline a comprehensive manifesto. Instead it is a very personal account: looking at people's lives that have inspired or influenced me; and looking at issues that interest me.

I profoundly disagree with those who argue that our problems will be solved by a new round of class warfare.

I believe that the call to capitalism – to grab what you can and never mind the consequences – will never do more than merely satisfy the material needs of a few.

The Britain in which I want to live would seek to join together both capital and labour as partners. More importantly, I would seek to address the much deeper alienation and sense of powerlessness which afflicts millions of citizens. Britain need not be a country where everything has a pound sterling rating. It could be a place where values other than utilitarian and monetary ones would matter; where the widespread feelings of individual helplessness and defeatism born of desperation are countered.

Should we be surprised that many have turned their backs on politics – labelling all politicians as crooks or cynics? Maybe not surprised, but surely we should all be anxious about the future health of our democracy? Daily I see the bitterness – and feel the hate – of young have-nots in Liverpool. To them the concept of an enterprise culture, or the social market, seem like a sick joke.

Yet there is another side to the coin. Our young people's response to starving Ethiopia displayed a generosity manifested in a gutsy determination and an enthusiasm which left Eurocrats and Aid officials reeling. 'Never mind the red tape, feed the people.' Whilst politicians in Westminster were cutting the aid programme young people demonstrated a commitment to a higher ideal. Yet translating that ideal into a wider political commitment will not be easy.

I grow daily more angry with the well-heeled comfortable response that tells me the time is not yet; that resources do not permit; that it can't be done. How often I wish that word 'can't' were expurgated from the vocabulary. Who says we can't have a fairer Britain; that power and wealth cannot be shared more equitably; that we can't do more in demanding justice for the powerless and alienated; that we can't enhance the rights of the weak; that we can't substantially reverse the debilitating arms race? There are just four years before we elect another government. Who says that before then we can't reshape a political agenda which sets forward an ideal capable of uniting and exciting millions of people?

Many people long to find an alternative to utility; an ideal founded on authentic human values. It is not only the young who are crying out for change. So many people are caught up in the world's suffocating bureaucracies and systems – ranging from the local planner to the world economic order; from the inertia of the housing department to the idiosyncrasies of the Common Agricultural Policy. All these people need new sign posts. This book is a modest attempt to chart a course, to steer a new direction.

INTRODUCTION – WHY BOTHER?

People get involved in politics for many and various reasons. In democracies it is usually because of a party. They are attracted by its policies or sometimes its leader. Every party is no more than a coalition of interests. On some issues, for example, members of the liberal wing of the Conservative Party may have more in common with the Liberal Party or even the Labour Party, than with their own party colleagues. At Westminster the whipping system may often thwart a putative rebellion. It might ultimately drive a member to despair. Usually, however, it succeeds in maintaining the facade of party unity. The discipline of a party is less an issue outside Parliament although, *in extremis* a party may act to protect itself from infiltration. It may try to remove people who simply wish to use it for their own ends and who are totally at variance with its principles. This was the case of the Trotskyite Militant Tendency, some of whose members have been expelled from the Labour Party.

'Non-political' people often complain that there is 'too much politics in our lives'. 'If only,' they say, 'we could get the politics out of education, housing, industry etc' . . . then everything would be all right. In truth, these are all intensely political issues – often hotly contested. But, like many, I mourn the passing of the 'Independents' from most local authorities. In Parliament far too many members are content to conform compliantly to the Party dictat. The refreshing approach and success of The Independent newspaper demonstrates that many have grown tired of the shrill and partisan subjectivity of its chief competitors. It is also why many have discarded the blind allegiance to political parties that prevailed in yesteryear.

My regret about the British system is its adversarial and combatative quality. Rubbish the other person's point of view simply because they said it. The opposite side of the House of Commons is the enemy. Our British party system has become a strait-jacket which often requires total obedience. It rarely makes allowances for differences of approach or for making use of collective wisdom or experience. Co-operation between parties or, bipartisanship, common in so many legislatures and parliaments throughout the world is spurned in Britain. We have the nerve to call this strong government.

Our democracy is a long way from the ideal of the ancient Greeks, but from time to time it has evidenced progress. Looking at the alternatives, on offer in the non-democratic countries, we should count ourselves lucky that we have the privilege of living in a democracy at all. But our grandmother of parliaments and our over-bureau-cratised institutions, are in need of rejuvenation. To achieve this we must stimulate and re-order our political parties. But what kind of parties do we want?

David Penhaligon used to quip in his lovely, down to earth, Cornish way that what the great British public really wanted was a 'stuff'em all' party. This would be a home for all the people who say 'You're all the same' party and 'You're all in it for what you can get out of it'. Though reviled and ridiculed inevitably the parties and politicians are only as good or bad as the people who put them there. It's easy to criticise and to complain, but if you really don't like the way things are, you will only change things when you start to bother. Doing nothing never changes anything. It is the ultimate irony that some of the loudest in their abuse and deepest in their bitterness cannot even be bothered to vote. Only two out of three people vote in local elections, four in five at general elections. Those people who don't vote should ponder on Edmund Burke's advice that 'for the triumphs of evil it is only necessary that good men do nothing.'

Contemporary issues and today's passing fashions and challenges can be seen more clearly against the backcloth of time. Worried about our cities, confused about our country and perplexed by the scale of the world's problems we can be forgiven for all too often feeling as overwhelmed as Robert Louis Stevenson's little boy who cried, 'The world is so big and I am so small, I do not like it at all, at all.' In approaching the great issues we all need weather vanes. Only then may we understand the signs of the time.

Political history and the calamities wrought by wrong-headedness need not propel us into a trough of despon-dency. 'History is the teacher of life' Cicero said. The lives of courage and achievement, to say nothing of the self sacrifice of many of our forebears can both uplift and clarify. History also has an uncanny way of repeating itself.

I have chosen to approach today's issues through the lives of several people who have influenced me: all are different but all are bound by a common ideal and a common humanity. We all need our heroes but it is important to see them, 'warts and all'. E M Forster warns that 'Hero worship is a dangerous vice, and one of the minor merits of a democracy is that it does not encourage it or produce that unimaginable type of citizen known as the great man. It produces instead different kinds of small men – a much finer achievement.' Great or small, we can all get our bearings from the people of the past. The thumbnail sketches that follow are about people special to me. They are important to me for the values and beliefs that each one had. Each possessed particular qualities. I believe that they are qualities that the next generation of Britain's leaders could do well to adopt.

Part One

WHAT KIND OF PEOPLE?

Chapter One

THREE GIANTS

Three giants, Wilberforce, Shaftesbury and Gladstone straddled the 100 years when Britain emerged from the industrial revolution to become a world power. It was the time when Britain, at last, moved from government by a few to a more representative form of democracy, when the masses moved from the country to the city and when Parliament had to face the many challenges posed by the new mobile urban class.

The growth of Liverpool illustrates that transition. As the 19th century began, Liverpool was no more than a fishing village, but by the century's close it had become a great city. Where once there had been green fields, bustling warehouses now stood. Tenements and back-to-back courts bulged with people and disease. There were areas of great affluence too. Liverpool's grand terraces and its majestic boulevards that led to the City's well-planned Victorian parks still stand witness to its former glory and wealth – initially financed from the proceeds of the slave trade. It was into a family of Liverpool slave traders that W E Gladstone was born. His father remained one of the fiercest opponents of the anti-slavery movement which was then being galvanised by William Wilberforce. The slave trade was arguably one of the earliest experiments with free market economics.

Wilberforce, a Conservative Member, believed slavery

to be profoundly immoral. It was an affront to God and to the dignity of man. For forty years he worked for the abolition of slavery. Wilberforce was a notable member of the so-called 'Clapham Sect', a group of wealthy and influential adherents of Anglican evangelicalism notable for humanitarian activities. It was so named because they gathered at the Clapham home of Henry Thornton, a close friend of Wilberforce's. It was here that Wilberforce lived whilst the Commons was in session. The sect, an early example of the organised pressure and prayer group, promoted missionary societies and the education of the poor, in addition to their campaigning for the abolition of slavery.

After years of parliamentary battles and many reverses, slavery was finally ended in 1833. Wilberforce, who had made the campaign his life's work, died shortly after. The fascinating thing for today's observer is that the Prime Ministers of the time, Canning and Liverpool for example, are hardly remembered, while Wilberforce, who never became a Cabinet Minister is a revered name.

The chief argument used by Wilberforce's opponents was, that if we stopped trading in slaves, other countries would simply take up where we left off. Today the same arguments are used to oppose the imposition of sanctions on South Africa, in support of the sale of arms to third world countries, and even to justify the undertaking in Britain of late abortions banned overseas: 'if we do not do it, someone else will?'

The Abolition of Slavery Act received its Royal Assent on August 28th 1833. One day later another historic piece of reforming legislation was enacted – Shaftesbury's Factory Act. The work of the two great Christian campaigners thus overlapped. Shaftesbury attended Wilberforce's funeral in Westminster Abbey on August 6th. As Shaftesbury's biographer, John Pollock, puts it: 'Thus the two crusades and the lives of two great social reformers touched briefly and symbolically . . . an end and a beginning.'

Like Wilberforce, Shaftesbury eschewed public office, preferring to promote his reforming legislation from the backbenches. His parliamentary career got off to a shaky start. He was elected to represent the 'rotten borough' of Woodstock in the unreformed parliament of 1826 – thanks to his uncle the Duke of Marlborough who controlled the seat. His banners carried the slogan 'No Popery' and he declared himself opposed to Catholic emancipation. He had taken this stand to placate his father. He later threw off the paternal yoke and spoke and voted in favour of Catholic voting rights.

The vote on Catholic emancipation in 1828 was forced by the famous by-election victory of Daniel O'Connell in County Clare. As a Catholic, O'Connell was barred by statute from taking his seat. The Duke of Wellington, himself an Irishman, bowed to the pressure and introduced the necessary reform legislation.

In today's climate of inter-denominational ecumenism such suspicion and open hostility seem years away. Yet, up until the passage of the 1829 Act, immigrant Irish Catholics in parishes like St. Patrick's in Liverpool 8 even had to build their churches in the architectural form of tithe barns. The disguise was required to prevent offence being given to members of the Established Church.

Despite the century and a half that have elapsed since Emancipation the process of achieving christian unity and equal status for christian churches has never been completed. The most famous examples of this are the barring of Catholics from the throne and the Bishop's benches in Parliament. Restrictions like these might only be removed when Britain introduces a Bill of Rights or with disestablishment.

In a City like Liverpool, where today's Catholic and Anglican Bishops, Derek Worlock and David Sheppard, act together and have broken down much of the sectarianism which once disfigured the City, it is easy to forget that in Shaftesbury's England, 150 years ago, there was a great deal of anti-Catholic prejudice which even today surfaces from time to time.

As recently as 1929, Liverpool's Protestant Party successfully blocked planning permission for the Roman Catholic Cathedral whilst Archbishop Beck, Derek Worlock's predecessor, wrote in a letter to The Times in 1949 that he could not say the Lord's Prayer with an Anglican. He also refused to give a joint blessing with the Anglican Bishop of Winchester on the grounds that the Bishop did not have valid orders and 'was only a layman'.

We have come a long way since then, and since Shaftesbury and his father argued about Catholic voting rights.

Shaftesbury, who was born in to a wealthy aristocratic family, was an unlikely champion of the poor. Yet ministerial preferments and the trappings of power held no appeal for him as he began a life's work of championing issues which the Government largely overlooked. He was a tireless crusader for the most unfashionable of causes. He founded or presided over a dozen societies ranging from the London City Mission to the Ragged Schools' Union, from the YMCA to the Church Pastoral Aid Society. He was an active patron of scores of other worthy causes like Dr. Barnado's and the National Anti-Vivisection Society. He was no paper patron either. Anyone who knows anything of Shaftesbury's life is simply staggered by the time and effort he dedicated to those causes in which he believed.

But his most enduring work was done in Parliament. He first won his parliamentary spurs in a Commons Committee considering lunatic asylums. He visited one institution himself – similar to the infamous Bethlehem Hospital (the truncated form of which, 'bedlam', has been used as a synonym ever since the beginning of the 19th century) – and, as he told the House of Commons later, 'I well remember the sounds that assailed my ears and the sights that shocked my eyes [in] that abode of the most wretched.' The mentally ill were treated primarily as a danger to society and existing legislation was designed to keep them well away from the minds and sight of the public. In the way that issues move on, today's debates in Parliament revolves around the provision in the 1967 Abortion Act which denies the physically and mentally handicapped the absolute right to life. When in 1828 Shaftesbury's County Asylum Bill and the Madhouse Bill became law, fifteen Metropolitan Commissioners were established by the new legislation. Shaftesbury became a Commissioner and was soon appointed Chairman – a position he held for fifty-seven years. Disability was at last afforded dignity and respect.

Shaftesbury is best remembered for his legislation regulating child labour. His first Factory Act in 1833 was restricted to the textile industry and provided that children under the age of nine were not to work in the mills and that those between the ages of nine and thirteen were to be limited to eight hours a day. It did not tackle the mines, however, and Shaftesbury and his backers knew that it could only be an interim measure. Still, it was an important breakthrough and paved the way for more effective legislation. The slavery of women and children in the mines was ended with the Mines Act of 1842, introduced again by Shaftesbury, after the report of the Royal Commission on the Mines pricked the conscience of the nation. But Shaftesbury's goal was to lift the burden of over long hours on the young; the 'Ten Hour Question.'

In January 1846, Shaftesbury introduced his Ten Hour Bill but two days later he resigned his seat in Parliament: he had been elected on a Protectionist platform to represent a rural constituency but had been persuaded to support the Anti-Corn Law League's campaign to 'Untax the bread of the poor!'. He resigned on that point of principle. He was able to tour the country in support of the Bill that had been taken up in his absence by John Fielden, the Radical

MP. The Bill became law in the summer of 1847 and two months later Shaftesbury was back in Parliament.

His great campaign to free children from the yoke of oppressive labour was inspired by his belief in the spiritual and temporal value of education. With all his social reforms, which are too many to adumbrate here, he was 'contending for the faith'. Without that faith all social improvement was irrelevant.

He succeeded his father in 1851 and took his place in the House of Lords as the seventh Earl of Shaftesbury. He was always known as 'the poor man's Earl'. His death in October 1885 saddened the whole nation. John Pollock, ending his biography, quotes Cecil Ashley, Shaftesbury's son, in a letter to a friend: 'When I saw,' he wrote, 'the crowd which lined the streets on Thursday as my father's body was borne to the Abbey – the halt, the blind, the maimed, the poor and the naked standing bare-headed in their rags amidst a pelting rain patiently enduring to show their love and reverence to their departed friend, I thought it the most heart-stirring sight my eyes had ever looked upon; and I could only feel how happy was the man to whom it had been given to be thus useful in his life and thrice blessed in his death, and to be laid at last to his long sleep amidst the sob of a great nation's heart.'

Wilberforce's emancipation of the slaves and Shaftesbury's social reforms created a spirit for the times. The four ministries of Gladstone and Disraeli's reforming government of 1874–1880 continued the trend and increased the role of the state in the provision of welfare and education. Disraeli called it One Nation Toryism and Gladstone, loathe to sanction greater state 'interference', conceded that the extension of education would provide the framework in which the individual would flourish.

Gladstone entered Parliament as a Tory and crossed the floor of the House in later years to join the Whig opposition. His leadership saw the birth of the modern Liberal Party which evolved from the traditional Whigs and the more recent Radicals into the National Liberal Federation in 1867. He and Disraeli were the principal architects of our modern party political system. The dominating statue of Gladstone in the central lobby at Westminster keeps a watchful eye on the parliamentary democracy he did so much to establish.

The democratic ideals of the ancient Greeks were a long time coming to Britain. It was in 1265, long after the collapse of the Greek city-states, that Simon de Montfort and his barons assembled at Westminster to challenge the authority of Edward I. Another four hundred years were to slip by before Charles I, on trial in the same Westminster Hall, was sentenced to death for the crime of treason against the State of England. His death in 1649 marked the end of the English monarch's claim to the divine right of kings. Following the brief period of Cromwell's republic the monarchy was restored and Charles II became our first constitutional monarch. The classic British fudge of a sovereign parliament existing beside a conferred monarchy was thus established.

Through these interminable centuries, the rights of the masses remained confined to feudal custom and practice. Full emancipation from serfdom required a further two hundred years of progress.

The industrial revolution and the enclosure of common land removed the quiescent masses from the country and the urban sprawls of Birmingham, Manchester and Glasgow, to name only the largest of the new, mushrooming conurbations were duly conceived. Outside rare pockets of affluence and elegance, row upon row and block upon block of congested, poorly planned and inadequately served 'houses' were thrown up to accommodate the masses. The working places of the new urban under class were worse. Blake's dark satanic mills were the graveyard of many unfortunate men, women and children. Human life was expendable. Many died, caught in unprotected machinery, or were crippled by back-breaking work. These were the Victorian vices to which Shaftesbury was to address himself.

. Meanwhile, as the nineteenth century opened, there was war – and just as World Wars One and Two and Vietnam ushered in political change so did the war with the French. The war-weary returned to Britain from the victories of the Peninsula War and Waterloo determined to seek change. The most famous illustration of the seething discontent was 'the Peterloo Massacre' of 1819. A large but peaceable crowd had gathered, on a Sunday afternoon, at St. Peter's Fields in Manchester to hear the great orators demand political reform. The authorities, in line with the repressive policies of the day, decided to disperse the crowd before John Hunt, a renowned agitator, was able to speak. They sent in a local regiment of Hussars whose zealousness left dozens dead and hundreds wounded.

Repression was a short-lived policy. The Great Reform Act of 1832 which extended the franchise and abolished the 'rotten boroughs', thus giving the vote to the emerging mercantile class of the industrial cities, was greeted with an enthusiasm that outmatched its radicalism. It was a touchstone issue though. Without it the Revolutions which gripped Europe in forthcoming years might well have engulfed Britain.

At a local level too, the municipalities of proud little boroughs and cities were being formed and as the century moved towards its climax famed politicians like Joseph Chamberlain became synonymous with the city councils which had provided them with their entry into representative politics. Perhaps in these days of obsessive centralisation it is worth reflecting that this was the nearest Britain came to capturing the Greek ideal of democracy based on the autonomous authority of the city-state. For Disraeli, the leading Conservative of the 19th century, 'centralisation was the deathblow of democracy'. Municipalisation and strong local authorities brought into the lives of the huddled masses the improvements that central Government could not contemplate. Sewers, street lighting, and municipal parks were the tangible benefits of local authority power. In Liverpool, the country's first public health inspector was appointed. The record of the appointment of Dr. Dalton still hangs in the office of the Permanent Secretary at the Department of Health and Social Security in London.

The further extensions to the franchise in the Representation of the People Acts of 1867, 1884, 1929 and 1967 ultimately established universal adult suffrage. It took a long time coming but at last this quiet revolution pitted, in the words of Gladstone, 'the masses against the classes.' Certainly by the time that the voting age was reduced to the age of eighteen in 1967 Britain could say it had come a long way from its ancient 'mootes' and feudal 'parlements'.

Perhaps the most significant change in the way British Governments are elected came in the Secret Ballots Act of 1872. Until then families were in danger of being thrown off their holdings and men lost their employment if they were seen, by voting in public, to go against the wishes of their landlord or employer. This infamy led David Lloyd George to recall his first formative political impression which was of the 1868 election:

'I was a boy at school then, and I was in the blackest Tory parish in the land. I believe that my old uncle who brought me up was the only Liberal in the village, though not the only Liberal in the parish. There were three or four in the parish besides him. One or two of them refused to vote for the Tory candidate, and two or three actually went further, and dared to record their votes for the Liberal. All of them received notice to quit. I remember that some lads who were at school with me in the same class, in a year or two had to leave the neighbourhood. I was very young but young lads do not forget things of that sort. I knew the reason why they left – because the great Squire of the Parish had turned their fathers out of their houses purely because they dared to vote for the Liberal candidate.

As a result they were turned out by the score onto the roadside because they dared to vote according to their consciences. It is,' he concluded, 'my first memory of politics.'

Secret voting at last enabled the populace to cast their votes free of intimidation, although today, in Labour heartlands, there is a new kind of intimidation and corruption. The municipal overlords frequently take punitive action against those who refuse to display their election posters. The notorious 'jobs for the boys' policies pursued by Liverpool's Labour masters was an outrage. This, in an area of massive unemployment, involved the local authority giving employment to those who had supported the party. Another ugly feature of modern elections in Labour inner city strongholds has been the levels of organised impersonation: the Northern Ireland disease where voters are encouraged to 'vote early and vote often'.

1872 at least removed the worst excesses and enabled male Britons to vote in secret for the candidate and party of their choice – it would take a further fifty years and the turbulence of a World War before women were enfranchised.

If these reforms enabled Britain to boast that it was the Mother of Parliaments then Gladstone and Disraeli must be recorded as the fathers of the modern party political system.

Gladstone's Liberal Party took its origins from the aristocratic faction of Whigs – often indistinguishable from their Tory opponents. It evolved a clear programme based on the philosophy of John Stuart Mill. Classic Liberal thinking placed prime importance on the liberty of the individual to act freely, save where in so doing, the rights of others are infringed. Gladstone, the consummate party politician, distilled the principles into practical politics. As he railed against injustices and oppression in the Balkans, atrocities in Armenia and championed the cause of Home Rule in Ireland he was asserting a morality which was based squarely on his liberalism and his strongly held Christian beliefs. For him, the right of self determination and the ascendancy of the individual over the oppressor was the stuff of liberalism. This has its echoes in the views of his modern heirs. Where we would part company, though, is in the application of 'self help alone' to the economy. Gladstone's economics were the precursor of the free market theories of today's Thatcherites. Gladstone, not Mr. Nigel Lawson, was the original tax-cutting Chancellor and despite, for example, the financing of the free education he introduced in 1872, he was implacably opposed to the interference of the State in the affairs of individual. Education, the classical Liberal would have argued, equipped man to compete and to help himself, and having helped himself, his altruism should inspire him to help others.

Unlike the New Right of the 1980's the Gladstonians of the 1880's did not have a fastidious view of the unerring value of economics. Victorian liberalism was a set of values not an obsession with crude monetary methods. Gladstone would have been repelled by the over reliance of modern politicians with treasury statistics and economic predictions. He would, I am sure, have shared G B Shaw's disparaging view that if all the economists in the world were laid end to end they would never reach a conclusion. Gladstone, the supreme moralist and ethical politician, would have rejected a view of money that applies no ethics, no morality, no responsibility. He would reject those views with the same vigour with which he would reject the iconoclasm of Labour's left who would impale us all on the rusty old stake of Clause Four Socialism.

Social Liberals of the early 20th century saw the limitations of the untrammelled market. They saw, unlike today's Thatcherite economic gurus, that markets could

not be left to themselves. They believed in the responsible
market: which today we might call the 'enterprise culture
plus': plus national insurance to protect the worker in times
of illness, plus the old age pension to protect the elderly in
their retirement, plus the legitimate rights of trade unions
to safeguard worker's interests, plus unemployment
benefits to protect the jobless and plus redistributive
taxation to pay for it all.

The Social Liberals were spurred by Seebohm Rowntree's study of poverty in the urban areas. The Quakers
investigated the condition of every family in York and
discovered that 80% of the children in working class
districts suffered the effects of privation and neglect. Lloyd
George contrasted 'the national degradation of slums and
widespread poverty and destitution in a land glittering with
wealth.' Arguing the case for his redistributive taxation
policies, Lloyd George said at a meeting of the Liberal
Christian League in 1910 that people would have to pay
to alleviate that need: 'Industrial life is now perpetuated
through pure greed', he commented, 'avarice and selfish
niggardliness are standing between the people of the
country and their highest interests.'

The new consensus of the Social Liberals was the combination of the rights of the individual, classic liberalism,
with the legitimate interests of those that the market
missed, social liberalism. This redefinition of Gladstonian
concepts and the fusion of late twentieth century social
liberalism and social democracy happily illustrates the
continued metamorphosis of our political parties. Politics
is like the sea – it is never quite free from movement. There
are times of comparative calm then there are squalls and
even violent storms. People who join political parties must
be prepared to be more than fairweather friends – facing
the tidal wave and gale as well as the days of perfect sailing.

The House that Gladstone built, the Liberal Party, could
be extended and redesigned at will. The flexibility of the
structure enlivened the politics of the day. Even in the days

of the Grand Old Man there was realignment. Liberal Unionists, rejecting Gladstone's principled stand on Home Rule for Ireland, left the Party and joined the Conservatives. In contrast to the rigid Marxist one party states British political parties were not to be set in concrete. The overriding imperative for Mr. Gladstone was the maintenance of a principle, not a party.

In 1879, Gladstone launched his famous crusading Midlothian Campaign. During the course of two weeks he travelled through North East England, the Borders, Central and Eastern Scotland. He was re-launching his own political career and also attempting to set the agenda for the forthcoming General Election. He succeeded and in 1880, Disraeli was defeated. During that barn-storming campaign and indeed throughout the total span of his long and distinguished career, Gladstone would have reached less people than his 20th century successor, Mr David Steel, will speak to just in one night. Whether Mr Gladstone could have thrived in Britain's teleculture is another matter.

Two years ago I distributed prizes at Liverpool College, the Headmaster, Mr Roy Haygarth, recounted that one hundred years earlier Mr Gladstone had officiated at the same event. His speech had lasted for close on three hours. A modern party broadcast which lasts for ten minutes is regarded as too long by bored viewers.

Mr Gladstone's heirs and successors might wince at the demogoguery and rhetoric of the Grand Old Man but physical and intellectual stamina, even into old age and his belief in what was right, enabled him to command the heights of Victorian politics for half a century. Mr Gladstone was the original conviction politician. He, Shaftesbury and Wilberforce used their convictions to ensure the passage of gigantic pieces of extraordinarily important legislation.

Chapter Two

THEN THEY CAME FOR ME

The Merseyside-educated poet Wilfred Owen, who was killed in action during World War One, used his poetry to argue that patriotism alone was not reason enough to commit a people and its resources to a cataclysmic world war. He believed that all a poet might do is to warn future generations of the pity of war. Whilst contemporaries, like Jessie Pope, tried to rouse national pride through the publication of her *Simple Rhymes for Stirring Times* (1916) and Kitchener appealed to Britain's youth to join the blood-letting on the fields of Flanders, Owen countered with one of the most memorable war poems of our times:

> If you could hear, at every jolt, the blood
> Came gargling from the froth-corrupted lungs,
> Obscene as cancer, bitter as the cud
> Of vile, incurable sore on innocent tongues . . .
> My friend, you would not tell with such high zest
> To children ardent for some desperate glory,
> The old lie: Dulce et decorum est
> Pro patria mori.   *"Dulce et Decorum Est"*

It is difficult indeed, writing in the 1980s, to see in what circumstances it would have been 'sweet' or 'fitting' to die for one's country in World War One. The horror of the trenches alone should surely have brought European leaders to their senses. Yet the same blood lust which fuelled the pre-War Arms Race, the narrow nationalism, the deep-rooted suspicions, conspiracy and intrigue all conspired together to perpetuate the war for five long years during which almost fifteen million died and twenty-one million were injured. The cost was $282 billion dollars.

Wilfred Owen was not a pacifist and in 1915 enlisted to fight. He won the MC for bravery, he was killed in machine gun fire in November 1918.

Owen deplored the pride which led to millions of young Europeans dying in the trenches. Comparing their sacrifice to that of Isaac by Abraham he writes angrily:

Then Abram bound the youth with belts and straps.
And builded parapets and trenches there
And stretched forth the knife to slay his son.
When lo! An angel called him out of heaven,
Saying, lay not thy hand upon the lad,
Neither do anything to him. Behold,
A ram, caught in a thicket by its horns;
Offer the Ram of Pride instead of him.

But the old man would not so, but slew his son,
And half the seed of Europe, one by one.
                'The Parable of The Old Man and The Young'

He saw the Great War for what it was and tried to issue a warning to those who would follow – not to wrap themselves mindlessly in the flag and to follow blindly patriot appeals to arms.

With the benefit of hindsight we can see World War One as an orgy of nationalism and patriotism. As the Liberal Foreign Secretary of the day, Edward Grey, surveyed the scene from his Whitehall Office, he rightly predicted that the lights would be extinguished throughout the continent of Europe. There were few voices that urged the making fast of our War machine; with many people torn by the dilemma of supporting Belgium neutrality which Britain had guaranteed.

Doubts about fighting in World War One dissipated in 1939. This time the nature of Hitler's totalitarian regime, with its daily outrages against humanity, were motivation enough. The life and death of the German theologian, Dietrich Bonhoeffer, is an illustration of how the commandments – even to love one's neighbour – may cause a person to believe it right to resort to violence and killing to counter tyranny. Bonhoeffer's intended tyrannicide was something for which he knew he would ultimately be answerable. He had to ponder the morality of attempting to take Hitler's life, and thereby risking the eternal damnation which murder must bring, or to try and kill a man upon whose instructions six million Jews were being murdered. In a different way, a young farm boy in the Sudentland had to face the dilemma about whether to enlist in Hitler's armies. Like Bonhoeffer, he too, had a burning Christian faith. This is what he wrote to his parents:

Dear Parents, I must give you bad news – I have been condemned to death, I and Gustave G. We did not sign up for the SS, and so they condemned us to death. You wrote me, indeed that I should not join the SS; my comrade, Gustave G., did not sign up either. Both of us would rather die than stain our consciences with such deeds of horror. I know what the SS has to do. Oh, my dear parents, difficult as it is for me and for you, forgive me everything; if I have offended you, please forgive me and pray for me. If I were to be killed in the war while my conscience was bad, that too would be sad for you. Many more parents will lose their children. Many SS men will get killed too. I thank you for everything you have done for my good since my childhood; forgive me, pray for me. . . .

The farm boy's response was different to Bonhoeffer's

but both, in their particular circumstances, were brave and morally correct decisions.

Bonhoeffer secured a position in the Abwehr in Berlin and began to plot Hitler's death. In 1942, he travelled to neutral Sweden where he secretly met with George Bell, Bishop of Chichester. Bell returned to Britain and acquainted Eden and Churchill with the determination of Bonhoeffer and others to launch a putsch against Hitler. Two years later after the attempt had failed, Bell was to complain that the British Government was doing nothing to encourage those in Germany who were seeking to destroy the regime. He received no response from Eden and of Churchill he said, 'He is living in a world of battles only, and seeing time with the mind of a child with regard to deep policy: for Home Affairs as well as for graver matters of Europe. And disaster gets nearer and nearer'.

For Bonhoeffer the disaster of discovery brought at first a prison cell at Tegel; remorseless interrogation by the Gestapo; meagre food; a dirty cell; the humiliation of handcuffs and separation from family and friends. In the last days of the 3rd Reich at Flossenburg Camp in April 1945, Bonhoeffer was executed, along with Admiral Canaris and General Oster. After watching him go to the gallows, the camp doctor wrote that in almost fifty years as a doctor he had hardly ever seen such bravery, composure or total submission to the will of God.

At a memorial service at London's Holy Trinity Church, Kingsway, Bishop Bell said Bonhoeffer represented, 'both the resistance of the believing soul, in the name of God, to the assault of evil, and also the moral and political revolt of the human conscience against injustice and cruelty. It was this passion for justice that brought him and so many others . . . into such close partnership with other resisters, who, though outside the church, shared the same humanitarian and liberal ideals. . . .'

When later on some fundamentalist German pastors appealed to the Bonhoeffer family to protest against the naming of streets after Dietrich Bonhoeffer, 'Because we do not want the names of our colleagues who were killed for their faith, lumped together with political martyrs'. Bonhoeffer's mother replied: 'I am sure it would not have been his desire to cut himself off from those who had perished for political reasons, with whom he had lived for years in prison and concentration camps.'

Bonhoeffer knew that he had been left with no choice but to fight and that, for him, to fight alongside political figures was right. His regret was delay. First the Gestapo had come for the Jews, and he did nothing. Then they came for the Trade Unionists, and he did nothing. 'Then they came for me!' All too often we are all guilty of trying to stand aloof – 'I don't want to get involved'. As many good men remained silent, Hitler's evil regime consigned millions of men, women and children to death. The scape-goating and slaughter of minorities is paralleled only by Stalin's atrocities from 1929 and Pol Pot's genocide in Cambodia. Should those who contend with dictatorships and evil tyrannies passively accept such monstrous subjugation of their liberties? In the next chapter I describe the non-violent Martin Luther King as an 'extremist for love'. Bonhoeffer is equally deserving of such a description. King practised non-violent principles which provided the impetus for change; Bonhoeffer, in a tyranny where all civilised values had collapsed, conspired to kill.

In our contemporary world it would be rash to condemn churchmen like the Methodist, Cedric Mayson, who was involved in the South African liberation movement and escaped after being tried for High Treason; or El Salvador's Archbishop Oscar Romero who was mown down by right wing militiamen for speaking out against injustices in Central America; or Father Jerry Popouieskou, murdered by Polish Communist agents attempting to suppress support for Solidarity, the outlawed trade union. All of them made different and brave responses to differing circumstances. Isaiah talks of beating swords into ploughshares (2.4) but Joel (3.10) talks of turning ploughshares into swords. Just as Old Testament prophets had their policy differences there can be wholly different responses to varying situations. A non-violent society must be our clear objective but not everyone lives in the comfortable surroundings of a parliamentary democracy where the pious espousal of such principles from long distances must rankle with men and women faced by the immediacy of violent or repressive regimes. In meeting his Maker, would Bonhoeffer have a clearer conscience for attempting to kill Adolph Hitler rather than if he hadn't tried?

Chapter Three

AN EXTREMIST FOR LOVE

Throughout the 1960's the ghettoes of America burned with brooding resentment and indignation as black men and women demanded civil rights and equal opportunities. At the centre of the movement was a man whose passionate commitment to change was to cost him his life. The disorders which swept through Britain's cities in 1981 at Brixton, Toxteth, Manchester, Hulme, St. Paul's in Bristol and in 1985 at Handsworth were, by comparison, minor disturbances. The conflagration and the string of riots which shook America, from the segregated Southern States to the pockets of poverty in Harlem and the Watts district of Los Angeles, ignited more than buildings. It stirred the deep yearning, that exists in everyone, to be rid of the shackles that oppress us. From a jail cell in Birmingham, Alabama, in April 1963, Dr Martin Luther King, Jr conducted his campaign to end the political slavery of black America.

In a letter to his fellow clergymen, King addressed the central issues. The Letter From Birmingham Jail took its inspiration from the apostle Paul's letters written during periods of confinement in Roman jails. Written on scraps of paper it was smuggled out and addressed to eight clergymen who had called King's actions in confronting Alabama's racist laws, 'unwise and untimely'. King had earlier organised the successful boycott of buses in Montgomery

– where blacks had been forced to ride in segregation at the back of the bus. Now, against shops and stores in Birmingham that ran segregated lunch counters, King had led a non-violent protest march through some forbidden streets. The authorities arrested him. King later wrote that he had never been truly in solitary confinement: 'God's companionship does not stop at the door of the door of a jail cell. I don't know whether the sun was shining at that moment. But I know that once again I could see the light'.

King was no alabaster saint. Flawed in several respects, those failings became an obsession of the CIA's director, J Edgar Hoover who appears to have made his life's work the laying of traps to discredit King. Files on King joined those he kept on President John Kennedy on the fifth floor of his headquarters, and filled four rooms. Perhaps it is precisely King's susceptibility to the passions of the heart and his, at times, deep self doubts that make him so appealing to those of us who come from the same 'failed again' tradition of Christianity. The late David Watson described the Church as congregations of sinners. King had little time for judgementalism, perhaps realising that the man who never made a mistake, never made anything.

King's letter followed sharp criticism that he had been sticking his nose into Birmingham City's domestic affairs. His fellow clergymen regarded him as a trouble-maker, an outsider. King countered by comparing himself with Paul, who had left his village of Tarsus and carried Christ's gospel to the far corners of the ancient world, 'So am I compelled to carry the gospel of freedom beyond my home town'.

King's denunciation attacked the double standards that had caused the local church leaders to condemn the demonstrators of local blacks, but not the conditions which gave rise to them. He went on to compare the violence against the demonstrators with the non-violence he preached and which the demonstrators had practised. King drew considerable inspiration from the Ghandian resistance to the British Raj. In India, King had studied deeply the breaking of the Salt Laws and how the corrosion of colonial rule had hastened independence. In the Southern States he aimed to create a similar non-violent tension which would be a prelude to change. Such leadership would enable them to rise from the dark depths of prejudice and racism to the majestic heights of understanding and brotherhood.

Yet King's idealism was not of the preachy variety. He knew that freedom is never voluntarily or willingly given by the oppressor; it had to be demanded by the oppressed. The contrasting approach of the Muslim Black power leader, Malcolm X, and the non-violent King, offered America a genuine choice. The same alternatives exist today in South Africa and in Britain's black and poor-white ghettoes and our response to today's injustice, alienation, and acute poverty will determine the future shape of our own cities and country.

In his Letter, King powerfully addressed the age-old injunction of the conservative who will tell you that the time for change is not yet:

Perhaps it is easy for those who have never felt the stinging darts of segregation to say 'wait'. But when you have seen vicious mobs lynch your sisters and brothers at whim; when you have seen hate-filled policemen curse, kick, and even kill your black brothers and sisters; when you see the vast majority of your twenty million Negro brothers smothering in an air-tight cage of poverty in the midst of an affluent society; when you suddenly find your tongue twisted and your speech stammering as you seek to explain to your six year old daughter why she can't go to the public amusement park that has just been advertised on television, and see tears welling up in her eyes when she is told that Funtown is closed to coloured children, and see ominous clouds of inferiority beginning to form in her little mental sky, and see her beginning to distort her personality by developing an unconscious bitterness towards white people; when you have to concoct an answer for a five-year-old son who is asking: 'Daddy, why do white people treat coloured people so mean?'; when you take a cross country drive and find it necessary to sleep night after night in the uncomfortable corners of your automobile because no motel will accept you; when you are humiliated day in day out by nagging signs reading 'white' and 'coloured'; when your first name becomes 'nigger'; your middle name becomes 'boy' (however old you are); and your last name becomes 'John', and your wife and mother are never given the respected title 'Mrs'; when you are harried by day and haunted by night by the fact that you are a Negro, living constantly at tiptoe stance, never quite knowing what to expect next, and are plagued with inner fears and outer resentments; when you are forever fighting a degenerating sense of 'nobodiness' – then you will understand why we find it difficult to wait.

King's anger with the segregation and the evil Klu Klux Klan came from the deep experience of facing daily the pain of racism. His anger with extreme right-wing forces implacably pledged to fight change turned to frustration when he talked about the white moderate of liberal disposition. They admitted the need for change, but while their tone was different, like the conservatives, they too advised waiting for a more convenient season.

American Blacks could not wait and one by one the constitutional and God-given rights which they had sought for 240 years became theirs. Yet twenty years after King's death the fight against innate prejudice and discrimination which legislation alone will not counter continues in America and elsewhere. In our own British cities we still have to come to terms with institutionalised racism – the sort that led a young black woman in Liverpool to remark to me once, 'We came here 150 years ago at the time of the slave trade; since then we have moved just half a mile up the road!' Lack of job prospects, failure by authorities to take affirmative action, substandard homes, insensitive policing, and second rate schools all conspire together to create a hidden racism every bit as evil as the out-front segregation of King's Southern States.

But if our own racism is discreetly swept under the carpet the position of blacks in South Africa can hardly be similarly concealed. Our country's refusal to impose full economic sanctions, our muted condemnation of apartheid, our pious hopes that one day South Africa might reform itself all conjure up St. Augustine of Hippo's famous plea, 'Lord make me chaste, but not just yet!' 'Lord end apartheid, but not just yet'. Rarely have I felt more ashamed of my country or of the Parliament of which I am a member than on the day we refused to impose full sanctions on South Africa.

Twenty-five years ago, when Dr King was attempting to rouse the moral conscience of his nation, he lamented, 'We shall have to repent in this generation not so much for the evil deeds of wicked people but for the appalling silence of the good people.' Once again, people did not want to be dragged in, 'to get involved'.

In South Africa today, as we ignore the calls of Bishop Desmond Tutu and the Rev Alan Boesak for full sanctions, we idly hope that the Pretoria Government's peripheral reforms will one day lead to change. The truth is that to hold on to power the right-wing Nationalists will go on ruthlessly suppressing the townships and crushing the spirits of black people yearning to be free. Our silence continues to encourage South Africa's Nationalists thus enabling them to maintain their tenuous control by our acquiescence. Our silence is dictated mainly by financial considerations; £7 billion of British investment and $14 billion of American investment. We stay silent, too, as men like Paraguay's dictator, General Stroessner, operate a profitable re-export trade in arms to South Africa. We remain dumb as South African security forces (BOSS) operate in White South Africa's interests from our own country.

In 1985 at our Dundee Assembly, I invited my friend Donald Woods, a former South African newspaper editor to take part in our debate on South Africa. He was smuggled out of the country in the boot of a car, disguised as a Catholic priest coming to Britain where he published his book on Steve Biko. His life is portrayed in Sir Richard Attenborough's film "Cry Freedom." He cogently argued for a Gleneagles Agreement, not just covering sport, but economic, social and cultural links as well. This would undoubtedly be the most effective way to pressurise South Africa into repealing the remaining 317 apartheid laws. Later in this book, I suggest a series of other initiatives the UK and Commonwealth might take.

It is now twenty-five years since the Sharpeville Massacre and two years since Crossroads. After twenty-four years Nelson Mandela continues to languish in a South African jail, Tutu is told what he may preach. Britain, meanwhile merely tut-tuts at the tyranny of a nation whose law and constitution are moulded on Nietzche's theories of racial superiority. Twenty years after the assassin's bullets ripped through King's body the spirit of the self styled 'extremist for love' must continue to light the way for a free Azania which one day will enjoy full freedom and human rights. By failing to stand alongside the blacks of South Africa in this struggle we should ask ourselves what our own black citizens will make of our inertia.

Chapter Four

WE THINK OF THINGS THAT MIGHT HAVE BEEN

Most people of my generation are able to recapture the time, the place, the very moment when they heard of John Kennedy's assassination. The English ruminated on the senseless violence and the sheer waste of a man in his prime – whose promise still remained greater than his administration's mistakes. For a boy being brought up in a Catholic home by a mother from the West of Ireland far deeper emotions were stirred.

Kennedy's forebears had arrived in America from County Wexford after the potato famine of 1848. These immigrants three generations removed, were reviled as 'the scum of creation'. Hatred of the starving new arrivals manifested itself in 'No Irish need apply' signs erected by virtually all employers. All who derive from Irish stock have the vicissitudes of those times locked in to their collective memories. The oral and musical tradition of a nation that was almost wiped out by ruthless repression, starvation and despair has been handed on in much the same way that others pass on family heirlooms. Cromwell and the Black and Tans blur to make Irishmen and their descendents prisoners of their own history. While the modern young Irishman is confidently taking his place along side his European counterparts and is at last placing his country's past firmly behind him, events of yesteryear dominate the psyche of the Irish diaspora. Nowhere more so than in the United States where generous donations pour in to NORAID and the IRA out of a false sense of romanticism which no self respecting Irishman would ever accord terrorists and gangsters. On a visit to Cleveland, Ohio in 1981 I vividly recall being lambasted by a young American who compared Northern Ireland with Vietnam and refused to believe that the British had not killed millions of people in the province.

Ireland's new confidence has come with its membership of the European Community and through the leadership of Fine Gael's, Dr. Garret Fitzgerald. As Taoiseach from 1981 to 1987, and particularly through his pioneering of the All Ireland Forum and the subsequent Anglo-Irish Agreement, he has transformed Ireland's view of itself and its place in the world.

Twenty-five years ago there was little of that confidence – and the election of an American from an Irish background as President of the United States was cause for great rejoicing. To the same community his assassination brought the grief usually reserved for the closest of kith and kin. I can only recall one previous occasion seeing my mother in tears. Kennedy's death plunged us all in to a gloomy depression.

Yet the practices of John Kennedy's administration were in many ways as dubious as those which came to light in the congressional hearings following Richard Nixon's Watergate and Ronald Reagan's Irangate. The Cuban Missile Crisis, the handling of the Berlin crisis – during which the wall was erected, the authorisation of an assasination hit squad in the Caribbean (christened 'Murder Inc.' by Vice President Johnson), the stepping up of involvement in Vietnam (16,732 military personnel by October 1963 and more on the way), and his choice of close friends reveal at times a man of flawed judgement.

Kennedy's greatest redeeming feature was his brother

Robert. Arguably, his assassination in 1968 robbed America and the rest of the world of a far greater man.

Robert Kennedy served as Attorney General in Kennedy's administration. He cut his teeth in the investigation and the ultimate indictment of Dave Beck and Jimmy Hoffa, the crooked leaders of the Teamsters Union, a period which he referred to as his time: 'chasing bad men', and throughout his life he despised and crusaded against corruption.

His apprenticeship was served in less auspicious circumstances, under Senator Joe McCarthy. He worked for a time as part of McCarthy's anti-communist committee: a crusade which at times had all the venom and judicial fairness of the Salem witches trial. McCarthy was ultimately judged by the Senate, in December 1954, to have brought both the Senate and the USA in to disrepute. McCarthy had been prevailed upon by Kennedy's father, Joe, to take Bobby in to his team. McCarthy and Joe Kennedy came out of the same Conservative stable of machine politics. Joe had been American ambassador to Britain at the outbreak of World War Two and he had strongly advised Roosevelt to keep America out of the war and tried to persuade the British Government to learn to cooexist with the European Fascist dictatorships. He was known as ruthless – a charge later directed at Bobby Kennedy when he was appointed Chairman of his brother's Presidential campaign.

Ruthlessness and determination in politics are often confused. Kennedy's zeal for the causes in which he believed and devotion to duty came from deeper wells than simple self advancement. Those earlier battles against Trades Union corruption – and even his rash decision to embrace McCarthyism – gave him a cutting edge which manifested itself in a deep commitment to civil rights and social justice. He gradually shed the reactionary views of his father and began to be respected for his own liberal credentials as he stepped somewhat reluctantly from his brother's shadow.

Using the power which was his as Attorney General, Kennedy – the rich boy from a privileged background – placed his office and talents at the disposal of the powerless and dispossessed. Nor was it all talk – he discovered that only ten black lawyers worked in his Department of Justice: within two years this had risen to over 100. He also pointedly commented that none of the 6,600 agents employed by the CIA were black. Hoover, the FBI director, had said privately 'everybody knows that negroes' brains are twenty per cent smaller than white people's', revealing a deep rooted racism that still persists amongst many public officials today. Kennedy confronted this head on.

Kennedy became close to Martin Luther King during this period. King articulated the burning rage and sense of exploitation which black America felt – and about which even Kennedy, with his pleas for logic, reason, patience and good will seemed insufficiently concerned. A few extra jobs in the Justice Department, and even the passage of anti-segregation and discriminatory measures would not be enough. When it came to the crunch: as Freedom Riders challenged segregation throughout the Southern States, and black student James Meredith successfully enrolled in Mississippi's all-white Oxford University, Robert Kennedy provided the moral back-bone and the political force to see integration through. On the night King was assasinated Kennedy spoke to a black audience and told them, 'What we need in the United States is not division; what we need in the United States is not violence or lawlessness, but love and wisdom, and compassion toward those who still suffer within our country, whether they be white or they be black.'

In his political testament, where he announces his candidacy and intention to run against President Johnson, he inscribed a dedication to his parents and to his wife, Ethel, after whose name he had written the Old Testament textual reference, RUTH 1:16.17, 'Entreat me not to leave thee, or to return from following after thee: for whither thou goest, I will go; and where thou lodgest I will lodge; thy people shall be my people, and thy God, my God.'

He was a practical politician who tried to turn his Christian ideals in to politics that ensured that the Kingdom came on earth as well as in heaven, unlike today's American fundamentalists who fall in to the trap of believing that salvation of the soul is incompatible with social justice when, of course, as Kennedy saw, it is not a case of one or the other. On one occasion when he discovered that his children were not understanding the meaning of sermons, he berated the pastor telling him that his sermons should be like his own political speeches, 'simple and clear, going directly to the point.' When the pastor facetiously suggested that Kennedy should send over one of his speech-writers to help with future sermons he apologised but told the pastor: 'You should not be talking about God up there so much. I want to know what God is like down here, how He is concerned with what we do here. I want to know how my life should be lived here and now.'

This was the basis of Robert Kennedy's belief and he tried to do something about it, his discovery of the plight of the poor America he had never even known existed gave him the opportunity to prove himself. Once, as Senator for New York, during a visit to Bedford-Stuyvesent in Brooklyn, a huge slum that contained the most depressed black community in America, he was told by community leaders that he was merely another white politician who would shed a few tears and never be seen again. His response was to enlist the aid of business leaders and bankers to set up the Bedford-Stuyvesent Corporation to bring investment, jobs and amenities to the area. He made sure that black community leaders had a leading role and also amazed local Republican politicians who suspected it was just a political project by including them too. He considered it his finest achievement and admitted that he would rather devote his time to Bedford-Stuyvesent than continue as politician. Today the area is virtually unrecognisable, more than 1,500 new homes have been reconstructed thousands more have been renovated, millions of dollars in mortgages have been made available to help residents to buy their homes, there are many black-owned small businesses and many larger businesses providing work for local people. There are also social services, parks, and other recreational facilities including the Billie Holliday theatre.

Today's political landscape is populated by people who seem to always appeal to the lowest common denominator and who moralise and prescribe political remedies from the comfort of their armchairs. Having come out from the shadows of his father and his brother, Robert Kennedy appealed to people's highest ideals, raised their aspirations and through his practical political actions put flesh on the poetic invocation of Aeschylus, that we 'should seek to tame the savageness of man and make gentle the life of the world'. President Robert Kennedy would have ended the war in Vietnam, inspired millions the world over, and given hope to blacks, Hispanics and other powerless minorities. It is tempting to paraphrase Robert Kennedy himself to think of things that might have been, and then ask, why not?

Chapter Five

BEYOND THE HEROES . . .

During the summer of 1968 Martin Luther King Jr. and Robert Kennedy were both assassinated. Those events, the Vietnam war, African famine and student demonstrations all over Europe made many people think about politics. My own political interest had first been roused by the 1966 General Election. To a fifteen year old, the parties seemed much of a muchness. On council estates like ours there was generally much rejoicing that Labour had consolidated its 1964 win – an election which had ended thirteen years of Conservative rule.

My family had been rehoused from the run-down East End where I was born, to one of London's many overspill council estates. The people who lived there, including all the neighbours in our block of flats, voted Labour. For my father, a shop floor worker at Fords, voting Labour was a habit.

These were heady days for Labour. Our local candidate campaigned on the slogan 'Launch *Moon Man*' and to commemorate his victory one of Eric Moonman's supporters christened her baby 'Launch'. Harold Wilson meanwhile promised to launch Britain into 'the great white heat of a technological revolution' and to modernise the economy and our country. The promise soon paled. Within a year or so there were clever car stickers which posed the question, underneath photographs of Harold Wilson and Edward Heath, 'Which twin is the Tory?'

Disillusionment rapidly sets in when the expectation so overwhelmingly exceeds the reality. It is especially difficult for parties from the left who come to office on a mandate for change: and so often with the hopes of idealists pinned to them. Harold Wilson's government seemed to lurch along, stumbling over industrial legislation and taking political positions which smacked of pure opportunism. He was the ultimate political acrobat regularly contorting himself to appease the power of the trade unions or to preserve party unity. The socialists who voted Labour felt cheated and the social democrats felt too dependent on the more militant left. Arguably the process of realignment which took many of Wilson's stars – Shirley Williams and Roy Jenkins for instance – into the Council For Social Democracy, began here. The SDP is also where Eric Moonman finally landed.

Realignment – perhaps based on the balance of power which has eluded liberals for so long – was the theme being offered by the Third Man of the 1966 election. Jo Grimond was the Liberal leader. For a teenage observer not yet understanding much about politics, Grimond seemed to be offering a vision of the kind of country in which I wanted to live.

The Liberals had only a handful of seats in Parliament and few votes in the country. Disparagingly my father caricatured it as a party of lost opportunities and its leader someone who would always be the bridesmaid, never the bride. Despite its phenomenal success in a by-election at Orpington some four years earlier, when Eric Lubbock had stormed home in a previously safe Conservative seat; and another by-election win the year before, when Parliament's youngest member, David Steel, had secured victory in a Scottish Borders seat, the Liberal Party seemed light years away from securing office. And yet, politics surely was not simply about the cynical manipulation of power?

1967 had come and Labour's Home Secretary, Jim Callaghan, introduced his now infamous Commonwealth Immigrants Act. Responding to racist campaigns organised by the National Front, Labour tore up the right of Ugandan Asians to hold British passports. It seemed inconceivable to me that a country could go back on its word and push through Parliament – in twenty-four hours flat – a Bill which removed rights which had previously been conferred. David Steel was one of the leading voices raised in protest and in his book, *No Right To Enter*, he trenchantly argued against the Callaghan Bill. Enoch Powell in a notorious and hate-ridden speech raised the temperature further by prophesying that there would be rivers flowing red with blood, caused by racial tension. Immigration and race relations were on the political agenda and the National Front was gaining ground. Labour pandered to prejudice and failed to take the issue head-on, fearing a backlash from many of its own supporters.

But the late 60s were also the time of Liverpool-inspired Beatles music, of flower power, San Francisco hippy communes and love-ins. This was the colourful contrast to America's bloody involvement in South East Asia. The Vietnam War dragged on and a wave of anti-Americanism swept Britain. In the autumn of 1968 I joined the Young Liberals – nicknamed by the popular press the Red Guards – and dutifully went to demonstrate against the Vietnam War, wrote letters to the press, and in common with others of my generation, I became more and more angry about the pictures of bombed villages, and pointless killing.

President Kennedy's assassination in 1963 had been followed by the succession and then election of his deputy, Lyndon B. Johnson. It was Johnson who bore the ire of my generation. The chants went up demanding 'LBJ, LBJ how many kids have you killed today?' The war continued to escalate. Challenged by Kennedy's anti-war younger brother, Bobby, who had declared his candidacy in the upcoming Presidential contest, LBJ announced at the end of March 1968 that he was throwing in the towel.

By May, Martin Luther King, Jr was dead, and on June 4th, after winning the California Primary, Robert Kennedy was also dead. Bobby Kennedy had remarked on the news of King's death: America must 'replace that violence, that stain of bloodshed that has spread across our land, with an effort to understand with compassion and with love.' It stood well as his epitaph too.

The violence of these deaths and the violence of Vietnam parodied the flower power and talk of love and co-existence. The troubadors of the time sang of the eve of destruction and Bob Dylan warned the mighty that 'the times they are a-changin'.

Violence was not the prerogative of the American Army. Earlier in the year the little country of Czechoslovakia had dared to talk of liberalisation and to loosen the screws of communism. For his troubles, Alexander Dubcek, the Czech Prime Minister, was forced from office and given a humble job in a remote part of the country. The Russian tanks rolled into Prague and the Czechoslovak Spring turned into a Cold Long Winter. It still grips that sad country today.

Once again we demonstrated, although this time many of the groups from the left who had been in Red Lion Square and outside the American Embassy were conspicuous by their absence – and unusually silent when socialist excesses were the target. Today they demonstrate about South Africa and Central America but say little about refuseniks and dissidents in the USSR or the violent removal of independence from Afghanistan and its subsequent repression.

It wasn't necessary to look at far away Vietnam or Czechoslovakia to see violence engulfing countries. Closer to home, across the St George's Channel, Harold Wilson was about to send the troops to Northern Ireland after months of unrest and civil disorder. They remain in Ireland to this day.

The general violent climate of the times, double standards on human rights and domestic policies made me angry and determined to get involved in politics. These events were compounded by the horrible war in Biafra – the Ethiopia of its day. Starving children with swollen bellies cut a pitiful sight as television brought into our comfortable homes the awfulness of famine and the pointlessness of war. Angry and frustrated, I recall dragooning school friends into an all-night walk around our school's playing fields to raise funds for Biafra. It may not have raised millions or even have saved many lives, but it was a personal attempt at direct action. Thousands more were doing likewise. I was quickly learning that you do not have to wait on international diplomacy and lethargic institutions. It was possible to do something yourself.

The Old Man of Hoy

This feeling of wanting to be involved was something which Jo Grimond had seized upon in developing as his own the theme of devolved decision-making through participation, involvement and consultation, 'If politics is about power and if Liberalism is about people, then we are for power to people', he declared. Although I didn't know a single Liberal, let alone any detailed policy, I did want to do something about the things I wanted to see change in Britain and beyond. Grimond seemed to offer a way, so I recruited a friend who came along for company, and together we found the dusty church hall where weekly the Young Liberals met. I joined up.

It was then October 1968. Jo Grimond had repeatedly been urging his Liberal troops to march 'towards the sound of gunfire' – and to 'bring Liberalism off the side lines and into the ring'.

Twenty years later Liberal forces still strive to make Jo's

dream of a radical realignment of the non-socialist left into
a reality.

The intervening skirmishes, defeats and victories, the
changes of tactics and generals have left us war-hardened,
though at times war-weary too. The gunfire still beckons,
but the sound is clearer. Our Dad's Army of the 60's has
become a far more professional outfit.

An Unlikely Hero

Grimond is an unlikely hero. A patrician from the Eton
and Oxford stables, he can be an awkward man. On
returning from the Second World War the former Army
major stood for Parliament in the remote Orkney and Shet-
land Islands which had long been part of the traditional
Liberal fringe. He lost in 1945 but stood again in 1950. He
won the seat then and went on to represent the Islands
until his retirement from the Commons and subsequent
elevation to the peerage in 1983. He and his wife Laura,
the grand-daughter of the great reforming Liberal Prime
Minister Herbert Asquith and a great Liberal herself, live
just outside Kirkwall.

Like Jim Wallace, his successor as the local MP, Jo
Grimond was not an Orcadian by birth, but quickly
became the mouthpiece of the Islands. Both men strongly
identify with local people and have a passionate commitment to their interests and for preserving their unique way
of life. Jim Wallace will often be found wearing a special
Island tie which depicts a map of the Shetlands, while
somewhere down below there is a small box containing the
rest of the UK. This is a neat reminder to those cartogra-
phers and others who will often tuck the Islands away in
some obscure part of the atlas. Jim Wallace quickly tells
you that his constituency is nearer to Oslo than London.
This remoteness and independence are a clue to Grimond's
success and long tenure.

Grimond became leader of the Liberal Party in 1956. He

followed Clement Davies who had seen the Party's national vote drop to 730,546 (2.6%) and its number of MP's fall to six by 1951. The joke then was that the Liberal Party held its meetings in the back of a taxi. Only Grimond himself had been elected without the help of a local electoral pact. The Party did not fare much better in 1955 taking 2.7% of the total vote. Churchill had offered Clement Davies a seat in the Cabinet which, had he accepted, would certainly have seen the end of the Liberal Party in Parliament. Just as the National Liberals led by Sir John Simon had been swallowed up by the Conservatives in the 30's (as had the nineteenth century Liberal Unionists before them – and maybe the Owenites of the future) so would the Liberal Party have been quickly consumed. Bravely, Davies chose the lonelier road of seemingly futile opposition. At a meeting in the early 1950s at Manchester University Davies admitted: 'I can offer you nothing – only hard work and suffering.' The Party which had given Britain five Governments, leaders of the calibre of Gladstone, Asquith and Lloyd-George, and which had introduced reforms like free education, the old age pension, national insurance, crushed the power of the House of Lords, and much more besides was in a pretty sorry state. It could no longer even lay claim to great thinkers like Beveridge and Keynes, who had, at least made the Party a power house of ideas before the war. Its principal role was to keep alive liberal values which were constantly being undermined and eroded.

There is an element of the romantic about British Liberals – riding out on chargers in fresh pursuit of the Holy Grail at regular intervals. It is good to be reminded of the daunting odds which faced Grimond thirty-three years ago as he faced the wastelands of British politics – split in half as they were between the two class-based parties commanding between them over 90% of the popular vote at elections. Finding the Grail must have seemed the remotest of possibilities. Grimond's achieve-

ment appears quite tame today. Most young voters would
be forgiven for not knowing who Grimond was, let alone
what he accomplished. Yet for me, part of an older generation, the reconstruction of a great Party, the honing of
ideas into a tangible prospectus and the leadership that
required remain profoundly inspiring. There were no
Cabinet posts, ministerial limousines or financial rewards
for Grimond. His was a labour of love and duty. That
Grimond never grew bitter as he watched lesser men take
and hold the great offices of the land should be an example
to today's career politicians who, too often, aspire to *be*
things rather than to *do* things.

Grimond was a party builder without being a narrow
party man. He joked that he never let the Party's newspaper, *Liberal News*, anywhere near his constituency lest
people learned what his policies were. He showed a modest
sense of self deprecation and humour which delighted and
inspired his hearers. He is also mischievous. At one of my
final by-election rallies in 1979 he spoke just before Party
leader, David Steel, and announced with a twinkle in his
eye that he had been brought all the way to Liverpool 'to
get an audience for David Steel!' Earlier I had told the
same audience that we laid no claim to be better people
than our opponents – just that our way of doing things
was better. 'Not true,' quipped Grimond later, 'we *are*
better people than our opponents!'

In 1981 at a meeting in Llandudno, North Wales, at
our annual Party Conference, it was Grimond, with Steel,
Shirley Williams and Roy Jenkins, who persuaded the
Liberal Party to embrace the concept of an Alliance
between Liberals and Social Democrats. Jo told his hearers
that this was the manifestation of the vision he had some
thirty years before. This was the vehicle which would
realign British politics. If young men have visions, that
night in 1981 must have seemed like the conclusion of an
old man's dream. Dr David Owen was to remark in 1987
that neither of the Social Democrats who spoke had sought

permission from his Committee, nor had either of their speeches been checked. Both had broken the injunction not to speak on Liberal platforms. He complained that it was at this meeting much against his wishes, that the Alliance was born. It was to take the Liberals and their allies on to eight million votes in 1983 and to 7.3 million votes in 1987. That night in Llandudno both Williams and Jenkins generously paid tribute to Grimond whom they saw as architect and layer of realignment foundations.

Chapter Six

A NEW PARTY FOR A NEW COUNTRY?

Election '87 – What Went Wrong

1987 could have been a great year for the Alliance. The members of both the Liberal and the Social Democratic parties that joined together for a rally at the Barbican in January could be forgiven for being optimistic about the future. By-election victories at Greenwich and Truro further bolstered our enthusiasm, and big gains in the local elections in May whetted our appetites for the General Election we knew lay ahead. But 1987 saw the Alliance fail.

Not since 1970 had we fought a General Election where the result was so wide of the expectation. While I remain convinced that our basic message was right. On the Sunday before the Election, at a North West rally in Rochdale, I argued that our campaign lacked conviction and clarity. Ironically, Jo Grimond had offered us some characteristically wise advice at our Barbican rally. 'Don't let us have a scatter gun approach to policy,' he warned. 'Let us cool it on policy, say what is essential and get it across to the voters so everyone will know by the election what kind of animal the Alliance is.'

Unfortunately, by June 11th the only animal that the public could associate us with was Dr. Doolittle's 'Push-me-pull-you'. The root of the problem was that we had one leader too many. Now that one of those leaders has seemingly set his course for the political wilderness it is appropriate to pause and consider his contribution. Spitting Image may have decided that it has little further use for a puppet of David Owen but his caricature will be well remembered. We in the new party owe David Owen a great deal. That he has decided not to join our new movement, and quite possibly to have led it, is a matter of genuine regret. Not since Grimond had the centre ground of British politics had such an innovative leader. At times his policy statements sent shivers down Liberal spines but the rigorous intellect which forced him to take seriously proposals which were for a long time taboo in our circles was certainly refreshing. We shared many values and despite the much publicised splits on some issues there were reams of policy with which we agreed on both sides of the Alliance. His commitment to constitutional reform and open government, his concern for trade union and industrial democracy, his faith in the National Health Service and the social market economy, and his desire to break our choking two party system made him our natural ally. He stood with us as a genuine, though sometimes sceptical, friend.

Friends can often drift apart and that may be the fault of neither. There is no doubt that there were differences of opinion between Steel and Owen, and often between Owen and everybody else, and that those differences cost us dear in the election. Essentially we parted company on the need for a continuing British independent nuclear deterrent and David Owen's much vaunted admiration for Mrs. Thatcher.

Later in this book I set out my own approach to nuclear defence and disarmament and I don't want to go over the same ground here. Suffice to say that the British Liberal Party since the days of Grimond has always argued that Britain does not need its own nuclear weapon independent of NATO's huge arsenal. Indeed this unique position was a well known hallmark of Liberal policy. David Owen must have appreciated that difficulty. Our Joint Committee, established to look into Alliance defence and disarmament policy, was set to propose, in the late spring of 1986, a formula that managed to contain Liberal misgivings about the independent deterrent and SDP insistence on a policy which would be considered 'strong'. Given the circumstances, David Owen's advance pooh-poohing of that proposal was mischievous to say the least. The proposal was that the Alliance would be prepared to continue with the independent deterrent if necessary. But there was an important caveat: that as a decision to replace Polaris would not have to be made until the mid 1990's and because an opposition party could not be expected to make a decision about its replacement, or otherwise, so far in advance without reference to essential military documents we could legitimately refrain from choosing a definite weapon system.

The formula was wordy but worthy. Ultimately it was every bit as good as our manifesto commitment and I believe it could have been explained to an electorate clearly looking for a balanced policy for disarmament and defence. But for his own reasons David Owen shot the rabbit before the Joint Committee had time to pull it from their hat. Perhaps he perceived it as a tactical defeat which would undermine his credibility. For whatever reason, though, he scuppered our defence policy and began an embarrassing public review which culminated in fiasco at the Liberal Assembly in Eastbourne. The Liberal Party's decision then was not to unilaterally disarm, as was inevitably reported on the evening news that day and in the newspapers the following morning, but to insist that the policy that was to emerge phoenix-like from these ashes should not include a commitment to building a separate European nuclear pillar (the so-called 'Euro-bomb').

The damage done that summer to Alliance defence

policy and credibility jeopardised our General Election prospects. Six months' hard work went in to repairing the damage at a crucial time which would have been far better spent attacking Conservative misrule and asserting ourselves as the genuine party of constructive opposition.

That difference of opinion and David Owen's peculiar tactical awareness and sense of timing cost us dear. But what lost us thousands of votes and possibly dozens of seats, particularly in the North of England, was the public perception that David Owen was a willing bed-fellow for Mrs. Thatcher.

On the doorstep in Liverpool and throughout the North West time and time again I found that ordinary people could not bring themselves to support the Alliance because they feared that David Owen would put Mrs Thatcher back in, even if she had lost her parliamentary majority.

In fact we were prepared, officially, to enter negotiations with either of the other parties in the event of a balanced parliament. After all we offered ourselves as the party of sensible moderation and partnership. It would have been foolish to suggest that our desire to talk only extended to the Labour Party. However, at our Eastbourne Assembly, I argued that in order to talk to the Conservative Party a defeated Mrs Thatcher would have to be replaced. That sentiment was widely supported within the Alliance and among our potential voters. To take that position and then to talk up the prospects of doing a deal with Mrs Thatcher and simultaneously rubbishing the idea of being able to formulate a joint programme with the Labour Party caused confusion and antipathy amongst the electorate.

Dr Owen now considers himself free to tour the country extolling the virtues of Mrs. Thatcher in an attempt to drum up support for his breakaway group. It has been suggested by Tom McNally, a memer of the SDP National Committee that he will be 'washed up on the further shores of Thatcherism' That he was so beached in the full glare of General Election publicity did our cause more damage than we will ever know.

The final difference, and at the heart of the Alliance split, was between David Owen's view that our political system could bear multi-party politics and that a fourth party, or two smaller third parties, could survive intact until proportional representation gave them a realistic chance of achieving power. The majority of the SDP and all of the Liberal Party believe that the breaking of the two-party system needs all the strength and clarity of purpose which one party can bring.

Essentially these were not insuperable differences. Perhaps you could drive a car between them as our critics claimed. But you could and still can drive a bus between Neil Kinnock and many of his MP's.

The Alliance suffered from divisions, perceived and real. I don't deny that differences existed. That was the nature of the beast that we purposefully created. We offered a partnership of principle. Two political groupings who shared basic values and who were prepared to put their differences aside and work together as a symbol of the co-operation and fraternity that we advocated for the system and for our country. I make no apologies for that. It was a brave attempt. Ultimately, if we are to be judged by the harsh standards of success under our corrupt electoral system, we failed – although, despite everything, 7.3 million people (23%) voted for us. The country was not ready for the fundamental change of style and approach we offered and we did not have the money nor the opportunity to change minds. That's politics!

After the defeat we suffered in the 1970 General Election, where we polled just 7.5% of the total vote, the Liberal Party took stock. Out of that brief period of reflection came community politics.

Our political opponents belittle community politics. They complain that it is apolitical, that its concern is with cracked pavements and uncleared rubbish not high-minded ideals and dogma. Some think our belief in the concept is more cynical. Peter Tatchell, the self-styled rebel, wrote after his defeat at the Bermondsey by-election, 'Liberal "community politics" is a fundamentally dishonest evasion of the issues and a cynical vote-catching exploitation of people's grievances and frustrations.' (p.94 *The Battle for Bermondsey*. Heretic Books). It is neither. In a pamphlet produced by the Association of Liberal Councillors called *The Theory and Practice of Community Politics*, co-authors Bernard Greaves and Gordon Lishman write,

'The objective of community politics is not the welfare of the communities themselves. Communities are not in themselves an end. The end is the quality of the experience of each individual within them. The justification for community politics lies in the belief that the key to releasing the potential of each person as unique individual lies in bringing all individuals together in voluntary, mutual and co-operative enterprise within relevant communities.'

It is a way of demonstrating to people that decision making and the stuff of politics is not beyond their grasp. It is a way of re-awakening interest in your habitat, your community and your environment. To be blunt it is a way of kicking people in the backside and tempting them to take their share of power and responsibility.

It is also a focus for political activity. The strategy, officially adopted at the 1970 Eastbourne Assembly, has produced an army of activists and, now, thousands of councillors. But the Liberal Party must now learn that community politics is not enough. It is not a strategy for national power. In General Elections people vote for Governments and for a Prime Minister as well as for local MP's. Our community politics has failed to gain us the trust of the electorate in national elections. In 1987 we failed to offer the basic thing that is required by the electorate: an alternative government. Unless we can put ourselves forward as a Party, as men and women, capable and willing to manage our country then we are simply not credible and all our well intentioned candidates, regardless of their years of dedication to their communities, will never be more than spectators of political life.

So, as in 1970, we must start on a disciplined intellectual journey which will equip us to face the last years of this century. This is an enormous task. It is being undertaken, with varying degrees of reluctance, by all non-Thatcherites. David Steel was right to get us off to a quick start.

In this context it is clear that no bounce was intended. The only bouncing done was by the majority of the SDP's National Committee. Liberals held fire during the internal SDP debate not wanting to impinge on their discussion. We let many criticisms and insults go unanswered. I would like to put the record straight, finally, on one particularly important point: the timing of the merger debate.

On the Friday morning following the election, in the wake of the disappointing result, David Steel telephoned David Owen and told him of his view that merger of the two parties was now vital. David Owen then abandoned his pre-Election line that merger was a possibility and told a Plymouth press conference that he would oppose merger.

The SDP launched into their own ballot without any exploration or discussion of any kind with the Liberal Party as to what forms fusion might take and what might be the policy principles of the new party.

For this series of major misjudgements, culminating in his defeat by his own party members, David Owen has paid an inevitably heavy price. The minority 42% voted not for what he now calls 'amicable divorce', but for closer links of a kind never specified. And, in what was the last ever joint Liberal Assembly, at Harrogate in September, The Liberal Party overwhelmingly endorsed the view that a new united force should be created. This time the majority was slightly larger – 98% to 2%. A margin of victory that even the Politburo might envy.

Our new force should base its appeal on what I have already called the 'enterprise culture *plus*'. Yes, we believe in enterprise; there is nothing wrong with wealth creation. We must acknowledge that people want to work, earn money and succeed. They want to own their own homes, provide a good education for their children and depend on a reliable health service in their old age. People want and demand more than they ever did.

Expectations of standards of living are higher than ever before and not just in the South, the same is true of the North, and in the deprived inner cities. But as things stand, the needy are denied the things that the successful demand. Worst of all they are denied the prospect of success. Sometimes it's called the 'free market economy', but we should not allow the market to run roughshod over the poor, the powerless and the alienated. *Our* enterprise culture would be built alongside a concern for the bitter and the resigned; the people that the market has passed by; the very people that an unelectable Labour Party, which talks only to its tribe and never to the whole nation, will never be able to help.

The demands and aspirations of those millions forgotten by this government will not be ignored in our enabling and sharing society.

I state firmly that I believe in a redistributive system of taxation and that I am opposed to unfettered capitalism. Capital should not be free to dictate to labour. Richard Wainwright, the former Liberal MP, reaffirmed our Liberal faith in an article in *The Radical Quarterly*, he wrote:

'The Liberal approach, in the 1929 Yellow Book and elsewhere, derived from a belief, which seems now to have faded amongst some leading Liberals, that the distribution of wealth is badly flawed and must be tackled. Unsound patterns of land ownership, the effect of two wars in reinforcing monopolies and the failure of Labour governments to achieve serious re-distribution all combine to produce our present divided society, which becomes explosive as the Welfare State palliative crumbles. Where Labour has repeatedly failed, Liberals must tackle re-distribution of capital as well as income in a fundamental and far-reaching way.'

Our position must also strike a proper concern for the quality of life and for the value of the individual. It must assert our dependence on each other at local community level, in our country at large and in the world as a whole.

In creating that kind of country we must be prepared to work with others who share our objectives.

Lloyd George who is reputed to be David Owen's greatest political hero, was a great believer in Coalition Government. He was also unsentimental about party labels and unashamedly advocated realignment after the First World War, when Labour was establishing itself as a major challenger for power and the old parties suffered serious divisions. One change of party label from 'Liberal' to 'Coalition Liberal' did not preclude him from proposing further changes.

In his book, *The Goat in the Wilderness*, John Campbell described Lloyd George's attempt in the early 1920's to form a Centre Party of like-minded Liberals and Tories in a passage amazingly reminiscent of the current controversy in the Alliance:

'He, (Lloyd George) did not believe, however, that he betrayed his past either by leading the Coalition or by contemplating 'fusion'. In the post war world, pre-war divisions seemed to him irrelevant. In the new disturbed conditions he feared both revolution and reaction and thought that only a strong national Government could resist them.'

Too much introspection only hinders the way forward; Great Liberals like Lloyd George, and Gladstone before him, cared more about progress than the safeguarding of party power bases.

In 1988, can there be a re-alignment that is capable of creating a sharing, enabling society? Maybe. With the merger of Social Democrats and Liberals, we have the opportunity to build such a movement. It can be more than the sum of its two parts. We stretch out a hand of welcome to progressive men and women who wish to join in. They will come if they see that. What we argue for our country: tolerance, respect and diversity, we want for this new party too.

Part 2

WHAT KIND OF COUNTRY?

Chapter Seven

WHAT KIND OF COUNTRY?

The 1987 General election was not so much a contest, more a coronation. The period since June has seen continued disarray and ineffectiveness amongst opposition parties. This factionalism has led to the myths of the Thatcher years going unchallenged: and to the political agenda being shaped around the tenets of Thatcherism.

In 1981 *The Police* sang:

'Poets, priests and politicians
Have words to thank for their positions.
Words that scream for you submission
No one's jamming their transmission.'

The transmission of Thatcherite myths has yet to be jammed: the bogus claims that half a century of national decline has been halted; that a new consensus has been created; that the coming of the yuppies is synonymous with a new era of prosperity and meritocracy. The slick words of Saatchi and Saatchi sold the people of Britain a lie. The lie was compounded by the hijacking of St Francis of Assisi's psalm on the night of the 1979 election victory. Harmony instead of discord seems like a sick joke instead of a sacred and beautiful prayer. Our country has been ripped to tatters by needless confrontations which the Government has foolishly encouraged. Claims to have 'curbed' union power, have more to do with an economic recession and fear of unemployment, than with reasoned industrial policies. And as the opposition has argued amongst themselves, Thatcherism has surreptitiously altered the political landscape. But perhaps the characteristic of Margaret Thatcher's Britain which I most despise is the bitterness and rancour which have become the hallmarks of all her government's dealings: the politics of hate, the principles of self advancement; the elevation of grasping greed, and the intransigence and intolerance which she describes as a 'resolute approach'. The bitterness has seeped into every last vestige of British life.

I do not negatively oppose everything that the Prime Minister stands for, but it is important to see these years for what they really are. All opposition within her own ranks has been ruthlessly expunged. The Cabinet has been downgraded and these days it is more a fan club than a collective body critically examining policy. She has abolished tiers of government that stood in her way. She has ridden rough-shod over the political neutrality of the Civil Service; she has misused rather than reformed such instruments of government as the Official Secrets Act; and there is an unpleasing arrogance which John Biffen identified with her use of power. For saying as much he was sacked as Leader of The House – a job he did with panache and integrity.

Private affluence and public squalor. Unthinkable levels of unemployment. Industrial decline. For the first time since the industrial revolution, Britain becoming a net importer of manufactured goods. While Britain has become a low productivity and low skill economy we have squandered £100 billion of North Sea Oil revenue and funds gained by the sale of public assets instead of reinvesting in the future. And philistinism towards the values of the arts, the universities and the BBC. These are the hallmarks of the kind of country in which we now live.

Yes, some people are better off, but three reports in 1987

show what has been happening to those that Thatcherism passes by. The first revealed inequalities in health – with the poor having a shorter life expectancy and an inferior quality of life. The second stated that a quarter of the long term unemployed are deficient in literacy and numeracy and, therefore, to all intents and purposes unemployable. The third points to the 750,000 people waiting for a National Health Service operation, some of whom will die before they reach the top of the list. By denying the existence of a divided nation the Prime Minister is either blind of wilfully oblivious to the truth.

Even those who think they are better off are in for a shock. The collapse in share values exposed the ephemeral nature of popular capitalism. People are encouraged to borrow and to build up phenomenal debts. Credit cards and Micawberism are no substitute for prudence and thrift. In 1979, 2,500 homes were repossessed. In 1986, as the money ran out – it was a staggering 22,000. In what was a country of savers, we have created a country of borrowers. Millions are now servile, hopelessly in hock to an economy based on the principles of the pawn shop.

Robert Kennedy once talked of a 'ripple of hope':

'Each time a man stands up for an ideal, or acts to improve the lot of others, or strikes out against injustice, he sends forth a tiny ripple of hope.' He also said that the future belong 'to those who can blend vision, reason and courage in a personal commitment to the ideals and great enterprises of our society.'

Surely a commitment to a society which sets freedom first – but does not put compassion last – is what could transform Britain. Our country needs a freedom that protects the individual from the State but ensures that the community acts as enabler. We must bring together self-reliance, and participation, voluntarism and co-operation, and, above all, community. This banner could attract people in increasing numbers. These attitudes and ideals are ultimately attractive to the radicals and progressives who spurn the dead hand of the centralised State and believe that market forces are not enough.

Unwatered by the refreshing springs of altruism, generosity, compassion – or even that 'ripple of hope' – is it any wonder Britain has become a spiritual and social desert?

The late Earl of Stockton, and former Prime Minister, Harold Macmillan, understood well how deep the divisions go and where his 'never had it so good' years had brought us, when he perceptively observed, 'It breaks my heart to see what has happened to our country.'

The fight which lies ahead is about more than votes. It is about the soul of our nation and the spirit of our people. To turn dreams into reality will require teonine courage and unrelenting effort. It is a fight in which the crucial question is 'In just what kind of country do you want to live?'

I want to live in a Britain where progressive people realise that privilege – the comfortable side of an unjust system; where we defeat those who preach revolution, not by reaction, but by progress; where we champion the rights of others; show a reverence for the rule of law; and pay more than lip service to the high ideal of the worth and dignity of humanity.

Our enemy should be the personal misery of our own people; a country in which its peoples will be free to inherit their own history and their own identity; a place where the powerless and vulnerable, the voiceless and the alienated count for most. And our watchword must be the maintenance of liberty in a free society.

Chapter Eight

WHAT KIND OF CITY?

As the final results of the 1987 General Election were declared and the opposition conceded defeat, Margaret Thatcher held up three fingers to signify the start of her third administration. Then came the announcement that the third term would be blessed by new policies for the inner cities. Those dirty, decaying disintegrating cities had been noticed at last and were going to be subjected to the 'Thatcher treatment'.

Labour, who behave as if the cities were their personal fiefdoms, believe that the unspeakable conditions in many inner cities are all the fault of Mrs Thatcher's uncaring administration. Unemployment and crime statistics have soared whilst housing and rate subsidies have been depleted. Without the wicked woman's policies, the argument goes, the inner-cities would now be ideal places in which to live and thrive and people would be flocking back to them.

Conversely, the Conservatives argue that it is entirely because the dead-hand of the state, or the local council, has poked its extended finger into every pocket of the city's life that they are in this mess. Over-interference in planning, maladroit and insensitive housing and education policies have all conspired to drive the burghers away. The answer, say the Tories, is to bypass local government and to establish an alternative capable of fostering enterprise.

One of the options canvassed when Labour councils began to defy rate-capping legislation and levying illegal rates was that central government Commissioners would be sent in to run local authority affairs in place of the disqualified councillors. Fortunately it never came to that but the government's gauleiter has crept in wearing the carpet slippers of the Urban Development Corporation.

For any Liberal coming to this argument there is the same sense of frustration and deja-vu as experienced when listening to 'yah-boo' politics across the whole spectrum of political debate. Just as arguments centred on market economics versus clause four socialism; independent education versus state education; private sector versus public sector; or big bombs versus no bombs exclude perfectly legitimate, and often far wiser, third choices the present debate on the inner-cities is becoming similarly polarised. The pity is that there is a grain of truth in some things which both Labour and Tory say. In addition there are some specifically Liberal proposals that we fear will be excluded if the ideological battle lines are drawn between Gog and Magog.

Turning the inner cities into the scene of this Parliament's pitched battle will do nothing for the often deeply despairing people who live there. Liverpool has been a museum of horrifying example. The people of Liverpool have been caught in the crossfire between central and local government like World War One soldiers stuck in trenches not of their own making. This should be a warning to those who seek to impose and those who say they will oppose – no good will come out of the bickering for those who grow weary of battles being fought over their heads. Jo Grimond's dictum that 'if politics is about power and if liberalism is about people then we are for power to people', is not a bad starting point. But today, it goes deeper than that. Power must first go to the powerless; power must be given to the alienated. The power to control and shape your own present and future is more important than subsidies or other substitutes.

I prefer living in a city. I was born in a city – in the London Borough of Tower Hamlets. As a child my family were rehoused to an overspill council estate (many of which have worse problems than the inner cities – a point recognised by the *Faith In The City* report). I cut my political teeth in the inner city in the Birmingham Ladywood by-election of 1969 – a famous Liberal victory. For the last sixteen years I have represented people in the inner city. I suppose I must declare some self interest – and a right to speak – in a debate which looks like turning into a dialogue of the deaf.

What of the Labour Party's approach? They are right when they argue that by and large the market economy has passed the inner-cities by. For every young upwardly mobile newcomer in the booming South East that buys a gentrified terrace house there are many, many more old downwardly spiralling and immobile people imprisoned in fading terraces and caught in the poverty trap. Market economics is simply not enough. Government has a duty to help the poorer people that the market leaves behind. In the 'enterprise culture *plus*' there must be adequate funding to maintain basic services, to provide health care and social services, and to embark on capital projects – preferably the labour intensive schemes which are the least inflationary – in areas of rampant unemployment.

In Manchester's Hulme area, male unemployment among the 12,000 population is 65%, and among blacks, who comprise a third of residents, it is 80%. In parts of my Liverpool constituency unemployment stands at over 50% and in the *Bullring* tenements at the back of Lime Street station I know few families who have work. For the young in these areas the situation is especially bitter and debilitating. For people like this the market remains permanently closed.

Labour, like anyone else, can correctly identify the prob-

lems. Yet it has had its chance to implement solutions and
has failed miserably.

Look at the vast municipal Bantustans that stretch
aimlessly from the cemetery to the railway line or the canal.
Look at the strips of motorway that split and litter our
inner cities; the high rise virility symbols that were erected
because everybody else was doing it; the Civic Centres and
other grandiose municipal status symbols that became the
over-riding political priority whilst communities tottered.
Steeped in their arrogance, that at best was paternal and
at worst despotic, they smashed down humble homes,
destroyed communities and shanghied people to places
they didn't want to go. The Liverpool musicians, Jacque
and Bridie, put it like this,

> 'Don't want to go to Kirkby,
> Don't want to go to Speke,
> Don't want to go,
> From all we know,
> In back Buchanan Street.
> We'll miss a lot of little things,
> Like putting out the cat,
> For there's no back door,
> On the fourteenth floor,
> Of a Unit-Comus flat.'

It wasn't just the lack of a back door. It was the lack of
everything else. There were no shops, few amenities and
even the brewers took their time in getting there. In a place
like Hulme, or Glasgow's Possil Park, the tell-tale signs are
still to be seen: no banks or building societies, and no one
delivering door to door. In Merseyside's Cantril Farm –
known locally as Cannibal Farm – and in nearby
Netherley, spine blocks and cluster blocks, just fifteen years
old (with forty-five years of debt charges left to pay) stand
abandoned or already bulldozed as the inner city solutions
of the 60's become the desperate problems of the 80's.

Liverpool's Labour masters christened their housing and planning policy 'the total approach'. The 'final solution' might have been more fitting.

The consequence of this strategy has been to bleed the cities of the people they need to let them flourish. The forced exodus starved the cities of ratepayers and consequent rate support grant (determined on a per capita basis). As decline set in the mobile also took flight – actively encouraged by this Government to travel to the prosperous South East in search of work. The forced and voluntary exodus created a nation of Dick Whittingtons and starved the Northern cities of the entrepreneur and the self-starter.

Inner London, a desert surrounded by an abundant oasis, suffers similarly – and is too often forgotten. Ken Livingstone has had cause recently to admonish his colleagues in the Parliamentary Labour Party whose ignorant outpourings on the South East have failed to recognise the plight of the inner city boroughs.

That most of London, the South East and now East Anglia are booming is uncontestable. While Liberals in Blackburn demand action to deal with decaying sites and abandoned buildings their Liberal activist colleagues in Berkshire campaign to stop green fields being churned up by developers and volume builders. This corner of the country is in danger of over-heating. House prices are rocketing (the most recent survey suggests that the price of the average house in the South East rises £53 per day), cars and lorries choke the old roads, new office developments spring up on every street corner. The pace of life, and the tensions that run with it, quicken incessantly. Yet the quality of life for those caught up in the rat race diminishes. There might be a boom but the South East is in danger of suffocating itself.

Meanwhile back in the inner cities the overriding sense is one of stagnation. Reduced funds, compounded by rate-capping and by lunatic limitations on the use of council house receipts, stymie initiative and hasten decline.

Looking at the patchwork quilt of decay and permanently half-completed development I am tempted to think that we are in need of an eleventh commandment: thou shalt not bulldoze (until you can be sure of a replacement). I lack confidence in the new-look Labour Party. The city bosses are mainly still in their place and, with some honourable exceptions (Pat Lally in Glasgow for instance who has ardently supported the de-centralisation of housing management) they remain largely unrepentant and ready to prescribe another set of centrally inspired remedies. The Labour paternalist knows best.

The Tories think, too, that they know best. On winning the election, Margaret Thatcher said, 'From Monday we have got a big job to do in those inner cities . . . because we want them too next time.' Yet within eight weeks the Government's approach was said to be 'audibly creaking'. Their policies on education, housing, urban improvement and local government were not 'particularly conducive to confidence in the future'. This was the view of the Conservative Party's Bow Group.

Essentially her Pauline conversion to the needs of the inner cities has caused the Prime Minister to do two things. First, she has fallen in to Labour's trap. She believes that the Urban Development Corporation, like paternalistic local authorities before them, can legitimately superimpose solutions without taking any account of local preferences. There will be Task Forces, City Action Teams and UDC's. They will make some useful initiatives and I freely admit that the Merseyside Development Corporation's International Garden Festival and Albert Dock Development have been successful. The Festival's three million visitors were welcome to our city although few long term jobs came from it. Even the triumph of land reclamation will be lost unless central or local government accept the cost of maintaining the site – the private sector's attempt has been abandoned amidst bankruptcy and scandal. The Albert Dock – with the Tate of the North – is the most exciting development I can remember in the City. Yet, once again the failure to involve local people in any meaningful consultation and the failure to discriminate in favour of using local labour mean that these excellent initiatives seem irrelevant, remote and inaccessible to local people. By cutting out the local authorities, who argue that they could have achieved the same results if they had nothing else to do and were given the funds that were made available to the UDC's, the Government is storing up trouble for itself and creating a seething resentment and unnecessary jealousy. Whitehall emissaries will have to learn how to work in partnership with local councils, local businessmen, voluntary organisations and local people, or else they will learn that the natives can turn cannibal.

The other thrust of the Thatcher approach to the cities is based on the opt-out. The basic problem with this is that the sink-school or the hard-to-let estate will simply be by-passed while the more self-sufficient become islands of excellence, cruelly exacerbating the already sharp social and class differences which exist in our present system. The divided nation will be further fractured and its cities and communities divided into no-go and up and coming areas. A further opt-out will occur as people try to avoid registering for the poll tax – effectively opting out of democracy altogether effectively institutionalising an underclass. This may cause the have-gots to rally around Mrs Thatcher's standard and she may even realise her objective of firming up her vote in some city seats – perhaps securing a permanent majority – but at what cost to community, neighbourhood and family life? The opters-out will ultimately become part of another country comprising an underclass of the alienated and disillusioned.

Such divisiveness has absolutely no appeal for Liberals. Our whole approach to confronting the blighted and neglected parts of Britain requires as a prerequisite the close involvement of those whose future is at stake.

There is a great deal that can and should be done to raise and sharpen the profile of the individual local authority.

On the flip-side of the coin local authorities would have to be more accountable to the people they represent. A local income tax based on the ability of local residents to pay should be introduced instead of the Government's proposed poll tax and the present rating system. Proportional representation would ensure that local representatives were in tune with local people. When local people know that their vote can change things and can feel the cost of local democracy through a local income tax they are more likely to pay closer attention to the machinations of their councils.

I strongly believe we need to involve people in local decision making. Alienation, powerlessness, the feeling that you cannot contribute are the most demoralising things the disadvantaged people of the inner city must face. Involvement is the key. It is not a universal panacea however. Economic solutions are also required. Having a job not only gives you some self respect, it also puts money back in your pocket so that you can exercise economic power. Liberals are often first to criticise socialists for their sublime faith in economic dogma: the belief that all evils can be cured through economic reform. But I have much sympathy with the authors of the Church of England's report, *Faith In The City* when they say:

> 'If the problem of urban deprivation lies in the funda-
> mental structure of the economy (as we believe it does
> in large part), the public policy response is clearly open
> to the charge of being inadequate and superficial.'

Economic decline has hit all of Britain. But no one could deny that the inner-city (along with the satellite housing estate) has been hit the hardest. The inner-city has been the first to pay the price for the restructuring of our indus-trial and economic systems. The irony is that those in the inner city were always the most vulnerable and are clearly the least able to pay what has been exacted.

I shall look closely in the following chapter at creating the jobs needed to bring about the re-generation of the inner cities. What needs saying here is that macro-economic solutions dictated by central government and imposed on local people are not welcome. Again, involvement is the key. Of course the Government must spend public money and regional development agencies are helpful but the answer must be to grow the enterprise culture from the grassroots.

Other issues which directly affect our inner-cities are of national concern. I also intend to look more closely at housing, education and law and order in later chapters. Britain's cities *can* be rejuvenated and transformed. All that is required is will and commitment.

Chapter Nine

WHAT SORT OF WORK?

'Every election is a time of decision. But this General Election on June 11th face the British people with choices more sharp than at any time in the past fifty years.

The choices are between Labour's programme of work for people and Tory policies of waste of people: between investment in industrial strength, and acceptance of industrial decline; between a Britain with competitive modern industries, and a Britain with a low tech, low paid, low security economy increasingly dependent upon imports . . .'.

The opening lines of the 1987 Labour manifesto remind me of a similar choice offered by the Liberal Party in 1929. *We can conquer unemployment* was the bold title of its manifesto. No party since has offered an unambiguous promise of such magnitude.

The economist John Maynard Keynes inspired the Liberal Party, of which he was a member, to make that claim. For many, unemployment had become the twentieth century's great social scourge. Keynes appeared to provide the solution. Economic intervention was the key. Government investment could boost growth – and keep unemployment low.

Nearly sixty years later unemployment is once again the

scourge of many communities and in some parts of Britain it has reached epidemic proportions.

In a census of contituencies, published in 1986 nearly 300 constituencies had single figure unemployment. By contrast in some other parts of Britain unemployment ranges between forty and fifty percent.

People in deindustrialised Britain deeply resent the ostentatious luxury of the affluent, employed areas of the country. The destruction of the North's industrial base and the creation of wastelands is comparable with the punitive policies of William the Conqueror who 900 years ago earned himself the title 'harrier of the North'.

Unemployment not only divides, it disaffects; unemployment is having nothing to do and in the context of our country, than can mean having nothing to do with the rest of us. Unemployed people are a ready-made breeding ground for political revolutionaries, heroin pushers and the criminal fraternity.

The social consequences of unemployment are enormous, for young people especially. In some places they face fifty years on the dole. It's not entirely due to unemployment but juvenile offences have doubled in the past twenty years, and more than half of all those offences are committed by people under twenty-one. Most are unemployed.

Misery and despair are national characteristics once again, as they were in the 1930s. For the Labour Party the solution is expansion financed by government intervention. In fact the same Keynesian message – with industrial growth as the solution – has been repeated for every year since 1929.

Since World War Two controlling unemployment has been top priority for the British Left. Keynes's ideas provided their strategy. Conservatives too were no strangers to the Keynesian fold. In common with all European governments – the postwar period found them pursuing the god of central economic planning.

In the 19770s the economic consensus began to break down. Unemployment began to rise. Shocks to the world economy, such as the oil crises, suggested to many that the old order was collapsing. The new economic crisis, they claimed, could not be solved by traditional Keynesian methods.

The end of Keynesian consensus pushed the Conservatives to monetarism. Frustration affected the Labour Party too. Their policy-makers were not unaware of the breakdown in economic consensus. But, as their manifesto revealed, thinking up anything new was too difficult and the same old solutions are offered still. The Alliance also relied too much on pump priming and traditional remedies – important though some of those initiatives may be.

Economic expansion, or producing more, used to be synonymous with reducing unemployment, but has this connection finally broken down? Is a high level of unemployment now inevitable? And therefore should we abandon the reduction of unemployment as a worthwhile objective? In the words of former LSE Director, Ralf Dahrendorf:

> 'Unemployment is only the outward sign of a much more fundamental reduction of work in modern society. This trend is irreversible.'

Relentless growth as a solution to unemployment is now neither the answer or even a possibility. Some reduction in unemployment is possible with Government stimulation of the economy. But with machines replacing jobs, accelerating expansion will be necessary to mop up rising unemployment. Thus a society geared to continually expanding production – as a means to conquering unemployment – has a hard task on its hands.

Government expansion no longer provides the key. But there *are* alternatives – to both stagnation and growth. A revolution is taking place in the technology that produces our goods. It is an opportunity to forge a very different society. Now is the time to decide what sort it will be. . . .

Questioning the nature and purpose of work is fundamental. Complete automation offers the possibility of a leisure society, where only a few people will have to do only a little work. Is this what we want? Some very confused answers can be heard. Whilst the unemployed demand more work, many in work demand more leisure. At the same time workers are prepared to do even greater hours of overtime. So when people ask for work – what is the basic need they are trying to satisfy?

Most people's lives are spent in work or recovering from work. Yet making work more rewarding and fulfilling seems ever far from the political agenda. Economists and politicians tend to see work not as an end in itself but simply as a means. Work is simply seen as an opportunity to pay for your leisure time. But there's more to it than this.

People seek out work in some sense as a means to self-fulfillment. Yet from the highpaid to the lowpaid this need for *good* work is not being satisfied. It is of no use reciting the glories of full employment unless you can be convinced that the jobs you'd like to see created are actually worth doing. Are some jobs really worth having?

New technology creates the possibility of paying for leisure with decreasing levels of work. But is a leisure society what we really want? The economist philosopher, Schumacher, in his book *Good Work* (which followed the more widely-read *Small Is Beautiful*) argues that work is a necessary part of human life, each of us needs to feel we're contributing to society. He defines human work as having three purposes:

First, to provide necessary and useful goods and services.

Second, to enable every one of us to use and thereby perfect our gifts like good stewards.

Third, to do so in service to, and in cooperation with, others, so as to liberate ourselves from our inborn egocentricity.

He quotes Albert Camus:

Without work, all life goes rotten, but when work is soulless, life stifles and dies.

Despite the motto which appears on Liverpool's crest: DEUS NOBIS HAEC OTIA FECIT (God has provided for us this leisure), the unemployed of my city don't want a leisure society. They want a role to fulfil. But even those in work aren't immune to finding life meaningless. The choice should not simply be between no work and a mass of mindless tasks. We must create *good* work which liberates people by involving them in their community.

How then can the unemployment issue be tackled if a leisure society is not the answer and if Keynesian expansionism is neither practical or desirable? The alternative to this dichotomy requires the building of a new economy within the old. Initially we should challenge the old work ethic – which suggests that people are doing wrong if they don't have a full time job. Given limited work opportunities, what is available should be shared out. Those who do find satisfaction outside the formal economy – for example spending more time looking after their family, shouldn't be frowned upon. I'd like to see a major reform of the tax and benefit system, not only to make part-time work and work-sharing more practical but to encourage it. We have a crude system of work sharing at the moment. It's called unemployment. 87% have work and 13% do not. It is also ludicrous that more overtime is worked here than anywhere else in western Europe – while more than 3 million are jobless.

New forms of work need to be created. All around us are tasks which cry out to be done. A programme of environmental reconstruction, for instance, is sorely needed. Constructive and creative jobs can be created which don't rely on expanding production, giving us more than we need, and consuming more of the planet's resources.

'Quality not quantity' is an overused phrase, yet it sums up the kind of economic reconstruction needed. The quest for producing as much as possible has often meant putting quality to one side. Many things we consume are both wasteful and unnecessary. An appropriate use of new technology offers the chance to re-emphasise quality and to create real consumer choice.

New processes, if directed properly, will allow production to be decentralised to smaller firms. Smaller size creates greater potential for promoting cooperatives where important decisions are shared by workers and where producers are close to their consumers. It is in the small firm that cooperation can work most effectively. The current scheme which encourages the unemployed to set up in business for themselves should be expanded. Small-scale production encourages skills and provides greater opportunities – real participation – to reinvigorate work as a stimulating activity.

Our very approach to unemployment must be more small-scale and sensitive to local needs. Superimposed national solutions have failed in the past and will fail again. That is why we must tailor our response to community and regional needs. A year ago in Manchester I helped launch a regionally based programme called *Worksearch*. It is worth looking at this approach to unemployment.

It was a project that aims to gather data on the unemployment problem in each region of Great Britain, assess the scope for expansion and put forward realistic, costed proposals for getting people back to work. In the North West a successful seminar was held at which the main priorities were identified.

For many years the North West has been going through

a period of painful change. From 1979 the situation has become critical. Between 1981-1985 the manufacturing sector lost 49,000 jobs net, 390,000 people were affected by redundancy 1979-1985. In the same period unemployment rose from 204,000 to 450,000. *Worksearch* proposes a programme to tool up the North West for the 1990's and a crash programme to create 90,000 jobs.

The North West is second only to the South East in terms of population and contribution to GDP. It is in an area with a population approaching that of Sweden. We cannot afford to write off the entire North West, or any other region of our country.

The North West has social, economic and physical problems the equal of those of any region yet public investment per capita has been twice as high in Scotland than in the North West. This is equivalent to a £2bn under investment in the North West over the last 5 years.

Government has set up no effective machinery to co-ordinate regional development. Its successes have been isolated and of limited effect. *Worksearch* proposes an elected Regional Council charged with training strategy, industrial development, investment in public utilities, tourism and health and the spread of new technology to all sectors of the economy. The scrapping of the Regional Economic Councils and the Metropolitan County Councils was premature and regional government is precisely what is needed.

Government has withdrawn money, independence and above all, trust from local authorities. Genuine local government is necessary for effective regional growth.

Government has shown an obsession with short term cash cutting. Its initiatives such as Youth Training Scheme and Manpower Services Commission's in the Community are under researched and under-resourced, it's high time they were under scrutiny. 35% of Youth Training Schemes fail to meet the Manpower Services Commission's own standards. Take up rates are less than 70%.

Government has failed to appreciate the depth of the

reforms, needed in Education and Training. There can be no hope for the North West unless it can fully realise its human potential at every level. *Worksearch* proposes a concentration of effort towards helping new small firms grow. It also proposed a 10 point plan for small businesses including the introduction of business and enterprise into the school and college curriculum, decentralised buying by large firms trying to break into the export market, such as 'Buy British Shops' abroad. Our message is that more people need to plan a positive and creative part in the economy. The right kind of premises are needed but they are not enough. There is a co-operative at Wigan which is refurbishing a Mill as small workshops and Liverpool's Docks New Enterprise Workshops in the disused south docks are examples of where the right climate has been created to enable people to realise the untapped spirit of enterprise which still exists even in the most run down areas.

The *Worksearch* proposals for the North West include: the restoration of grants to industry to 1984/85 levels, a £12m Industrial Credit Scheme, a whole new programme to help very small businesses expand, a new range of incentives and assistance for application of microelectronics to products and processes, a leading roll for Universities and Polytechnics in the development of leading new industries.

Worksearch report identified there is a need for increased public expenditure of £570m. This extra investment, which would create 95,000 jobs, would be specifically targetted at the following areas:

Alleviate Distress: £60m would be spent on social services, particularly for the elderly. £55m on health, particularly preventive measures and transfer of patients from large inhumane institutions, £115m on house renovation to deal with unfit and unsatisfactory housing.

Cost Saving £40m would be spent on school repairs to save bigger bills later, £10m on energy conservation.

Tooling up for the future: £100m would be spent on education and training, £20m for technological research and development in centres of higher education. A doubling in the number of Information Technology Centres. A major curriculum review to give children an understanding of industry and enterprise. At the present time only 20% of small firms in the North West make any use of microelectronics.

Worksearch proposed efficient expansion, proper cost benefit testing of capital projects, use of innovative combinations of public, private and voluntary sectors, regardless of the effect on individual empire building. We do not just want more of the same, we need new ideas, invention and far sightedness.

Our proposals are realistic and have been tested on the Treasury Computer Model. They would not give rise to rampant inflation or unacceptable levels of public borrowing. The Strategy has been accepted by a wide range of opinion as both sensible and achievable.

Implementing *Worksearch* inevitably involves a real cost. It would mean no money for short term tax cuts; It would require those in work to accept reasonable wage rises. Those in work need to give those out of work a fighting chance.

Worksearch was mainly undertaken by volunteers in their spare time. Its proposals would give some hope to the 7 million of that Region. Its counterparts all over Britain would hold out an alternative to the dole.

Everyone – employee, employer and union – must be involved in working out the solutions to unemployment. By-passing the Unions won't work. With 3 million unemployed the Government have temporarily silenced the Unions through fear, but solving industrial unrest or creating new jobs cannot be about destroying trade union power. Large powerful firms are by no means preferable to large powerful trade unions. Its more about breaking down firms into manageable sizes where employers and workers can be partners. Despite new technology, smaller-scale production could be more labour intensive. Improving the *quality* and *nature* of work means to increase the *quantity* of *good* work.

We *can* conquer unemployment. But not overnight and not without some radical social changes – in the way we distribute wages and in the way our firms are structured. Our attitudes to work also need a radical re-evaluation. There is an old, apparently Haitian, proverb that says: 'If work were such a good thing, the rich would have kept it all to themselves.' We have in this country what is often called the Protestant Work Ethic. This is based on Paul's Epistle (2 Thessalonians 3:6–13) which contains the words: 'If a man will not work, he shall not eat.' But Paul's words must be read in context. The whole passage is about those *who will not* work. But the Protestant Work Ethic has been so strong that we have lost sight of precisely what he said. After all, why should we glory in tedious and repetitive work? Our society has placed too much reliance on the need for and value of work for work's sake. Traditionally a job gave self respect. In the post-Industrial world we now live in we must be prepared to respect people regardless of whether or not they have a traditional job.

The full employment that I envisage would be less immediate than that offered by the Kinnock manifesto. But it would be full employment in a much wider sense of the word – an opportunity for work that really fulfilled people – utilising the talents which each of us has been given. It would be based on the sharing of opportunities and the linkage of solutions to personal and local aspirations and needs.

Chapter Ten

POVERTY AND A GOOD SOCIETY

Mrs Thatcher often places great emphasis on the quest for 'Victorian values.' She usually manages to forget, though, the Victorian vices. Endemic poverty is on the increase in Mrs Thatcher's Britain, and the scourge of poverty which affected so many of our people a century ago is still very far from being eradicated.

Who are the poor? First, define your standards. Poverty can be either absolute or relative. If poverty is defined in absolute standards – that is, consumption of necessities – then the numbers of the poor have declined from about 20% in 1953 to about 2.5% in 1973. But in relative standards – in other words, relative to some measure of income in the general population – there has been no change. The net income of the poorest groups of our citizens has remained remarkably constant as a proportion of median income over that period. The poor have stayed poor – and since the 1979 election, have usually managed to sink even further into poverty. It was Abraham Lincoln who correctly observed that a nation cannot survive half slave and half free. In Britain there are gross discrepancies between oceans of affluence and islands of poverty.

Defining relative standards of need is itself difficult, of course. The most readily identifiable measure of subsistence is the level of supplementary benefit – fixed by Parliament each year as the safety net below which no one without income from full time work should be allowed to fall. For a 'typical' family consisting of a married couple with one child aged under 11, and one under 15, the benefit entitlement would come to £75.35 – and rent and rates up to a reasonable level would be paid by the local authority – assuming, that is, that their overloaded bureacracy can cope with the mass of claimants.

I doubt whether there are many people who would like to try and bring up a family on less than £11 a day. Yet in 1981 4.8 million people lived on this margin of poverty. Even more staggering, a further *2.8 million* lived – or tried to – *below* the officially-defined poverty line.

Furthermore, there is plenty of evidence to show that it is impossible for many families to make ends meet on these levels of supplementary benefit. Studies have shown that deprivation increases markedly if income falls below 140% of supplementary benefit – and this was also the level of income which the Breadline Britain survey by LWT showed was the very minimum on which most people thought the poor should have to manage. 7.3 million British citizens have incomes between 100 and 140% of the Supplementary Benefits level. A grand total of *16 million* people – of whom 3¾ million are children – live on or below the margins of poverty. That's almost 30% of our entire population and half a million people are living in homes that still lack a hot water supply or other basic amenities. Such figures, it might be thought, would be enough to stir the Government into action. Yet during the first four years in office (and the government have refused to publish figures more recent than this, probably because of their sensitive nature), the total number of people living on or below the poverty line increased by 47%, nearly half as much again. Unemployment was the main culprit. Since 1981 the situation has worsened further. The tax burden on the low paid has remained at a higher level, and although some cuts in benefits were restored in November

1983, other benefits have been abolished or cut further. Most importantly unemployment has risen to tragically high levels, and despite the recent falls, remains higher than at any time between the end of the war and the onset of Thatcherite austerity in the 1980s. In my own constituency there are areas where over half the people are out of work. Perhaps surprisingly, however, it is not the unemployed who comprise the largest section of the poor. Of the 9.1 million poverty-stricken non-pensioners, 2.6 million were unemployed. In contrast, 3.8 million were in work. These are the low paid.

The implementation of the Fowler Social Security Bill in April 1988 will certainly not improve matters, and is likely to make things a lot worse. Indeed, the review that proceded it was given a definite brief to reform social security *without an overall increase in government expenditure*. So any increases in one kind of benefit have to offset against cuts in others. The 1986 Social Security Bill is therefore not a redistribution of wealth, but rather a redistribution of poverty. One of the many cuts included in the Bill was the total abolition of Single Payments for people without such basic items as beds or cookers. These were replaced by a discretionary 'Social Fund', which in most cases will not give grants but loans, to be repaid out of already breadline incomes.

What is low pay? In 1983, the last time when Official Government figures on households in poverty were published, the gross weekly earnings necessary to attain a net income (subtracting taxation, national insurance, travel to work expenses, and so on) equivalent to the Supplementary Benefit entitlement – and that was £66.25 for a family of four – was £105.45. 680,000 people in work actually earned *less* than that equivalent. Another 3.1 million earned up to 140% of that level. Nearly a third of those became poor during Mrs Thatcher's first four years. . . .

Working families suffered from a relative fall in wages,

an increase in taxation and national insurance, and a cut in the real value of child benefit.

Contrast the plight of the low paid with the conditions of the most well off. In 1978 the lowest paid 10% of male workers had earnings which were just over 2/3 of the average ie 68.1%. By 1983 this had dropped to 64.1%. Over the same period, the relative earnings of the highest 10% of male workers had *risen* from 157.7 to 169.7%. Successive tax cutting budgets have made the rich richer and the poor poorer.

And, lastly in this chain of appalling statistics, there are the changes in the distribution of pay over the last 100 years. In fact, we will have to look hard. As the Department of Employment has itself said 'the distribution has changed little, particularly at the lower end, over the period from 1886 to the present day.' In fact, in 1886, the lowest paid 10% earned a *higher* proportion of the median (68.6%) than they did in 1981 (64.1%). Here indeed are Victorian virtues – or vices. But it must be borne in mind that stability does not mean inevitability. In the case of women's earnings, statutory intervention in pay in recent years has resulted in significant improvements relative to male earnings. Wage levels can be influenced; either to show improvement, as demonstrated by the Equal Pay legislation, or to the detriment of the low paid, as recent policy has shown. It is a question of political will and political priorities.

What are the consequences of low pay? First, self-evidently from the statistics, it is a major cause of poverty and all that is associated with it. Low pay may mean poverty in childhood, parenthood and old age. It is those who have had the least opportunity to build up resources because of low earnings who suffer most hardship when their incomes are further reduced or earnings interrupted, such as during sickness and unemployment. The low paid have little opportunity to accumulate savings, occupational pension rights or assets which help to prevent poverty during old age. This life cycle of poverty was first observed by Rowntree eighty years ago but remains no less widespread today. Other features of poverty Rowntree would have recognised include the pensioner so poor she bought catfood to eat herself, or the street people sleeping rough on the streets of London in cardboard city or underneath the arches. Low pay has serious consequences for the employer as much as the employee. The establishment of minimum standards of pay (and conditions) within industries has usually been welcomed by employers in order to prevent firms seeking short term competitive advantage through wage undercutting. Nevertheless, in sectors where firms are small and unorganised and where unions are weak, the whole industry may have come to rely on cheap labour. In these industries there is generally poor investment in training or capital equipment and little incentive to maintain a stable workforce. Productivity is poor and staff turnover high, with the result that overall efficiency suffers.

The final consequence of Britain's low pay problem is that the Government is failing to meet international commitments concerning minimum standards of pay. The Council of Europe concluded as early as 1981 that the UK was not conforming with its commitments under the European Social Charter – specifically, 'the right of workers to a remuneration such as will give them and their families a decent standard of living.' In other respects the Government has directly disowned its commitment to provide fair standards of pay. In 1983 the Conservatives renounced the International Labour Organisation Convention 94 concerning fair wage clauses in public contracts – the first Government ever to take such action in the 65-year history of the ILO.

Renouncing this Convention allowed the Government to rescind the Fair Wages Resolution, originally conceived in response to a report on sweated trades under the 1891 Conservative Government. It was designed to heighten the standards of contract work done for central government by stipulating that firms offer workers the accepted pay rates for their trade. In 1946 the Labour Government extended its scope to cover other conditions of employment. In rescinding this elementary form of wage regulation the Government is setting back nearly one hundred years of progress. Among the reasons why they followed this course of action was to allow them to contract out services such as NHS cleaning, local refuse collection, and so on. The firms which tender for these contracts are often able to offer low prices because they pay their employees absurdly low wages. Subsequently, of course, they may raise their prices (having held them artificially low to obtain the contract), though without raising wages.

I don't intend to go much further into the responsibility of this Government in causing poverty, but the rescinding of the Fair Wages Resolution, the abolition of Schedule 11 of the Employment Protection Act, the attacks on wage councils have all been part of the process. The real question is what should we do to stamp out our own domestic poverty? For 20 years I have subscribed to a Party whose constitution insists that none shall 'be enslaved by poverty, ignorance or conformity.' Almost since the Party was founded, Liberals have been at the forefront of the fight against poverty. The foundations of the welfare state were laid by Lloyd George and the great reforming Liberal Governments of 1906–14. Another Liberal, William Beveridge, was responsible for the framework of our current social security system. In 1944 in the House of Commons in his maiden speech, Beveridge thundered against the giant evils of squalor and poverty. In keeping with this, the 1990s must see a new major attack on poverty. The first priority must be to repair the damage done since 1979, for every category of the poor. For pensioners, I would abolish the earnings rule for retirement pensioners, restore the link between pensions and earnings, uprate pensions more frequently, pay an additional credit to those not receiving the full benefit of the '75 pension scheme, and make a generous increase for those over-80, including those receiving a non-contributory pension. In 1971 the Age Concern Manifesto pungently asserted the needs of elderly people in a manifesto: 'The elderly need to have sufficient income to meet their needs for social physical and emotional well-being; accommodation which ensures their right to privacy and the retention of their own material possessions; and the freedom to exercise those preferences and prejudices which express their individuality and sense of the past. They need easy access to transport to enable them to supply many of their own wants and to pursue their personal inclinations. They need the security of knowing that, in the event of an emergency, they will not be put at risk through the failure of essential domestic supplies or shortage of basic food stuffs whether living in residential institutions or their own homes, they need the kind of help, care and domiciliary support which will help them to obtain the maximum degree of independent living in spite of increasing infirmities or disabilities.' For families, I want to see a real increase in child benefit to cover real costs more adequately than at present, improved assistance for one-parent families, including widows, the extension of invalid care allowance to married or cohabiting women, and fair treatment of war widows. For the disabled, there should be a comprehensive and unified disability income, a disablement cost allowance as well as mobility and attendance allowances, and simpler and more sensitive methods of assessing entitlement to disability benefits. We must aim to reduce delays, and end the degrading and humiliating household duties test. Most importantly, job creation plans would put many people back to work – the initial commitment would be to reduce unemployment by 1 million over the first two years – and thus take them back out of poverty. We must help the low paid by restoring the lower rate of income tax which the Conservatives have abolished, and lift tax thresholds. But most importantly, we should integrate the tax/benefit system, including, among other factors, a statutory minimum income – thereby eventually abolishing the category of the 'low paid' altogether.

I have long been in favour of the integration of the tax and social security systems into a 'tax credit' scheme. Thorough reform of the system is needed for two reasons. First, because the original Beveridge plan of a welfare system has been amended on a piecemeal basis so that the structure no longer has any overall coherence – 44 different, but overlapping, benefits are now available to those who succeed in penetrating the DHSS bureaucracy. Second, because there are simply too few resources devoted to the present system overall. Any society calling itself civilised, yet in which almost 30% of its members live in poverty, is in desperate need of reform.

A tax credit would replace the present complex system of tax allowances and welfare benefits. If an individual receives no income, then this tax credit is automatically paid out to them – thereby effectively establishing a minimum income for all, young or old, sick or healthy, in work or out. Any earnings the individual manages to bring in are assessed for tax liability, and the liability offset against the credit. If the tax credit is greater than the liability, there is a payment to the individual. If the liability is greater than the credit, the individual pays into the system. The withdrawal rate of credit is less than 100%, thus ensuring that the citizen benefits to a certain extent from any earnings he or she is able to find – unlike the present system, where withdrawal of benefit and tax liability combined can often be greater than the increase in earnings. This is the 'poverty trap', in which by earning more, the family actually becomes worse off.

So, the tax credit scheme would abolish the poverty trap. Additionally, it would enormously simplify the tax/benefit system, and reduce collection costs. The amount of the tax credit would be flexible to take account of need – larger credits being allowed for the elderly, the sick or the disabled, or those with dependents. It will cost us more, of that you can have no doubt, but it would mean a fairer Britain and a happier country. A new Beveridge-type redistribution of income is necessary for the eradication of the frightening evidence of poverty we can see in Britain today. That must be a major political priority. This attack on poverty is basic to our strategy for creating in Britain a more united and caring community. I believe Britain must be an efficient and competitive society. That is the enterprise culture. But in addition we must seek a civilised community using the resources provided by a revived economy to guarantee to all the security and self-respect that are every citizen's right. And then 'distribution shall undo excess and each man shall have enough'.

Chapter Eleven

HOMES FIT FOR HEROES

The first housing problem I ever took up in 1972 as a student running for election to the local council was that of Mr and Mrs Livsey who lived in Liverpool's Prospect Street.

Mr Livsey was born in Prospect Street. It could have been in one of many similar streets in central Manchester, Glasgow, Cardiff, Birmingham or Leeds. In fact, Mr Livsey's home was in inner city Liverpool and had been home for fifty years. His father had been born there as well.

Back in the 1940s and 1950s thousands of folk like Mr Livsey had struggled to collect their coppers together and managed by hook or by crook to buy the homes they had rented for years. Mr Livsey's home was his prized possession and like so many others, he regarded it as insurance against old age and destitution.

From time to time minor repairs and improvements had been done, all without the aid of grants. With the help of friends in the trade he had built a lean-to bathroom and WC. It saved the walk down the yard to the outside loo.

But Prospect Street and the other little streets round and about were ear-marked for a road-scheme and speculative development. Mr Livsey's home was part of the rolling programme.

The council, always anxious to be fair, offered the residents 'full market value'. One of Mr Livsey's neighbours received £750. No one had received enough for a deposit on a new house and anyway most residents would have been too old for a mortgage.

The council had considerately decided that the people of Prospect Street would be offered a tenancy in one of the new estates on the outskirts of the city. Before making Mr Livsey an offer no one bothered to ask what he thought about the move.

In fact, Mr Livsey loathed the idea of becoming the council's tenant; he thought the rents were too high; he ridiculed the design: 'It's like a rabbit warren; I'd need a compass to get me in and out.'

He despised the humiliation of having to apply for a rent and rate rebate and the inevitable supplementary benefits he would need when at 65 he had to stop working: 'It's like charity. I've always paid my way.'

He saw himself becoming reliant on the hand-outs of some officious bureaucrat: ' . . . like a little Hitler; treats you like scum'.

Like Mr Livsey, the lady who had kept the corner shop for as long as anyone could remember would be out of a job. He himself would be deprived of his livelihood because his occupation was opening the gates at the abbatoir for early morning lorries. Quite apart from the expense of travelling by bus there simply wasn't a bus that left the estate early enough to get him to work.

So, in one fell swoop the council were taking his home, his job, his friends, his childhood haunts and the security that he was counting on for his wife and himself in their old age. They were changing his whole pattern of life, destroying his self-respect and pushing him into pawn.

All this to get some land for a developer who hoped to make a killing; all this to get some land for a new road scheme that the planners later abandoned because they decided they could no longer afford it; all this to create just another barren, empty space.

The council had waged a war of attrition against a whole community, painstakingly and deliberately running down a whole neighbourhood. Pubs, shops, even churches, had been closed. The street lamps were all out; the pavements were not maintained; the street sweepers, missed out Prospect Street.

Vandals and thieves had looted adjacent houses; lead had been ripped off the roofs. Where childhood friends had once lived, Mr Livsey encountered meths men, vagrants and rats. The ugly derelict eye-sores were tinder boxes and death traps for his children who were growing up amid dereliction and decay – in the corpse of a community that had been murdered.

All this had been done by the planners and the experts. In a blitzkrieg of raze and rise, these smash and grab merchants destroyed family life and security when they bulldozed the humble homes of our inner cities.

For the sake of Mr Livsey and thousands more like him we must develop a system of planning that shows sensitivity and concern for the wishes of those whom decisions affect. We must all become planners: playing our part in the shaping of our towns, our cities and our countryside.

Politicians must interpret the decisions of the experts and the computers in terms that people can understand. The planner must not be like the rich man in Tolstoy's fable who is prepared to do anything for the poor man except get off his back. That is the beauty of the co-op where 'everything is held in common' (Acts 2).

More Than Bricks and Mortar – The Housing Co-operative

Outside the rain fell steadily. Arc lights, mounted high on the buildings, cut through the darkness. Their glare was reflected in the pools of water collecting in the broken tarmac of the courtyard. Groups of youths gathered on the sheltered balconies, occasionally exchanging high-pitched shouts or screeching whistles.

The block's small youth centre was packed. Residents had gathered to hear about their prospects for rehousing from the deputy chairman of the city's housing committee, who was also their ward councillor. Two years before they had been promised that new council housing estates were to be built close by. Since then there had been a change of government. Plans for new housing had been cut. They were not pleased.

Caryl Gardens was one of Liverpool's largest tenement blocks. In the 1930s its construction had been praised as a model of all that was best in working class housing. Separated into ten sections, some facing each other and others overlooking a central yard, its 350 flats opened onto short balconies connected by stone staircases mounted in turrets which climbed up to six storeys high. Each had a tiny bathroom and kitchen, as well as bedrooms and a living room. In a city with some of the worst slums in Europe this had once been paradise indeed.

A strong community spirit had been part of life in the tenement block. Older residents looked back with fond memories to the days when no-one bothered to lock their doors, when the women kept the balconies spotless while the men went to work. If children misbehaved the greatest fear was that neighbours would tell their parents. People were poor, but they shared a sense of belonging and the security of being amongst friends and family.

Times had changed. Unemployment in 1981 was higher even than in the 1930s. Liverpool's South Docks, just a few hundred yards away, had closed entirely ten years before. Manufacturing industry was reeling under the effects of the Government's economic policies and longer term changes in the pattern of trade. Each day the *Liverpool Echo* reported new job losses. Crime had risen to the point where insurance companies refused to provide cover at any price for householders or shopkeepers.

Fear had replaced fellowship, particularly amongst elderly residents. People were frightened of being alone, of the constant threat of a break-in or burglary, of a violent attack in the darkness where lights had been vandalised and left unrepaired.

Standards had fallen. Those who cared were no longer prepared to clear up after those who did not. Dog excreta littered the balconies. The staircases stank of urine – animal and human. A stream of foul language, abuse and invective from both child and parent alike might be the response to a complaint about the former's behaviour. The cosy flats now seemed restricted and out of date. Coal fires had been replaced with gas heaters, bringing with them new problems of damp; condensation turning clothes mouldy in bedroom wardrobes.

Residents wanted something better. They wanted to move out, and they came to the meeting with suspicion. They were Labour. The councillor was Liberal, and they had all been told that that was as near to being a Tory as made no difference. Anyway, he was an outsider, had been to university and spoke with a posh accent. Few of them had voted for him.

He knew that a straightforward and honest approach was the only way to deal with a meeting which could otherwise be aggressive and unpleasant. So he spelt out the facts as seen by the city's Liberal administration.

First, that new council houses had indeed been planned for a neighbouring site, although not enough to rehouse more than a quarter of Caryl Gardens' residents. Now none were to be built. The Conservative Government had cut the council's housing investment programme and the council was concentrating its remaining resources on the refurbishment of existing properties, especially those with outside lavatories and lacking other basic amenities.

Second, that despite this setback every resident would be rehoused. They would be top of the list for a move to existing properties as they came empty. The geography of the city's housing meant that if they wanted to live locally they would probably have to settle for a flat of their choice. To get the tenancy of a house they would almost certainly have to move away to a more suburban part of the city.

Third, those people in work should consider the possibility of buying a house. Payments towards the purchase of terraced houses in Liverpool were not always that much more than those of council rents, and the city would provide a 100 per cent mortgage facility so no capital was needed.

Fourth, anyone determined to live locally in a new house might consider the idea of forming a housing co-operative. The Liberals thought it so important for the future of the city to try and re-establish strong communities that they would adjust their main housing priorities to find the money to finance housing co-operatives.

The more vocal residents made it clear that they did not think much of the options put before them. But amongst them were people who had long wanted to move to a different area, or who knew that they would not have qualified for a new house in any case. The meeting broke up, residents filing out into the rain grudgingly accepting that the councillor had at least put the options before them honestly. A few stayed behind to ask him individual questions.

Amongst them were a group of women who asked: 'What were you saying about a co-operative?'

An impromptu second meeting began and the councillor tried to explain.

Housing co-operatives can be formed by any group of people. Each member buys a £1 share which is their only financial stake. This gives them one vote and an equal right to express an opinion or participate in the making of decisions. Once registered as an Industrial Provident Society they become legal bodies, able to negotiate for funding and sign contracts but responsible for sound financial management.

There are two types. In an ownership co-operative the members collectively own and manage their properties, perhaps building them in the first place or purchasing them from a landlord and carrying out rehabilitation and modernisation work. Management co-operatives by comparison are responsible only for decisions affecting the day to day running of existing properties which remain in the ownership of the landlord, usually the local council.

By 1981, when the meeting in Caryl Gardens took place, Liverpool already had more than a dozen ownership co-operatives. The first had been formed in 1972 by the Shelter Neighbourhood Action Project. Based in the Granby Street General Improvement Area it worked to improve existing terraced houses, trying to keep the community together through local control of allocations.

Liberal policy in Liverpool during the 1970s aimed to halt the demolition of older properties, and instead fund housing associations to buy and improve them. Eventually the city came to have the largest programme of housing renewal in the country, with 31,000 properties in designated improvement areas. Rehab co-ops fitted in with this policy, and there were ten carrying out work in Liverpool 8 by this time.

The first new-build housing co-op, Weller Streets, had been formed in 1977 by residents of a slum clearance area who wanted to keep their community together. With funding from the Housing Corporation, their 61 unit housing scheme began to be developed less than a mile from Caryl Gardens in the autumn of 1980.

Meanwhile the Liberals had given their backing to a number of other new-build co-op schemes in various parts of the city, most of which had had their applications for funding turned down by the hard-pressed Housing Corporation. They had a common desire to re-establish lost communities, but not all met the council's strict criteria of housing need. The Liberals gave them a guarantee of financial support for new building in an effort at pump priming, to encourage a continued flow of interest in co-ops.

So the councillor was able to suggest that the women from Caryl Gardens talk to people like themselves who had practical experience of co-ops. Thanks to the work of past years there were also professional organisations in the city which could provide expert guidance.

Chris Davies was the councillor, and that meeting was the beginning of the Grafton Crescent Housing Co-operative. The next time their young councillor met the group it was in the offices of their professional advisers, Co-operative Development Services (Liverpool) Limited, and he was able to promise them full support from the city's ruling Liberal administration.

The co-op had elected a chairman and other officers, and it came as a surprise to learn that these were all men, none of whom had been at the original meeting. One of the women commented. 'We had to make sure they got involved. We can't succeed unless we all pull together.' They were good tacticians!

The co-op's name was Grafton Crescent which somehow seemed a bit pretentious at this early stage before plans for the 30 houses had even been prepared. 'Well, we wanted a bit of posh!', said one lady with a grin. And why not? Regaining a sense of community pride was one reason for the group coming together.

Liberal backing for co-ops in Liverpool was first expressed in the late 1960s when Cllr Roger Johnston moved a city council motion giving them support in-principle. Rehab co-ops were funded alongside housing associations throughout the 1970s, and Cllr Trevor Jones attempted to establish a management co-op on a new council estate in Kensington – only to have the idea destroyed in 1976 by the arrival of a Labour administration which would have no truck with the view that ordinary people should have the right to determine who did their repairs.

But it was not until 1980, with Cllr Richard Kemp as

housing chairman, that the promotion of co-ops became a mainstream part of the Liberals' approach. He initiated the policy, and Chris Davies developed it and started to shape a series of adhoc initiatives into a coherent policy.

An article in the *Architects' Journal* (September 1982) described the situation:

Something incredible has happened in Liverpool – arguably the most important step forward in British housing for decades. Without anyone in the rest of the country really noticing, an era spanning 60 years of paternalistic public housing has quietly come to an end. . . .

Liverpool City Council . . . funds the people who need new housing to organise the design, construction and management of it themselves through self-generating, self-reliant co-operatives. . . . When the houses are built, the co-op members become tenants of their homes, paying standard fair rents, but they are also collectively the landlord, responsible for management and maintenace.

The need for participation by tenants in public housing has been talked about for years. . . . But the Liverpool new-build co-ops are totally different. The tenants are not being asked to participate or be involved – they are actually and firmly in control.

There was an explosion of housing co-ops between 1980 and 1983. Fourteen, ranging in size from 19 to 150 families, received local authority funding for design work to proceed, and there were many others in the pipeline at a formative stage.

A bandwagon was rolling. The biggest difficulty in the way of establishing co-ops – lack of practical local knowledge about them – had effectively been overcome.

Their expansion was so rapid that detailed discussions were commenced to establish long term policies, aimed at ensuring that new co-ops seeking finance from the city council took their members on the basis of housing need, and to determine how vacant co-op properties were to be re-let with the council's involvement but without damaging the integrity of the co-op by introducing people who would not co-operate.

Liverpool's housing problems were immense, and the money available to tackle them very limited. Whichever party was in control none had succeeded in improving the maintenance and caretaking of estates and blocks of flats – and there was fierce opposition from the trade unions to plans for change which would give the tenants a better deal. Having only minority control of the council made it impossible for the Liberals to act resolutely in this respect. Meanwhile vandalism, decay and neglect were accentuating every other difficulty, making life a misery for thousands of people.

Further promotion of co-ops was certainly the wish of those of us committed to dealing with these problems by encouraging the involvement of tenants in the decision-making which affected them and in the raising of standards and sights. But only a limited number of new-build co-ops could be financed, and it would take decades before they could change the shape of the city's housing.

The answer had to lie with management co-ops, in which tenants would take responsibility for the running of their own estates. But there were none existing in Liverpool, strong opposition from both Labour and the unions to the very idea, and a genuine doubt over whether anyone would want to take responsibility for run down housing which the council had failed to manage properly.

The Eldonian Community Association provided the solution. Representing the people in part of the South Vauxhall area, a close knit, working class and strongly catholic community of tenements and depressing walk-up flats, the Eldonians were hard-headed, determined, practical and positive. They wanted housing improvements but also to keep their community together. Realistic about the council's financial problems, they were always prepared to explore new ideas if this would help achieve their objectives.

An early meeting to discuss the tenement rehousing programme had led to the formation of the Portland Gardens Housing Co-operative, effectively a new-build scheme. By no means everyone in the area could benefit from it, and Chris Davies floated the idea that a Tenants Trust should be formed to improve and manage existing flats in the Burlington Street tenements.

The council had recently sold Myrtle Gardens, a large tenement block close to the university, to Barratts, as an alternative to pulling it down. The builders were hard at work converting the place into a complex of secure and comfortable flats for sale. If flats like these could be improved to such a standard that people would want to buy them, could not the same be done with similar flats for rent? Previous improvements had often been seen as a poor investment, the flats rapidly becoming as unpopular as before. But with tenants' self-management perhaps this could be changed.

A draft agreement for a Burlington Street Tenants Trust was prepared. To last initially for a four year period, the trust would become responsible for the day to day management of the flats, including caretaking, repairs and allocations. As a stimulus the council would provide capital for major improvements to be made under the direction of the trust and its own architects.

We hoped this would prove the breakthrough, leading on towards the further development of a housing policy aimed at encouraging Liverpool's tenants to take control. As experience with the new-build co-ops had proved, once practical examples were underway other schemes could follow in their wake. Tens of thousands of properties could be renovated and managed by tenants' trusts.

The Eldonians' committee consulted the community as a whole. They wrote to Chris Davies with the result:

The residents of the tenements in Burlington Street, Eldon Street and Limekiln Lane have now all met and discussed in detail the Management Scheme.

Everyone was given the opportunity to attend and we had a 70% attendance at the meetings. There was a unanimous and favourable response to the Schemes. Now we need a City Council Resolution to start negotiations between Council Officers and our association.

We are now with our advisors working on a management agreement and we will discuss this with your Officers later in May.

The letter was dated 3 May 1983. It arrived on the day that the Liberals lost control of the city council.

Liverpool's housing policy was changed immediately and fundamentally. There was to be no place for co-ops or for tenants to have control over their own housing. Funding for co-ops was immediately cancelled, and only those schemes which had already signed final contracts with the council were able to proceed.

The Eldonians put their views very forcefully in a community newsletter with the headline: *PORTLAND GARDENS HOUSING CO-OP. WE'VE BEEN BETRAYED!*

The Labour Party are destroying people's dreams hopes and wishes by refusing to back housing co-ops. Is it just because co-ops weren't their idea but schemes aided and encouraged by the previous Liberal controlled council?

How can a party who say they represent the working class be against housing co-ops? Surely one of the basics of socialism is workers co-operatives, so why are housing co-operatives so different?

Co-op houses are houses for rent, they provide homes for people who can't afford to buy but who wish to have more say in the planning, upkeep and rent of their homes. If people take on more responsibility for their housing estates – through co-ops – this is one way of ensuring the maintenance and upkeep of houses and estates, which in the long term means less outlay for repairs due to vandalism etc. And provides a better standard of rented accommodation for years to come.

When the Labour Party canvassed in the May council election no mention was made of their anti co-op housing views. . . . We've been betrayed!

Grafton Crescent was amongst those co-ops which had obtained contractual commitments from the council before May 1983 and was able to carry on building. It was completed in May 1984. Two others, Shorefields and Mill Street, succeeded in gaining alternative funding from the Housing Corporation. The rest, including Portland Gardens Co-op, were 'municipalised'; the council taking over the architects' plans from the co-ops and building the houses as traditional housing estates.

Initially a sceptic, the Eldonians' chairman, Tony McGann, said some months later that 'It's the best thing that's happened to this community. It's got everyone working together and looking to the future.'

Once the idea had caught on they refused to accept defeat.

Their membership joined the local Labour Party en masse, and became the most vociferous critics of the Militants tactics and the party's local housing policy. One of their number, John Livingstone, a devout and committed christian, is now a local ward councillor.

And they campaigned vigorously to gain the land and Housing Corporation finance to build a new 150 unit co-operative housing scheme on the site of the former Tate & Lyle sugar refinery close to their homes. They lobbied everyone from councillors to government ministers, gaining friends in high places fighting off attacks from the city's new administration. They even enlisted Archbishop Derek Worlock to go into battle on their behalf at a Public

Inquiry. And against all the odds they won! In 1987 it was announced that they had gained all the backing they needed and overcome all opposition. The scheme was underway.

In Liverpool and elsewhere, Liberals have shown themselves to be strong supporters of the co-operative movement. At its best it demonstrates attitudes and action which we regard as close to the ideal, as a model for society as a whole. It is probably a reflection on the failure of the Liberal Party to present its views clearly and coherently in the past that this has taken some people by surprise.

So why am I such a strong supporter of the co-operative idea? Part of the answer lies with our strong belief in the need to create genuine communities, in which people of different abilities can work together towards a common goal, supporting the weak as well as allowing the strong to take initiatives.

Some of these sentiments were expressed in a letter from the Dingle Mount Housing Co-operative appealing, for city council backing for their plans:

> The membership, as the name suggests, are all from the Dingle area of Liverpool 8. 90% live in tenement flats and are currently included in the 'Tenement re-housing programme'. The remainder live in varied accomodation ranging from multi-let flats to maisonettes.
>
> The Co-operative's member content is varied, we have pensioners, couples with children, couples with grown up families, and single people. We have also catered for health cases, we have a blind person, wheel chair cases, and some members who are housebound. These people need specialised housing, the type that a Co-operative Housing Scheme can provide.
>
> Although our area has its problems, its our home and we wish to remain in it with our families and our friends. We are a thriving community and have all the facilities we need locally. Many members have lived in the area

all their lives, why should they be uprooted and moved
to areas where they do not want to go and where they
will certainly not by happy?

Pensioners' bungalows are at the heart of the Grafton Crescent scheme so that they can be overlooked by residents in
the surrounding houses – a good example of deliberate
design to ensure that the elderly are not left isolated.

Individuals should have the right to the maximum possible influence over the decisions which affect their lives.
For those who can afford it there is a lot to be said for
home ownership – mortgage commitments notwith-
standing.

But what is there for those who cannot afford to buy? Is
it to be nothing better than welfare housing, in which those
without jobs are denied all responsibility and pushed from
pillar to post at the mercy of the bureaucracy in housing
offices and social security departments? Or should these
people have the opportunity to contribute to their
communities in a way which gives them dignity?

Most of the members of Liverpool's housing co-operatives will define themselves as working class. Few have had
anything more than a basic minimum of formal education.
Most have never lived away from the city. The income of
many comes from social security benefits and pensions.
With continuing high levels of inner city unemployment
their prospects for improvement are not good.

The full potential within human beings is hardly being
touched at present. That is why we must develop the role
of individuals within our society, raising their aspirations,
encouraging them to develop their talents to the full, and
believing that they have a contribution to make to others
in the community as a whole.

The Conservatives' materialist philosophy encourages
the strong to trample the weak in their desire for petty
power or a wish to purchase still more possessions. In the
long term (which is not far away) we are all dead, so what

is the true benefit of owning more and more goods yet having no community, living in fear and having to bolt doors and windows and fit the house with a burglar alarm?

When Grafton Crescent Co-op was formed, no member had previous experience. Their vision was a new house in the same neighbourhood. They joined with others and started to work together, learning about the law which controlled them, about housing finance and planning conditions.

They had to choose their own architect: placing advertisements, carrying out interviews, inspecting the work which each had undertaken in the past, and asking a crucial question: 'What is the worst mistake you have ever made?'

The creation of a housing co-operative is more than a matter of bricks and mortar. For the first time in their lives the co-op members were working with well-educated, middle class professionals. They were learning the jargon. No longer powerless, unable even to understand what the professionals were talking about, they were designing a housing estate, negotiating its funding and seeing it built brick by brick. And all the time they were gaining in confidence, providing support for each other and realising that by working together they could achieve more than as individuals acting alone.

The Eldonians are not only building a new village in the inner city to be administered by the villagers themselves, but are investigating the possibility of forming workers' co-operatives to produce goods, providing services and create employment for themselves. In the Basque country – overlooked by Madrid – it was a priest who helped establish a people's bank and then a series of workers co-operatives. The Mondrugon co-ops may be a model for cities like Liverpool where many people just want the chance to pull themselves up by their own bootstraps.

Liverpool's housing co-operatives have proved an inspiration. The movement has survived and grown despite the opposition of the Labour Party locally, and the schemes have been visited by almost every political figure of note: Grafton Crescent's members even playing host to the Prime Minister.

Undoubtedly their example helped bring about the changes in housing law embodied in the 1986 Housing and Planning Act which encourage the formation of co-ops to manage or take up the ownership of existing local authority housing. But it is not enough and I introduced a Right to Co-operate Bill in Parliament last year to try and give co-operatives more incentives and greater rights.

Since 1979 there has been a massive and welcome increase in home ownership. Those who remain in deteriorating rented accommodation are increasingly amongst the poorest in society. But as Liverpool has shown, the inability to own their homes does not mean the individuals cannot have control over them.

A massive expansion of the co-operative movement throughout Britain is possible. If every individual is to be valued, and not just those who enjoy prosperity, then the opportunity to realise it must be grasped with enthusiasm and political determination.

'Homes fit for heroes' promised Lloyd George in 1919. These days on some of our sprawling council estates you need to be a hero to go on living there.

The municipal empires often fester in neglect and indifference. We must challenge municipalism by handing over estates and properties to tenants co-operatives and to individual owners. In 1978 when I was Liverpool's Housing Chairman we gave Corporation tenants the right to buy. We gave away derelict land to developers, contracted to build low cost homes for sale with priority for existing tenants. We initiated self-build schemes. Later we gave away derelict hard-to-let blocks to private enterprise and saw condemned municipal slums turned into cheap, yet attractive, owner occupied houses; and our Action Area programme, the biggest in this country, saved row upon row of terraced housing previously threatened by Labour's bulldozer. This approach led to real housing diversity.

Militant stopped all this when they came to power. They set out to smash the housing co-operative movement. They arrogantly declared that the tenants and their homes should be under their exclusive control (a control which has lead to 8,000 council properties standing empty at this very moment).

I believe that diversification and gradual dismantlement is too slow a process. What should be done? The Government's White Paper on Housing, published in September 1987 should be given a guarded welcome. My colleague Simon Hughes MP, commenting on the White Paper's publication, said:

'Liberals share certain of the Government's objectives such as the need to break down the monolithic nature of the large estates and to give tenants much more control over their own lives. We also welcome an increased role for partnership housing. We agree too that tenants who have a right to buy should be able to enforce this without the present increasingly unjustified delays imposed by local councils and we share the Government's view that the level of rents should give landlords a reasonable return.' But the whole thing smacks of complacency to me.

One radical idea that increasingly attracts me especially, is simply to give away the blocks, streets and estates to those occupiers prepared to take over ownership and to form housing co-operatives. The outstanding loan repayments could be met nationally and a nation of co-operators and owners would be created over night. Occupiers then freed from rent burdens could use their money to maintain and repair their houses. We would see immediate improvements. Once people have a degree of control (control conferred through the fact of ownership) over their homes; once they are given a real stake in their communities; once they feel that they have something to look after and care for; then the face of our inner city housing estates would change to the good. The responsibilities of ownership will provide a shot in the arm. Now when a window gets smashed, and the current yearly bill for replacing Liverpool's windows stands at hundreds of thousands of pounds, tenants don't bother to ask who did it – they just wait for the 'Corpy' to come and replace it. Often the Council does not come out to replace it and properties start to decay as tenants grow weary of waiting. As the Eldonians and others have shown, that simply need not be the case.

Chapter Twelve

POLICE, CRIME, AND VICTIMS

Every year for the past 30 years crime has risen by an average of 6%. Far from containing the ever increasing rise in crime, Government policies have allowed the situation to deteriorate into near chaos. Recently the London Evening Standard highlighted the case of the Beatons, a couple in their 'eighties' who were viciously attacked in their own home in the St Martins estate, Tulse Hill. When no-one came forward as witnesses the police branded the Beatons' neighbours as cowards and the police themselves were attacked as they made house to house calls on the estate. With incidents like this occurring regularly, especially in inner city areas and with one serious crime being committed every 9 seconds, it is hardly surprising that the people of Britain are demanding to know when this madness will come to an end.

In 1988 every family stands a one in four chance of becoming the victim of a serious crime. Since this Government took power serious crime has gone up by 40%, theft by 25%, violence against the person by 31%, burglaries by 59%, criminal damage by 65% and offences involving firearms are up by 48%.

Mrs Thatcher cannot even claim that her Government is on top of the situation. Since she became Prime Minister the number of crimes solved has fallen from 42% to 35%

. Nearly three burglars in every four get clean away and only one vandal in every five is ever caught. Whilst crime is obviously worse in the inner city areas, even those in the country cannot ignore the rise in crime, for example the number of offences recorded by the Police has risen by 31% in Devon and Cornwall since 1980, 29% in Suffolk, 33% in Norfolk and 37% in Sussex.

These statistics are frightening enough but they may be only half the truth. A survey by the Centre of Criminology and Police Studies at Middlesex Polytechnic showed recently that in Islington, Britain's fourth worst crime area, there are twice as any crimes committed as are actually reported to the Police. Since 1979 the number of offences committed per Policeman has risen from 24 to 29.

In 1983 the Conservative manifesto calmly assured us that: 'Already street crime is being reduced and public confidence improved in some of the worst inner city areas.'

The people of my own constituency would find that claim very difficult to swallow since in Liverpool burglaries now occur on an average of one every nine and a half minutes. The burglary rate is three times the national average and two out of three crimes go undetected. Crime in Liverpool seems to pay! A survey published 18 months ago showed that Merseysiders believe that the priorities of the Police should be changed. The public wanted an improved emergency response, thorough investigation of crime, and the maintenance of a deterrent presence on the streets. Merseyside is a perfect testing ground for checking out the public's declared priorities. Not only do we have a massive crime rate but we also have the highest ratio of Police officers to public outside London: 3.10 officers per 1,000 members of the population. At £71.58 a year for every man, woman and child in the County of Merseyside, ours is also the most expensive force outside of London.

Merseyside has 4,600 police officers – of whom 1,900 are allocated to patrol work. Yet on average a mere 185 divisional patrol officers will be on duty at any one time.

Given that some of these will be in court, interviewing suspects and answering calls, the number of police officers actually on the street is further reduced (to about 2.7% of the force). In other words, the most bobbies on the beat at any one time will be 126 (and that includes the traffic and operational support divisions).

It's a long way from Dixon of Dock Green. The public say they want more police on the beat – but less than 3% of the local force are used for this purpose. The public want more time spent answering emergency calls – yet only 3% of their time is used doing this (compared with 6% interviewing informants, witnesses and suspects). All told, some 56% of police time is spent inside police premises. Nearly a quarter of their time is spent on paperwork and administration. The public also say they want more time used to investigate crime – yet 71% of CID time is spent inside the police station.

However, even more worrying, the police have far too little knowledge or contact with the areas they serve. On Merseyside 81% of officers live outside the divisions in which they work; 57% admitted to having neither friends or relatives inside the division and 47% said they spent none of their leisure time there. If some officers spent more time in the place which they police they might have a better chance of dealing with local problems. Not that I would knock the police. They have a difficult job to do which often requires great bravery. But they must realise that if they want public co-operation then they have to pay attention to the public – and give them the kind of police force they think is needed.

The Government has received plenty of warning about the inadequacy of their policies on law and order. Even the Chief Constable of Greater Manchester has admitted that; 'The day of reckoning will surely come. The Government cannot possibly say they have not been warned.'

My mind goes back to 1981 and the Toxteth riots. One Saturday morning a constituent of mine came to my advice centre. He asked me to come home with him and see the damage the police had done while searching his house the night before. The place looked as if a bomb had hit it. Two teenage sons were brooding in a corner. I wasn't surprised when a few weeks later it was one of these young blacks who was involved in the incident which triggered off the Toxteth riot.

After my visit to the Cooper's house I rang the office of Derek Worlock, Liverpool's Archbishop, and asked him to advise the local Chief Constable that unnecessarily heavy handed policing would lead to confrontation and violence. I also supported Mr Cooper's complaint to the Police Complaints Board. The problem of course is that the police investigated the police and (with the watchdog far too closely identified with the burglar) they came out on the side of the officers. Ultimately Mr Cooper fought his case through the courts and received compensation and justice, but at what price?

As a young city councillor – still a student in 1972 – I was arrested by the police. Coming home from a local church I was stopped by some young people who asked me about the lack of local amenities. A police panda car pulled up and before establishing who any of us were or what was going on I was pushed against a wall. The police took me to the local police station and charged me with obstruction under section 78 of the 1835 Highways Act. When it came to court and it became clear that they had arrested a local councillor talking to his constituents, the magistrate threw out the case. But if I hadn't been a councillor; if I hadn't been articulate; or if I had been black; I wonder what would have happened?

Yet I have also been grateful to the police. My own home and my car have been robbed regularly. Another time my face needed stitching up after someone threw a brick; and the regular threats and attempts at intimidation have all made me aware of how much we need a police force to maintain our liberty in a free society.

The way to restore public confidence in the police and to prevent rising crime is to get more bobbies back on the beat. In this way the police can be seen to prevent crime instead of merely responding to it. With a return to community policing and closer consultation between the police and the local community they serve, public confidence and trust can be restored.

I have consistently called for proper funding for our police to restore morale and to provide them with the necessary resources to prevent crime. We should also cut out unnecessary political interference by people who never miss a chance to knock the police.

Next we should encourage more people to set up neighbourhood watch schemes so that the public can become actively involved in crime prevention, further encouraging good relations between the police force and those they are supposed to serve.

We should also recognise the powerful link between crime and drugs, by taking tougher action against drugs barons; and by responding compassionately to the needs of young people who must be given the chance of a job, self esteem and self respect.

There is enormous ignorance about the relationship between drug abuse and the way addicts come to steal in order to pay the pusher.

In some parts of the country heroin abuse is not a casual vice but an epidemic. Enslavement to the pushers breaks body, mind and spirit; and for many brings the prospect of a squalid and early death.

DHSS research covering the whole country reveals that the number of addicts has risen from 3,000 in the so-called drug-crazed 1960s to probably 100,000 in the heroin-hooked 1980s.

Heroin constitutes a powerful pressure for crime. It wrecks families, friendships and communities. It can be cheaper than going to the cinema or the pub – for a little as £5, two young people can buy sufficient heroin for a night. The BMA claims that one in three secondary school pupils has experimented either with drugs or gluesniffing. In 1982, 238 young people along the road that leads to the ruin of their lives? There are surely many reasons, but one must be the attempt to cope with the stresses and strains experienced in grappling with the complex demands of modern Britain.

Prince Charles recently recognised the link between the futility, rejection, isolation and hopelessness of so many young people and the growing menace of drugs abuse and rising crime. But the Prime Minister dismissed his remarks as anodyne.

Dr Martin Plant, one of Britain's authorities on drug addiction stated recently, 'I feel very pessimistic. Until recently the UK was a drug backwater. I used to think that it would continue to be so while we had low unemployment. Now that there is no indication that unemployment is falling there is little hope of solving the drug problem.'

But, Government spokesmen have consistently denied that unemployment was anything more than just one among several factors.

They should abandon their prejudices and examine the facts. One in five of the Merseyside population is unemployed, and half of the local dole queue is under 30. Almost a quarter of the unemployed in my constituency have been out of work for more than five years. And as the dole queue has soared, burglaries, break-ins and muggings have increased in unprecedented numbers.

Against that background it is no coincidence that heroin abuse and drug addiction are increasing. Crime and addiction feed one another – it costs £200 a week for some addicts to stay on heroin, and they obtain that money by theft and petty fraud, or by becoming dealers themselves. The sheer boredom and frustration of life in an economic disaster area kills the work ethic and the sense of responsibility that holds a society together.

So what can be done to combat this problem? One

remedy must be to try and stop the heroin entering the country. Heroin smuggling has increased by 400% since 1979, yet acts in the civil service during the same period have decimated the customs service. As a direct result of Government policies, 3,561 officials have been shed yet closer port scrutiny is vital if drug imports are to be reduced. Similarly, the hard-pressed drugs squads should be strengthened as a matter of urgency.

The police should make a top priority, the pursuit of mafia-style drugs barons. I successfully helped co-sponsor a Bill through parliament which imposes life sentences on these racketeers. We now need retrospective extradition arrangements with countries who have given safe havens to the drugs barons.

There are a wide variety of potential preventative measures that could also be taken. Doctors should be more cautious about prescribing controlled drugs – and in general we should move away from an over-dependence of drug-taking. School children should be better educated in the dangers of drug abuse. The media should adopt a more responsible attitude. Voluntary organisations have an important role to play – and groups like the Merseyside drugs council should have more funds made available.

A more concerted and determined attempt to combat the growing menace of heroin must be made. I want to see more pressure exerted on producer countries; a restoration of personnel in Customs posts and an increase in the number of police in drug squads; and tougher sentencing against the organisers of the drug rings, but a more sensitive and compassionate response to those who become addicted as well.

But, above all, we want to see policies for our youth which will strengthen their self-esteem and self-respect, enhance their future prospects, and end the feelings of hopelessness and despair which drives them towards heroin.

At present young people feel very bitter. Alfred Lord Tennyson could have had them in mind when he wrote:

What shall I be at 50
Should nature keep me alive
If I find the world so bitter
When I am but 25.

Drugs, hopelessness and ugly surrounding all conspire together to reduce people's standards and their aspirations. If you dump people in a ugly environment don't be surprised if they end up doing ugly things. If you dazzle people through the TV with the unattainable don't be surprised if they start using TV's methods to obtain what they want.

Techniques of violence on television can often seem admirable to and be imitated by young people. Children are strongly affected by realistic events close to their world. We have not yet taken the intrusion of television into our lives fully into account.

Violence on television often creates the wrong kind of images and anti-hero figures in people's lives. The impression should not be given on television that violence does not lead to injury, as it often is. Similarly, dangerous situations which children could easily imitate should be avoided.

In too many television programmes violence has become the norm and that has de-sensitised children. Some 700 pieces of published research show a link between watching violence on television and enhanced aggressiveness among viewers. Channel 4 provided a red triangle against programmes to warn viewers that the programme could contain distressing sequences. Perhaps, that could be emulated by other television stations. Although even this is of little use if parent's take no notice of the warnings.

Programmes like the 'A' Team are broadcast mid afternoon and carry no warnings but violence is sanitised and made to appear perfectly acceptable.

Criminal techniques should not be used by television producers as a legitimate way of achieving objectives. Far too often that is the case in television programmes.

Finally in looking at how we can cope with contemporary crime we should provide decent compensation for the victims of serious crime and establish statutory victim support schemes in every local authority.

In 1982 I laid before the House of Commons a Bill which set out to do two things for victims of violent crime.

First, my Bill sought to establish statutory victim support schemes in every local authority. It would be their job to complement the work already being done by voluntary organisations which, with the best will in the world, are unable to provide comprehensive cover for the entire country. On Merseyside, volunteers such as Mrs Joan Jonker of the local Victims of Violence organisation, do an excellent job, but they are the first to point out the inadequacy of simply relying on volunteers.

Under the terms of the Bill, once the police have been notified of an offence, they would immediately get in touch with the victim support unit, which in turn would arrange a visit to the victim. No one should underestimate the value of help, comfort, advice and administrative assistance at a moment of great personal desolation. Yet, at present, apart from the police taking details of the crime, a victim is often left in isolation and fear, haunted by the prospect of their assailant returning. A much more practical and sensitive response is required.

The support unit would assess the needs of the victim and then co-ordinate the response – help perhaps from the DHSS in replacing stolen electricity or gas money or the rent money; perhaps a visit from the doctor if that is needed or a visit from meals on wheels or the home help service, provided through the social services department. The installation of a security system might be needed – something as simple as a lock on the door or a burglar alarm – or help in obtaining sheltered accommodation through the local housing department.

That type of immediate aid, comfort, support and help requires more than voluntary efforts could possibly provide, operating as they do without any major financial backing. One year, the pitiful government subsidy to the National Association of Victim Support Schemes was the princely sum of £23,000, which was divided between the national headquarters and 60 local schemes – about £380 per scheme. It was further estimated by Roger Berthoud, writing in The Times, that for every pound that is spent on offenders about 1p is spent on victims – a ratio of 100.1. That is a grotesque position. A great deal of sentiment is expressed about victims, but there is no point in being long on sentiment while short on cash. Parliament must make better provision to aid voluntary groups when they exist, and to make statutory provision where they do not.

Liverpool City Council initiated a pilot scheme to provide intruder alarms in the homes of 300 elderly people. We need more initiatives like this.

How we treat the vulnerable and the weakest members of our community is a touchstone of a civilised society. If more work was done to prevent crime – for example, by preventing easy access into elderly people's homes – much unnecessary cost in financial as well as human terms might be avoided.

The second area covered by my Bill dealt with the need to reform the present terms of reference, scope and practice of the Criminal Injuries Compensation Board and the Criminal Injuries Compensation Scheme. The reforms would include the disclosures of all relevant information by the CICB to victims and their legal advisers that would be helpful or necessary to the victim's application for compensation. There should also be a right of appeal from decisions of the Criminal Injuries Compensation Board, and local boards should be established for the sake of

accessability and to improve the promptness of investigation and decision. It cannot be right that two Merseyside
mothers whom I met had to wait 18 months for their claim
to be settled, following the tragic murder of their two sons.
They also told me that they had never had a visit from a
local authority welfare worker or social worker. One of the
families was forced to go to a finance company to get a
loan to pay for the funeral of the son.

The Government should also examine the ludicrous situation whereby a victim is unable to claim legal aid when
pleading his case before the Criminal Injuries Compensation Board. There is more than a touch of Gilbertian
irony in the present administration of the legal aid system,
whereby the offender can usually easily claim legal aid but
not the victim. Similarly, the victim should have complete
access to information about the injuries he sustained and
the circumstances in which the offence was committed. A
duty should be placed upon the courts to determine and
place on record the victim's injuries.

At present, it would appear that there is no such person
in law as the victim of a crime. A victim, in the eyes of the
law, appears to be a person who may or may not be called
upon to give evidence tending to convict or acquit the
person alleged to have committed an offence. If the person
is acquitted, the courts appear to have little further interest
in the matter, even if the victim has been gravely injured.
On the other hand, if the accused person is convicted, the
courts may or may not make a compensation order on
behalf of the victim. That cannot be done unless an application has been previously lodged. That really is too cavalier a way to treat those who have been on the receiving
end of the crime. Although we must pursue humane penal
policies we have allowed a unbalance to grow between
victim and offender. In England and Wales there are nearly
two and a half times as many cases of wounding every year
as there were 10 years ago. Robberies involving violence
have doubled in the same period. In London, where nearly

one-quarter of all English crimes take place, wounding has increased by 50%, between 1975 and today. Such offences are not confined to London. In Nelson, Lancashire, an 81 year-old woman was killed for the £5 that she had in her home. In Manchester a church service has been switched from the evening to the afternoon because of attacks on members of the congregation.

I end in Liverpool, with the stories of two constituents. One lady aged 80 years was attacked in her flat and raped. Her screams for help were ignored. The rape took place at 5 o'clock in the morning. By the time a neighbour realised that she was screaming the assailant had escaped. The 80 year-old lady was left physically injured and severely shocked.

The other case concerns a council tenant living on the Chatsworth Street estate in Edge Hill. He was a man without legs, confined to a wheelchair, he said of the break-in of his home: 'Someone came in the bedroom window and hit me with a cobblestone. He hit me five times. He took 40 cigarettes and the gold watch that was given to me when my legs were taken off.'

These are only two of many cases but their plight eloquently illustrates why this debate cannot be left to the 'law and order' lobby whose policies have so dramatically failed our country.

Chapter Thirteen

A LIFETIME OF LEARNING

In the battle to safeguard our children's future education is at the frontline. We all worry about the rising generation. How can we influence them? Media and television seem too far off and too neutral to control. The local school however seems just as influential. Here many feel that something is going wrong. But blaming beleaguered teachers is too easy. So often they become our scapegoats.

We're not satisfying the needs of teachers, pupils or parents. Teachers are tired of a government which has removed their negotiating rights, forced them to implement new exam syllabuses and ever more changes. Disenchantment amongst teachers runs very deep. Many are disillusioned with the education system itself.

Social security for sixteen year old school leavers is being removed. Yet currently they queue up to leave school. They feel unstimulated and resentful of education. An educational study on Merseyside found an absentee rate of 40%.

Parents are sensitive to pupil dissatisfaction. They feel unsure that their children will be prepared to face the world and unhappy that they are insufficiently involved.

The different criticisms of the education system mirror conflicting ideas of what education is actually about. The system needs to be a balance between learning skills and learning human values. Skills are needed because they allow people to understand the language of a society that is ever more complex – and allow them to find a useful role in it.

Values are important because the world is meaningless and bewildering without a sense of right or wrong, and life is difficult without a sense of purpose and a confidence in oneself. Balance between these two purposes is lost – but which aspect has become too important?

As work is only seen now as a means to leisure so a good education in increasingly seen only as a means to a job. Education is about the preparation for life. If life is only about material advancement, then providing qualifications to secure high-paying jobs is its objective.

This is a conservative view of education. It treats it in a narrow utilitarian way. In doing so it emphasises the skill aspect of education. The purpose of syllabus reforms are to make exam grades measure the skills that employers require.

Rising unemployment has strengthened the argument for the materialist approach. The hardship of unemployment has left few untouched. Who doesn't worry about their children's chance of a job? Pupils too have become employment-anxious – hence the rising interest in technical subjects.

Humanities are under the axe. When its a question of priorities the sciences are painted as the only essential subject. Survival in the twentieth century depends on our ability to inculcate scientific literacy. And if the arts and humanities can't be entirely eliminated – the utilitarian ethic dictates that they should at least become more practical.

But do such concerns make for a better education? They certainly don't make it more enjoyable. Whilst economic worries make for quieter classrooms, they don't stimulate much excitement, don't generate much imagination or capture much interest from school students.

Education is not only about fitting into life but about

understanding it. People face the world with incomprehension – how can the find a sense of purpose and a motivation to achieve if they fail to find values which make sense of the chaos? Education is firstly about broadening horizons – to help provide understanding and destroy ignorance of the world. Overspecialisation limits our children's access to the wide range of opinions and ideas that will stimulate them. Stepping beyond normal experience is the weapon against ignorance. Secondly, it's about creativity encouraged by fostering imagination and continual desire to ask questions. These together provide the basis for passing on values and standards.

This sort of education is stimulating. Its less about learning facts off by heart and more about challenging preconceived ideas. Knowledge comes alive when it gives understanding and answers questions. The ability to question and to recognise controversy should not be left till later on. It should be fostered from an early age.

Yet nothing can be passed on at all without leadership. For me its nothing worse than a tragedy to see the lack of morale and disheartenment among the teaching profession. If teachers feel broken, have lost *their* sense of purpose, their enthusiasm – how can they provide that essential charisma which young people need so much?

We should value our teachers. They can do more to improve educational standards than any other single factor. Instead of being our most important educational resource, teachers have become progressively more disenchanted and demoralised. Constant sniping criticism from government ministers; inadequate resources; slum conditions in schools, and finally the long and bitter pay dispute culminating in an imposed settlement and an end to negotiating rights, all these have combined to undermine teachers' confidence, reduce their commitment and destroy their morale.

Wrangling between unions and the frequent disruption of industrial action have damaged relationships within staffrooms and between schools and parents.

I would like to see an immediate restoration of negotiating rights; a professional salary for a professional job; a fair and effective way of settling disputes; and a new voice which can speak for the whole teaching profession on educational matters. Four specific things we could do include the establishment of a framework to restore teachers' rights to negotiate their pay and conditions, with an independent Pay Review Body to assist the process and a procedure for ultimate arbitration if negotiations fail; the acceptance that the status and salaries of teachers must encourage the recruitment and retention of able graduates, and reward good classroom teaching as well as management ability; development an appraisal system to assist in teachers' career development and significantly extend inservice training; the enhancement of the sense of professionalism amongst teachers by establishing a General Teaching Council (This should be elected by all teachers, rather than appointed by the unions, with representation for parents and industry as well).

But there's nothing more fundamental than teaching values. That's why overemphasis on science and cuts in arts and humanities, is so disturbing. The problems in our world are not caused by the lack of technology but by the misuse of it. Personal problems such as stress, loneliness, family disputes and divorce, drug abuse, violence and political unrest – none of these result from any failure of science. They are a consequence of collapsing human relations.

World problems – Third world famine, the global arms race, mass unemployment – these too don't have purely scientific solutions. Famine will continue until people learn to share the resources they have. East/West tensions will continue until trust between people is restored. And unemployment will continue until a new social system shares our workload more equitably. These are human problems – they can't be solved by merely scientific analysis. They require an understanding of other people, a sensitivity to the needs and concerns of others. They require values of love and understanding – to destroy the barriers of hate. When we were children we were told to 'love our neighbour'. These days they are encouraged to then ask 'how much?' Isn't this precisely what is going wrong in our lives, our communities and in our world?

What do world problems have to do with school students? Is not their greatest need secure employment? That's certainly important but world problems concern us all. Only by teaching young people to understand the world they live in and to feel they've got a role in it can we tackle the estrangement they feel.

It's part of personal development – at least as important as learning employable skills – to think more widely. No-one should silently pursue their individual career and life without thinking of the collective results of their actions. We daily see the results, the neglect, that is the consequence of ignoring other people, ignoring basic values of love and human concern. The lack of love is not just a global issue – it's a national issue, a community issue, a family issue; and a personal issue – because a cold heart destroys the soul.

Education has to prepare people to face the world of work but intelligent and aware pupils are just the individuals that are useful to employers as well as society. All aspects of education are important – and the balance needs to be restored. Strong science funding must be maintained – but here too the emphasis can be placed on the creative aspect.

Rather than restore balance Mrs Thatcher's education programme could further harm the system. One of the greatest barriers to creative teaching is the rigidity of the curriculum and in particular its examination-orientated framework. Those teachers that do have a more visionary approach – who aim to stimulate their pupils – find themselves hindered by the need to always work within the exam syllabus. The Government's new National Core

Curriculum will further rigidify the syllabus. Increased centralisation could also stifle independent initiative.

Similarly, an over rigid examination system encourages the teaching of conformity. Extending examinations to a younger age could seriously affect the progress made in primary and early secondary school education. We want higher quality education with higher standards not a return to learning by rote.

It is of course, easy to measure number of facts that someone knows. But more important than the ability to know a fact is an ability to question it. Inventive and enterprising minds are created by teaching people to question and take nothing for granted.

It is in our primary schools that we must lay firm foundations for our education system. At present they enjoy cinderella status and that, together with the controversy in the secondary sector, has left parents unaware that:

– the rising population of 5 and 6 year olds has led to many overcrowded reception classes;
– there is a growing shortage of teachers training in early childhood education;
– after years of cuts, many schools are in poor condition, need redecorating and repair, and are short of books and basic equipment;
– many of the stimulating aspects of school life that enhance children's educational progress – music, school journeys, visits to museums and theatres – have suffered drastically from cuts, as well as from the effects of the teachers' pay dispute;
– in-service courses for teachers – for instance to enable them to teach primary science and computing – are in short supply;
– research findings and parents themselves tell us that not enough is being done to help children who are falling behind in the basic skills.

For all these reasons I would like to see an urgent review of the policies directed at primary education. Local authorities must be given sufficient resources to maintain and equip schools adequately and schemes must be fostered to involve parents more closely in their children's education. I would like to see the establishment of an education ombudsman service to safeguard these rights; and an increase in the size and powers of Her Majesty's Inspectorate, so that it could act more effectively to bring about improvements.

Not just in primary education but throughout the service, Britain needs a strategy that addresses real educational needs. In the country I'd like to see education which would be a life-long process with access to the system for people of all ages. Recently there's been drastic cuts in adult education. This should be reversed, new technology and science would be promoted in schools – as part of creative approach emphasising their use and applications. The arts and humanities should be defended to promote a questioning and a broad outlook. But they too need to be more socially aware. Narrow specialisation need to be avoided – an interesting and more useful education comes from wide knowledge. These syllabus innovations would be encouraged at all levels but particularly by a decentralised structure – that allows parents and pupils to chose their schools but refuses to allow central government to dictate the curriculum. Education needs to be reinvigorated – to revive interest in the process from both teachers and pupils. That means parents need to be constructively involved – not to be set up in confrontation with the teachers but in a process of continual dialogue. If instead of this a school simply opts out under new Government proposals it will merely add to the distortions in our devastated state sector where over 90% of our children receive their schooling. But if our schools are demoralised and in need of a new direction what of higher education?

There is a desperate need for more graduates in Britain,

yet the situation is getting worse. Government plans are actually to reduce the number of students as the 18–22 age group falls over the next ten years. This is madness in view of the CBI's estimate that industry's demand for graduates will increase by 4% a year. We also know that there is likely to be an increased demand for teachers and other professionals in the 1990's.

Yet, the proportion of young people continuing their studies beyond the age of 16 is lower in Britian then elsewhere in the advanced industrial world.

The Government's policy of cutting higher education funding has also hit research. In terms of real purchasing power, civil research funding has declined by at least 10% over the last decade. Two fifths of Alpha-rated projects are now being turned down. Many of our brightest young researchers are leaving Britain.

The 'brain drain' is also affecting senior posts in universities and polytechnics; in many key subjects it is increasingly difficult to fill chairs, or to make junior appointments of the right calibre, in many key subjects, because of the relative fall in academic salaries and the shortage of funds for research.

To arrest the decline in higher education we must urgently set targets to increase the proportion of 18/19 year olds entering higher education: our ambition should be to double it by the turn of the century. We must reduce and eventually abolish fees for part-time higher education courses, in order to encourage more older students, whether working or unemployed, to study for a degree, (this measure would, among others, particularly boost numbers enrolled at the Open University).

We must commence a programme to remove barriers to access to higher education. For instance, between 15% and 20% has been removed from student awards and benefits under this Government. Even DES officials admit that student grants and benefits are insufficient to prevent hardship. There should be immediate restoration of lost benefits; the establishment of an index showing the real increases in student living costs and this should be used in calculating benefits and awards. Steps should be taken to lower the age of independence with the aim firstly, of enabling students who are 21 at the time they start their course to have independence. I do not believe that a state system of loans has a part to play in providing access to higher education; Indeed, overseas experience show that loans create more problems than they solve.

In the longer term student financial support should be integrated into the tax/benefits system, so that every student has a basic level of financial support with extra allowances for housing, travel, books and equipment; we should also encourage links between higher education and industry, in particular through increasing demand for courses from industry with the introduction of a remissable training tax; and establish a Higher Education Council to oversee planning and increase co-operation across the binary line and advise on the further development of policy.

These would be morale boosting and realistic targets. Instead of the thin gruel of education cuts; which are in danger of turning the clock back prior to the 1944 Education Act – and even before Gladstone's 1870 Act – we must reassert the aim of a country which has an enlightened and literate population; aims only realisable through education.

Sadly, education has become just another area where the Government has applied the principles of its divisive Manifesto of Greed. People in this country are in need of more than recipes for income success. The economic regeneration, the revival of entrepreneurship, that is so often talked about simply will not come from over-examined, self-seeking, and unco-operative youths – but instead from motivated, outward-looking young people. Turning our schools and colleges into battle grounds will never ever achieve that.

Chapter Fourteen

THE MANIFESTO OF GREED

Building a New Britain

We all dream of the sort of country we'd like to leave behind us at the end of our lives. That's what politics should be all about. Fulfilling our life long dreams. Not just a quest for personal power.

In 1979, but more particularly in 1983, Mrs Thatcher hijacked the mantle of individualism, of 'putting people first'. Her brand of individualism is one where giving power to the people means giving them money. Yet she has managed to move the debate onto grounds familiar to Liberals. In 1987 the Conservative manifesto stated:

> Our goal is a capital-owning democracy of people and families who exercise power over their own lives in the most direct way. *They would take the important decisions – as tenants, home-owners, parents, employees, and trade unionists – rather than having them taken for them.*

How did Mrs Thatcher capture the ground that belonged essentially to Liberals? In the 1970s Liberalism was a growing force. Its community politics – with a commitment to personal power – challenged the Labour Party's claim to care.

The alliance with the SDP was in one respect a step

back for the Liberal Party. The SDP was not an individualist party. Its emphasis was on moderate socialism. Its roots were in the post war Labour Governments to which individualists were so strongly opposed. Its idea was that moderate tinkering with the economy could keep the economy in shape. Yet the economic crises of the 70's showed fairly precisely that tinkering was not enough. It was this revelation that helped push the Labour Party to extremism. Thus the new Alliance failed to provide an effective alternative to Thatcherism. And the new conservative philosophy also had a distinctive appeal.

In common with the American New Right, the New Conservatism is an individualism that extends only as far as the family. It is a reassertion of Victorian Values. If the Government is to relinquish power then the family must take over. Parents are to be given increased power in schools, and their authority supported with a school leaving age which is effectively to be raised to 18; reduced student grants – making people far more dependent on their parents; reduced pay for those on youth training schemes; restrictions on bed and breakfast benefit payments – creating a twentieth century poor law; made it illegal to put pupils on school governing bodies; abolished all low-wage protection for the under 21. The new Job Training Scheme forces young people into jobs offering no extra pay in addition to supplementary benefit, with no guaranteed level of training.

The prosperity the Tories want to bring is to the head of the household. It is the man in the full-time paid job that will benefit from the privatisation hand-outs.

The 1987 Conservative manifesto was, then, a radical one. As I attempt to show, the changes it will bring if implemented will be far reaching. Towards a country very different from the present. But its a future that I have no great desire to share in. Our individualism is of a very different sort. Its about more than money. It was Gandhi who said: 'Earth provided enough to satisfy every person's needs, but not for every person's greed.'

The Conservative programme of the last General Election was nothing other than a Manifesto of Greed. It would be good to think that there are better values on which we can base our plans. We must do everything in our power to show that there are tasks other than material self-advancement which are worthwhile. And we must also show that a quest for purely individual satisfaction will never be self-satisfying. I still hold with conviction the notion of 'Power to the People' because it is the hopelessness and lack of fulfillment that is at the root of most people's apathy. But power over your own life is not about making yourself rich. Nor is it about destroying someone else to get there.

Taking account of human needs and calculating satisfaction is not about adding up pounds spent on a problem. This sort of thought process is responsible for misguiding many of today's policies. There is for instance a growing emphasis on the need for preventative medicine. That means we should be looking at the kind of things that are making people ill, not just picking up the pieces. If the National Health Service policy-makers weren't so keen on adding up the number of beds in their possession – then they might be able to pay more attention to people's actual needs – encouraging programmes for healthy living. Preventing illness rather than struggling to cure it.

In Liverpool I have been very impressed by a group of young doctors pursuing a 'holistic' analysis – that means looking at the whole of a person – body, mind and spirit. To them you're not just healthy if you're not ill. Healthy living is a way of life. Real preventative health care means tackling all aspects of our lifestyle that makes us unhealthy – not just giving out more valium prescriptions. If we live in an environment where despite quantitively high incomes some of our basic needs are not being met – then this constitutes neither a healthy life or a high standard of living.

We must ask ourselves the question are standards of living measured in money terms actually making us happier – fulfilling our basic needs?

In 1948 Britain's National Income was £10 billion, in 1986 it was £318 billion. Expressed as pounds per head it was £209 in 1948 and today stands at £5,617 per head. There has hardly been an equivalent increase in human satisfaction. There is no point in harking back to a pre-industrial golden age – it didn't exist. Science and technology have given us the ability to satisfy basic human needs as never before. Yet there comes a point when its not greater material consumption that is the human need. Other values are at least as important – like quality of living for instance.

Living on a low salary in this country can seem like a real nightmare – and it sometimes is. But in global terms even the lowest level of supplementary benefit is a lot of money. But then a high world salary doesn't compensate for your smelly damp house, for the rubbish and dogs on the streets, for the unhealthy food – stuffed full of grease or additives, for the buses that run late, for the scorn of people who say you're a scruff and that you're old enough to own a car and that you should have a better job. Maybe most of all for some it doesn't compensate for being alone – for being without friends in a big city.

When Liverpool's Beatles sang that 'Money can't buy you love' – they had it right. When a political party offers to make people rich – it attracts a lot of support – if the offer is convincing. But then a political party doesn't usually offer love either. Few people are actually inspired by a call to materialism. But who can blame them for responding to it in some way. Its really the fault of those of us who claim to offer an alternative. What we've failed to do is to show that we really can be that alternative, to provide for their needs. Politicians too often make the illogical step of assuming they are right – just because their opponent's policy is an evident evil. Right and wrong don't necessarily coincide with the conventional political spectrum. If the politics of greed is to be superceded – then the politics of need must be its successor. Our challenge is to tackle those problems, to fulfil those needs that when honestly thought about are actually far more important than purely financial satisfaction.

42% of the electorate in 1987 voted for 'more of the same'. Not a majority. Post-election analysis on the left explained the result as a consequence of an enlarged prosperous elite. That is years of economic growth had enriched so many people that they were now inevitably more Conservative-minded. Labour's Brian Gould has subsequently argued that only a more materialistic opposition would hope to succeed. Yet I have no wish to participate in Mrs Thatcher's game. The people who voted for her were not some new elite. They were ordinary people. Our failure was to capture their imagination.

Most of the electorate share the same sense of despair and lack of fulfillment although in different ways. This applies to many other than those affected directly by unemployment or inner city decay. Its not difficult to show that today's industrial society falls short of providing for many of our needs, both now and particularly in the future. Our greater challenge is to show that there is a way to fulfil those needs without taking away the self confidence which the enterprise culture has conferred. Our first assault must be on Western society's obsession with relentless consumerism.

Promoting Relentless Consumerism

In a damp house even the finest of wallpapers will peel off sooner or later. To most people the glamour of their town's colourful billboards is a curious symbol of a far-off world. Its almost like building a Habitat showroom at the bottom of a huge tower block. Its a world to which they have no access – and each image forms a bitter reminder of the real world. The glossy shine of consumer satisfaction may seem a more appropriate image for a prosperous town in the south east. Yet here too the world of TV middle class satisfaction bares poor resemblance to human living.

'The American Dream will be yours when you buy the latest from the range of Zanussi washing machines.'

That's not a particularly unusual example of American advertising. The hopes and aspirations of a nation it seems are bound up with creating a consumers paradise. In Britain we're not altogether immune from this feeling – advertisers have no shame in telling us or implying that happiness will be obtained from consuming their product.

It's all hollow. I've yet to meet the model family with the microwave that has found contentment from replying to the Sunday supplement ads. Advertising aims not to satisfy needs but to create them. And in fact most of us are convinced, and buy what they tell us, but that doesn't mean we're any better off.

The new town experiment showed that a brand new world wasn't necessarily an ideal world. The dream became almost a social nightmare. Whilst the values of the industrial age told the planners to build new, big, tall, efficient and fast; the human beings found that big schools and institutions meant the loss of the friendly community spirit, that tall building meant nowhere to play, loneliness and lifts never working, and fast ringroads meant a deserted and dangerous nighttime town centre.

The Thatcher years may have spelt disaster for the manufacturing industry. But the advertising industry which it supports has gone from strength, with over £5 billion spent on advertising in 1986 alone – more than £30 billion in the last nine years. It was the Conservative Party's success, apparently, to convince people that personal prosperity should be their target and that they could provide it. Yet they've hardly been hindered by the huge sum spent each year on convincing people that – not only is spending money on this and that product desirable – its also essential.

Gearing political policies to what people want is what democracy should be about. But what people want and what they need are different. Making too much of this distinction is a recipe for totalitarianism. It lets us think that we know better than other people. But on the other hand its worth wondering whether the values drummed into us each day by the media are actually helping us rationally decide what we need.

Not only are huge sums spent on advertising, they're also spent on packaging. Protection used to be the purpose of wrapping something up. Now its more about hiding what is inside. Instead of the product itself you just see a glossy outside cover. What about the product itself? Its sometimes as if the product and packaging have merged. The product becomes no more than its image – its colour, design, ad status. Actual substance seems to mean very little.

Doesn't all this packaging and publicity help to brighten up our lives? Doesn't the wallpaper cheer us up – even if it does peel off eventually? Unfortunately its a false way of living. You can't eat an egg thats hollow; and creating extra needs won't help satisfy the ones that were already crying out to be satisfied.

Advertising often draws a false distinction between products that are essentially the same. Why are there so many brands of soap powder – so expensively advertised – when they all do the same job? Schumacher's famous example is of two biscuit lorries that pass each other on the motorway, one bound for Scotland and one bound for London. How much transport costs would be saved if local producers produced for local consumers instead of cut throat competition between big, national, and international companies?

What's produced to look good doesn't usually turn out the best. The amount of additives in food – sweeteners, colourings, flavourings and preservatives – destroys the purpose of having any sense of taste. It should be to distinguish between good and bad foods. Many foods just don't have any good in them. Advertising has also placed a greater emphasis on image and prestige over and above reliability. It isn't considered important if something actually works or lasts a long time – what matters is that you buy it.

Even worse, people that have no money are constantly told that to be successful they must have this or that – often way beyond the attainable. It was Churchill, hardly a poor man, the grandson of a Duke, who observed that 'to have a little freedom you have to have a little money!' The worst of all worlds is to be tantalised by the products of the market, while the market itself passes you by; to be blitzed by sharp advertising without having the legitimate means to secure the product.

What is the price we're paying for our personal consumerism? The vision of millions of inward-looking materialists trying to spend as much as possible presents a picture of both self destruction and collective destruction. Its a picture of stress. The stresses created by the competition for wealth, keeping up with the next door neighbours, and not feeling inadequate in a world where owning a TV and a car are described as essential. Also stress caused directly by our high pressure consumption – personal illhealth caused by obesity, under-exercise, urban pollution, and drug abuse. Stress is also caused by HP and borrowing committments way beyond any real capacity to meet them. These are the side-effects of modern living – glued alone to our television sets, chewing food full of poisonous substances – we're only hurting ourselves. The major cause of death in Britain is either cancer or heart disease – both of these are primarily twentieth century diseases. Our ill-health is fatal.

An obsession with satisfying ourselves before others creates a poisonous vicious circle. None of us like our noisy polluted environment but because we only look as far as our own horizon we do nothing and we feel we can do nothing to stop the pollution that causes it. Huge numbers of environmental problems – destruction of beautiful natural resources such as forests, rivers and lakes, pollution of the air – they all result from failing to take into account the collective effects of individual actions.

The country that I dream of would be coloured not with the glossy and gaudy colours of an artificial world. Instead it would be coloured by the beauty of a natural world preserved and a man-made world of quality made to actually satisfy our needs.

Mrs Thatcher's agenda is a false one. It is just not true that people are happy chasing the prosperity placed on offer. The happiness of endless enrichment is illusory because its not addressing our real problems. Obesity and glut is also just downright wrong in a world where millions are starving.

The economic state I'd like to see would not be about creating an advertisers paradise. The sort of recovery I envisage would not be about cynically exploiting peoples aspirations for a better place in life. Instead I'd like to see a curbing of this industry and the shameful way it exploits women's bodies to sell its wares, and has no hesitation to advertise the drugs that have harmed so many people's lives. I'd also like to see curbs on the additives that are put into foods and an education campaign to restore people's sense of what is healthy.

More fundamentally I'd like to see greater consumer and employee control over the policies of our manufacturers. In that way quality not total sales can be an aim – and preventing pollution can be a greater priority. The kind of hand-outs that we should be giving are not extra shares in the auction of our national assets but rather handouts of power to be able to choose what we consume – and hand-outs of quality.

There's got to come a time when politicians and all of

us will gather the courage to say that less prosperity not more should be our aim. In 1972 the Lifestyle Movement was founded by Canon Dammers, Dean of Coventry Cathedral. The slogan of this small movement has been to 'Live more simply that all of us may simply live.' I'm no example of how to live a simpler lifestyle but that doesn't change the reality that consuming less will probably provide the key for a better quality of life and for sharing resources more fairly in the world. It is on this basis that we should set our new agenda. Dr Jorgen Lissner leaves us with ten compelling reasons why we should make a break from personal consumerism and choose a simpler lifestyle:

1. As an *act of faith performed for the sake of personal integrity as an expression of personal commitment to a more equitable distribution of the world's wealth;*

2. As an *act of self-defence* against the mind-polluting effects of over-consumption;

3. As an *act of withdrawal from the achievement-neurosis of our high-pressure materialistic societies;*

4. As an *act of solidarity* with the majority of humankind, which has no choice about lifestyle;

5. As an *act of sharing* with others what has been given to us, or of returning what was usured by us through unjust social and economic structures;

6. As an *act of celebration* of the riches found in creativity, spirituality and community with others rather than in mindless materialism;

7. As an *act of provocation* – ostentatious underconsump-

tion to arouse curiosity leading to dialogue with others about affluence, alienation, poverty and social injustice;

8. As an *act of anticipation* of the era when the self-confidence and assertiveness of the underprivileged forces new power relationships and new patterns of resource allocation upon us.

9. As an *act of advocacy* of legislated changes in the present patterns of production and consumption in the direction of a new international economic order;

10. As an *exercise of purchasing power* to redirect production away from the satisfaction of artificially created wants towards the supply of goods and services that meet genuine social needs.

People sometimes misquote the Biblical injunction and say that 'money is at the root of all evil!' Of course it is the love of money that is at the root of our troubles not the money or the market. We have our enterprise culture in Britain but we have allowed it to dictate to us instead of using it to create a good society and a happy country.

Chapter Fifteen

THE WAY WE RUN OUR COUNTRY

There is usually a great yawn when anyone mentions constitutional reform. Proportional representation, constitutional reform, devolution, freedom of information 'Bill of Rights' – or even the reform of our great grandmother of parliaments – are guaranteed to produce a glazed look across the faces of any audience. And yet it does get to the very heart of what's wrong with Britain.

Our Parliament is like a Gentleman's Club – where new member's are only grudgingly accepted. Any company which ran its affairs as we do would quickly go bankrupt. Cyril Smith once described it as the longest running farce in the West End.

The problems begin with the way in which Parliament is elected. Two thirds of the country may not vote for a party but the first past the post system allows them to form a Government – with two thirds of the seats in the House of Commons. This leads to arrogance by the Government party and frustration on the opposition benches. In turn that leads to division, confrontation and plain nastiness. If parties had to learn to work with one another – as they do in countries that have fair electoral systems – it would strengthen our democracy. First past-the-post is a very weak system. This is especially true in local government.

There is a very good case for at least trying out proportional representation at local level.

The electorate in the area of a local council – county, region, district or borough – is not being asked to elect a Government. They are being invited to choose men and women to deal with the problems of their communities. How much better it would be if they had an electoral system which gave them the opportunity of having their views accurately reflected in the council chamber.

Examples of electoral distortion are not at all hard to find in local government. In Liverpool in 1984, 90,000 voters supported Labour and 100,000 against them – yet a Militant administration with a majority of 15 on the City Council was formed with dire consequences. And again in 1987 the Alliance outpolled Labour comfortably but were denied office because of the concentration of Labour seats in the de-populated wards of the City. In another election, this time in Edinburgh, 66,000 voted for Labour and over 100,000 against – yet Labour had a Council majority of 6.

But distortions do not only occur on Labour-controlled Councils. In 1982, in the London Borough of Sutton, the Conservative Party won just over 50% of the vote. I fully accept that this would entitle them to control of the Council. I do not accept that it entitled them to the 82% of the seats they actually won. In nearby Surrey the Conservatives won over 2/3 of the seats on less than half the vote, and in the London Borough of Richmond in 1987 the Alliance took 52% of the vote and 94% of the seats.

How can anyone pretend that such outcomes are justified? Can it really be right not to have any representation at all of minority interests, or to have only a derisory level of representation? How can it be right to have total, virtually unchallenged, power over the affairs of any local community?

If the majority of people do not vote for a party why should that party be given absolute control of a local Authority? In many communities it leads to local government

being weighed down by unimaginative councillors who are
either preaching the class battles of the hunger marches;
or still fighting the political battles of low rates versus lower
service provision for the poor and needy. This distorts
people's wishes and gives false powers to unrepresentative
people.

That these powers are often abused is all too evident.
Rigged agendas, denial of the right of democratic debate,
and the appointment of council officers on the basis of
their political views – this has happened in authorities
like Liverpool where the majority parties are grossly over-
represented. In many Town Halls officials know that their
entire future is dependent on their relations with the
members of a single political party. In these circumstances,
the majority party may come to believe it can get away with
virtually anything. The report of the Royal Commission on
Standards of Conduct in Political Life had this to say:

> The local authorities most vulnerable to corruption have
> tended to be those in which one political party has
> unchallenged dominance. Not only are such authorities
> at particular risk because of absence of an effective oppo-
> sition which can scrutinise their decisions, but investi-
> gations and the making of complaints in such areas may
> also be inhibited by the feeling that there is no way
> round the party machine.

The old parties like to keep it this way. Their power at
any price complex is summed up by the cryptic message I
saw daubed on the wall of a North East England council
office, 'All power corrupts; but absolute power is even more
fun!'

One way to counter the party machines is through the
introduction of the single transferable vote system into
local government elections everywhere. Under this system,
voters elect a number of councillors for each ward. They
would number the candidates in their order of preference

on their ballot papers, and can transfer their lower preferences between parties, within parties, or even to independents. They can vote for just who they like, and will be
sure that, whatever the choice, their vote will not be wasted
– unlike the present system – since if their first choice
candidate is not elected, their vote will transfer to their
second choice, and so on. Evidence from other countries
which already use this system show that it results in the
election of more women and more representatives of ethnic
minorities. It results in a higher turnout – a factor of
especial importance for local government. Evidence from
opinion polls in this country show that this system – or
any other system of PR is supported by a large majority
of our population.

I think Dr Rhodes Boyson MP was right when he said:

There is a similar disappointment for the people who
voted Conservative in Stockport, North, and those who
voted Labour in my constituency. They might ask what
the point is in voting. Whatever people may think of the
person who represents them, it is a funny system. People
vote and then find out that they are not represented.

A fair electoral system for local government ensuring that
everyone is represented – would be a start in giving our
Country a balanced democracy truly reflecting the wishes
of the people.

Yet, after 'Spycatcher' and the Westland Affair it is also
clear that Britain needs to establish tough new investigative
select committees, backed up by freedom of information
legislation. At present we run the risk of suffocating in our
highly secretive system.

Secrecy is a national disease in Britain. The case of Clive
Ponting was perhaps the classic example of our determination to keep the public in the dark about how and why
decisions are made. Instead of encouraging the public to

take an interest in how their country is governed we tell them to mind their own business.

Ponting leaked secret documents relating to the sinking of the Belgrano. Within a month of his acquittal at the Old Bailey, Ponting's Apologia surfaced in our book shops. It was published without warning as a way of avoiding injunctions from the Ministry of Defence.

'The Right To Know' is a catalogue of events – how the Official Secrets Act came onto the Statute Books in the first place; what successive Governments have done to consolidate it; and the attempts which have been made to reform it. It is also a diary of a man who acted first as game keeper ('Many prosecutions under the Official Secrets Act passed through my office on the way to the Director of Public Prosecutions') but later turned poacher ('It did not cross my mind that I too would become a "case" to be dealt with in the same way!') Clive Ponting's case revealed a great deal about the incompetence and inefficiency of the civil service. He is also scathing about the way resources are squandered and departments see themselves above parliamentary scrutiny or public accountability.

An inordinate number of activities in Britain are currently deemed to be secret. Even the day-to-day running of the White Fish Authority is classified information, no doubt jealously guarded by a crabby-mannered civil servant sitting in Whitehall waiting for his inflation-proofed pension to come in. Even gardeners at Hampton Court are asked to sign a form promising not to reveal the secrets of the compost heap. Should they divulge to you details of the methods used to cultivate bigger and better begonias you had better watch out – no doubt you could become an accessory and had up too!

Ponting's case should have made the Government rue the day they ever decided (against the advice of their officials) to bring a clumsy prosecution. Yet not satisfied with turning 'Right To Know' into a best seller they went one better with Peter Wright's 'Spycatcher'.

As Clive Ponting says; 'Secrecy conditions the Whitehall climate about the provision of information. Information is seen as something to controlled by Whitehall and allowed outside only when it is politically convenient.'

Politicians, as well as the public, are also regularly treated to a process of disinformation and are strung along. Talking about how Whitehall deals with its Ministers and maintains the status quo rather than have to face the irritating business of change: Ponting admitted that 'The hidden consensus behind elegant drafting is that the current system is satisfactory but that a small change has to be made to avoid something worse – public access to information!' Anyone who has served on a House of Commons Select Committee knows exactly what he means. Clever, delightfully phrased statements, peppered with civil service gobbledygook, are designed to keep the over inquisitive Member at bay. Their answers are also designed to tell you precisely nothing and to hold the line; at all costs hold the line. Never place at risk the accepted orthodoxy. We may smugly smirk at Irangate hearings in Congress, but the sad truth is that in Britain such corruption would be hidden from view.

If, by chance, an over zealous, back-bench MP gets a little too close to the truth then the answer is to classify whatever it is he wants to know. Even if, as with the Belgrano the information was not classifiable, don't let minor details like that worry you. Argue the opposite and scare the public by telling them that subversives like Clive Ponting are really only enemy spies out to undermine the State and aiming to place at risk the lives of British servicemen.

It doesn't sound a very convincing argument. And despite the best efforts of Mr Justice McGowan, the Jury in the Ponting case did not think it very convincing either. McCowan contended that the Government and the State are one and the same thing. The Jury, and I suspect the great British public outside, took a different view. The universal approbrium in which the public holds politicians necessarily does not extend to their own Member of Parliament – for whom they still have significant respect and regard. Asked to put them in some sort of pecking order, the Jury and the public, saw Parliament, not the Government, as the guardians of the interests of the State. The Ponting Jury did more to reassert the rights of Parliament over the Executive than the House of Commons has dared to do in 70 years. Ironically, the earlier failure of *The Guardian* newspaper to protect Sara Tisdall – the civil servant who gave them information about the timing of the arrival of Cruise missiles – badly undermined the Freedom of Information cause. If *The Guardian* had stuck to their guns the ensuing court case might have been a major watershed.

In 1920 a Liberal MP, Sir Donald Maclean, spoke passionately against Section 2 of the Official Secrets Act; 'I find it difficult to confine my language to this Bill within the range of Parliamentary propriety. It is another attempt to clamp the powers of war on the liberties of the citizen in peace.' It had been a Liberal Government, which nine years earlier, without any debate in Parliament, had enacted Section 2. A reforming government should replace it with a Freedom of Information Act.

A fair electoral system and a more open approach would transform Parliament. These reforms, together with devolved decision making and a Bill of Rights, would be the basis of a new constitutional settlement. I want to see the structures of government made to serve our people, not the other way around; and I want our country to have a democracy up to the job of governing 21st century Britain.

Chapter Sixteen

WHOSE COUNTRY, WHOSE FAULT? – IRELAND

'I forgive the men who murdered my daughter'
—GORDON WILSON of Enniskillen

We ask 'What kind of country?' but for many people there is one part of our country which is usually ignored. I would strongly argue that our most pressing domestic problem is the continued carnage in Northern Ireland. Two and a half thousand people have died and another twenty-four thousand have been injured since the present troubles began nearly twenty years ago. I write now in the aftermath of the atrocity at Enniskillen. Ten days after the bombing I visited that town and was struck by the extraordinary spirit of forgiveness of Unionists I met. It was not just the almost beatific forebearance of Gordon Wilson, whose daughter lay dead in the rubble alongside him, but a general spirit of reconciliation. This is quite remarkable given that from the perspective of Fermanagh Protestants the IRA campaign resembles nothing less than a planned campaign of extermination. That Poppy Day massacre on 8th of November, 1987, may well be forgotten, along with countless other horrors. But as an example of the Christian virtue of forgiveness it will stand out like a beacon amidst the bitterness, viciousness, sectarianism and strife that has

engulfed Ireland for most of twenty years and for as long
as most people can remember. In the House of Commons
I said that the most lasting memorial to the dead of Enniskillen would be political progress towards true
reconciliation.

As a result of Enniskillen, Northern Ireland is once more
in the news but out of four thousand people interviewed
by Gallup at the time of the 1987 election just ten (one
quarter of one percent) listed Northern Ireland as the top
election issue. Important but distant conflicts in Nicaragua
and South Africa frequently rate more public interest.
Debates in Parliament about Northern Ireland are sparsely
attended and Northern Irish business is pushed through in
a most undemocratic way using unamendable orders. Party
manifestoes usually contain little more than a polite but
passing reference. All too easily politicians live behind the
clapped out rhetoric and empty sloganeering – 'NO
SURRENDER' is matched by demands for a United
Ireland; and calls for British Troops out are capped by the
assertion that Ulster will Fight and Ulster will be Right.
To the British observer Ulster seems unable to say
anything other than 'No' and with democratic politics in
suspended animation there is a growing tendency for
British to simply say 'let them get on with it.'

The average Briton is bewildered by Northern Ireland
and ignorant of how this troubled part of the British Isles
became locked into its hate-ridden conflict.

Robert Kee, in his magnificent 'Ireland: A History' sets
out the seeds of conflict, and concludes that the blame for
today's tragedy should be laid at the door of history. Up
to a point this is true; but it will require today's politicians,
not historians, to chart new ways forward.

The political relationship between England and Ireland
stretches back 800 years. Nicholas Breakspear, a monk
from St Albans, had been elected Pope. As Adrian IV he
acceded to Henry II's request to be allowed to send an

English army to quiet the unruly Irish. 'Troops Out' is not a new slogan: the first English troops arrived in 1170.

For the first 400 years, until the Reformation, effective power lay in the hands of the local Earls. The signal for real conflict came in 1534 when the Earl of Kildare rebelled against Henry VIII, who attempted to replace both Catholic Pope and doctrines.

For the next 70 years English influence was at its most effective in the Pale of Dublin – everything 'beyond the Pale' was Catholic Gaelic territory. Nowhere more so than Ulster.

The Earls of Ulster led the resistance against Protestant England and in 1603 they were defeated by Queen Elizabeth's forces, James I determined to prevent any further uprisings and from 1610 to 1630 the English 'planted' Protestants on land confiscated from the Irish. The new Plantation settlers surrounded by the dispossessed and embittered Irish immediately became a security minded community. These days the Royal Ulster Constabulary has 11,000 personnel and the security services in their various guises remain one of Northern Ireland's major employers.

The next phase of the conflict began when the Charles I came to the throne. Before long he and Parliament were in a dispute culminating, in 1642, in the English Civil War. This was a signal for Catholics in Ireland to stage an uprising. Protestants were slaughtered by the score: at Portadown 100 men, women and children were hurled into the river and clubbed to death.

In 1649 Oliver Cromwell came to reek vengeance and at Drogheda and Wexford thousands of Catholics were massacred. Cromwell gave the rich lands to his soldiers and banished the Catholic landlords to the poor West. He wrote 'I am persuaded that this is a righteous judgement of God upon those barbarous wretches, who have imbrued their hands with much innocent blood.' This would not be the last time that God's name would be called in aid of violent and brutal acts committed on both sides.

In 1660 the Monarchy was Restored with Charles II. The Church of Ireland, with very few adherents, became the established church. Ironically, this turned Ulster Presbyterians, who mainly came from Scotland, into dissenters along with the majority Irish Catholic population. This helps explain the pro-Crown but anti-English attitude of Ulster Protestants which continues to this day. It is one of the reasons why the naming of the Hillsborough Accord as the Anglo Irish Agreement was so unfortunate. Words mean everything in Northern Ireland and in a place where conspiracy is thought to lurk everywhere a British-Irish Agreement would have been marginally less provocative.

In 1681 the Crown became concerned about Irish Catholic loyalty and, determined to make an example, they arrested and subsequently executed the peaceable Archbishop of Armagh, Oliver Plunkett. The comparisons with Archbishop Oscar Romero executed in El Salvador some 300 years later are inescapable. Plunkett's death became a rallying point; the hunger strikes being the most recent.

By 1688 William of Orange, a Dutch Protestant prince, had been placed on the throne of Britain and the Catholic James II fled to Ireland. Protestant settlers resisted his Catholic army and thirteen apprentice boys successfully led the 13 week resistence during the Seige of Derry, defying the Jacobite Army. Against the wishes of the commander, Robert Conoy, they refused to hand over the garrison. They insisted that there would be 'No Surrender'. In 1690, William's troops arrived in Northern Ireland and at the Battle of the Boyne James II was defeated. The supremacy of Protestantism continued until the Irish Free State was declared in 1921.

The intervening centuries brought famine and destitution. In the potato famine of 1845–48 a million died and a million joined the exodus to America. The centuries were marred by seething resentment and English disinterest. English politicians and civil servants failed to comprehend or even care about Ireland's historical grievances. Twenty years before he became Prime Minister, Gladstone wrote to his wife: 'Ireland, Ireland that cloud in the West, that coming storm, the minister of God's retribution upon cruel and inveterate and but half-atoned injustice.' Gladstone's disestablishment of the Church of Ireland, his land reform, the provision of education and his attempts to introduce Home Rule were the first great attack on that half-atoned injustice, His Home Rule Bill of 1866 was defeated and Gladstone split the Liberal Party in the process – doing so because principle came first and party considerations last. Edward Carson led the fight against 'Home Rule' as he called it and in 1912 formed the 100,000 strong Ulster Volunteer Force that pledged to defend Ulster by force if necessary. This has its echoes in the 1980's displays of fire arms and gun licenses by the UVF's modern heirs.

Militant republicans in the South responded with the Dublin Easter Rising of 1916. The leaders were executed or interred without trial and the Irish Republican Army was born. Their heirs in Northern Ireland continue the bloodshed to this day.

In 1921 the Irish Free State was finally formed but Northern Ireland's six counties remained a part of the United Kingdom. Sir James Craig, Northern Ireland's first Prime Minister boasted at Stormont that we have 'a Protestant Parliament and a Protestant State.' For the next fifty years the third of Northern Ireland's population who were Catholic were discriminated against and treated as second class citizens.

In 1968 this led to the formation of the Civil Rights movement; and in 1969 the coming of British troops – who on arrival were cheered in the streets by Catholics believing they had arrived to establish a system of fair representation.

Two years earlier, in 1966, the leader of the Ulster Liberals, the Reverend Albert McElroy, who was also Moderator of the Non-Subscribing Presbyterian Church of Ireland, had written:

Stripped of all pretensions our local politics are about sectarian bitterness. This is bad politics and worse religion. Religion is about the meaning of life, the nature of man and his eternal destiny. Politics is the application of these principles to the life of human society. Religion and politics in this sense are inseparable. It is only when religion is misused by politicians to exploit religious differences that the association of the two is false and evil.

McElroy was part of Northern Ireland's small ecumenical movement. He trenchantly attacked what he called 'anti-Catholic neurosis'. In June 1969 he made a prophetic speech when he said: 'Worse still, the optimism of a year ago has given way to the polarisation of political and cultural life along traditional narrow sectarian lines . . .

This situation is fraught with great danger. Things could easily return to the tragic conditions of the 1920's and 30's. As usual the innocent, the ordinary people on both sides would pay the price and a new legacy of hatred created.' – Within two months the present 'troubles' that led to the troops being sent had erupted.

Although McElroy believed in a united Ireland he recognised that the only worthwhile unity is the unity Churchill once described as the 'unity of hearts'. He knew his history and believed that a heritage of politics based on the monopolisation of political power by one party, not just for fifty years but since before the Act of Union, could not survive.

For every Englishman ignorant of Ireland's history there is an Irishman reliving the siege of Drogheda or the Battle of the Boyne. The Irish are prisoners of their own history: captives of events that anywhere else would have been long forgotten. And the history lessons that they teach differ according to the teacher.

Liam McCloskey was a Catholic INLA hunger striker. He was imprisoned in the Maze. He was part of the 'dirty protest' and was 'on the blanket'. No one will quickly forget the protests at the Maze. First, in December 1977, prisoners refused to wear prison uniforms and wrapped themselves in blankets. Then, in March 1978, they refused to leave their cells – never washing or shaving. Human excrement was smeared over the cell walls and thrown out of the smashed windows. The men lived and slept in their own filth for months. The hunger strikes began in 1981 and on May 5th 1981, Bobby Sands, died. That and nine other deaths, on top of the history of the last 16 years persuaded the Government that the status quo was not an option.

McCloskey had begun his hunger strike in 1981 immediately after Bobby Sands' death. He starved himself for 55 days. Then, when he had lost his sight and his hearing, he renounced violence and gave up his fast. No one had fasted so long and survived. During his fast he read the Bible – the only book available – and he determined to become a Christian. He is now based at Derry's St. Columba House working for the reconciliation of the two traditions within Northern Ireland.

During a prayer meeting at the 1987 Liberal Party Assembly he recalled how he had been taught one version of Irish history which excluded all reference to atrocities committed against Protestants. He was to find that the Protestant paramilitaries in the Maze had been taught the same but in reverse. As Northern Ireland's integrated schools have understood, history must not be manipulated in this way. School's like Belfast's Lagan College have dual heads of history and religion to ensure that teaching is objective. Unless all schools and teachers learn to disengage Loyalist and Republican bigotry from their teaching yet another generation will be schooled in the traditions of intolerance, prejudice and bloodshed.

Northern Ireland must now look to the future and learn to bury its past.

Martin Luther King in his 'Strength To Love' points the way:

A third way is open to our quest for freedom, namely non-violence. Through non violence we shall be able to oppose the unjust system and at the same time love the perpetrators of the system. We must work passionately and unremittingly but may it never be said that we used the inferior methods of falsehood, malice, hate and violence.

Inferior methods are not acceptable in Northern Ireland which is part of a parliamentary democracy and therefore open to change without the gun. Violence and those who deal in it must be unequivocally repudiated. Change must come from men and women in the Unionist and Nationalist traditions learning to co-operate with one another. The Labour Party and others like Lord Whitelaw who have met with Sinn Fein, the politicians of the IRA, have been quite wrong to do so. The job of democrats is not to sustain or lend credibility to those who use violence to maintain their tribalistic and sectarian positions. This is something which Northern Ireland's brave non sectarian Alliance Party have understood and courageously they seek to unite this fractured community.

The Nobel Peace prize winner Solzhenitsyn well understood the nature of violence. He wrote: 'Violence can only be concealed by the lie. Anyone who has once proclaimed that violence is his method is inevitably forced to choose the lie as his guiding principle.' The lies, the distortions and past injuries perpetrated by paramilitaries and their political backers must be set on one side. The way forward must centre on mutual forgiveness for past injuries and through the building up of the common ground.

Liam McAnoy, a prisoner I met at the Maze in 1984 who, like McClosky has renounced violence, put it like this in a letter to me: 'Justice requires, just as peace demands, the pacific co-existence of both communities in mutual respect and in equality of rights. Violence and the talk of civil war makes the attainment of co-existence more difficult.' Or as the Rev. Ray Davey, the founder of the Corrymeela Community said at Westminster Abbey in 1980: 'Truth demands that we be willing to look at another's point of view when it is opposed to ours and to try to understand it.'

The future cannot consist of rabble-rousing marches and displays of triumphalism. It cannot consist of intimidation and threats of maiming and murder. If Northern Ireland politicians simply go on demanding an eye for an eye or a life for a life, their corner of this country will be littered with the blind and dead. For Christians, especially, this is a scandal, a by-word among nations. The community has a right to expect Christian leaders who preach of love, forgiveness and reconciliation to speak with one voice on at least some of the issues facing the Province. Northern Ireland enables men the world over to caricature Christianity and to equate tribalism with Christian values. That is why the work of Corrymeela, the Rosstrevor centre for Christian renewal groups like the Maranatha Community and St Columba House in Derry are so important. They will keep changing men's hearts. So will integrated Christian education – which the Churches have laggardly in supporting.

In addition to a personal change of heart a fundamental political choice now faces Northern Ireland.

Either Unionists can now create a relationship with their fellow citizens, a relationship which recognises the legitimacy of the two traditions and the need to share power and responsibility, their actions will lead to the end of the Union, probably re-partition, and another, perhaps fatal, twist in the cycle of violence.

For the Catholic members of the community there must be a radical reappraisal too.

Unlike Shylock, who demanded his pound of flesh, old grievances, the demand for revenge and old hatreds must be put to one side. There can be no room for ambiguity or acquiescence in the use of violence; a violence which attempts to push unwilling people into a single state.

Catholics will have to decide what is more important to them in the immediate future: redrawn boundaries and worn out slogans, or justice and reconciliation in Northern Ireland. In particular they must face up to the over-riding need to play a full part in the North's institutions, including the Royal Ulster Constabulary. It is a great paradox that at a time when the RUC is being probed for the use of 'shoot to kill' policies, it has courageously and impartially been upholding the Anglo-Irish Agreement. But if Catholics are to have confidence, every last vestige of sectarianism must be stripped from the RUC and every citizen – nationalist or unionist – must give the RUC their whole-hearted support. To that end it is disappointing that the Code of Conduct promised for the RUC has still not appeared. The symbolism of this will be crucially important. Security and militancy measures on their own are incapable of defeating terrorism. That is why security and justice must go hand in hand. Catholics must support and join the RUC and the prison service but there must be an underpinning of the legitimacy of the RUC by involving the Irish Garda in joint policing and security. A joint Security Commission should be established, joint training of security personnel undertaken the English Prevention of terrorism legislation (which is perceived by many to be 'anti Irish') replaced by joint British-Irish laws, and the one judge Diplock Courts replaced by three judges' courts. I would like to see all terrorist cases on both sides of the border tried in mixed courts of Irish and British judges. Given the eccentricities of individual judges who wouldn't prefer to be before three?

The Anglo-Irish Agreement is much hated by Unionists. The British Government were wrong to shroud the Agreement in secrecy and to ignore moderate Unionist opinions. But the Agreement comes up for review in 1988. This time Unionists should ensure that they are fully involved.

Building on the Agreement we should establish a British-Irish parliamentary tier where parliamentarians from all parts of the British Isles might meet regularly, and in Northern Ireland itself the Unionists and Nationalists must learn to work a responsibility sharing, devolved assembly. They will have to learn to shape their destiny together. This is the one way in which Unionists can ensure that they are not frozen out of future decision making.

In the longer term the alienated nationalist must be able to look towards Dublin while simultaneously the fearful Unionist can look towards Westminster. Such a confederation is surely the fulfillment of the Old Gladstonian ideal and offers justice and hope to all. We can make a start by forging a confederation between Ireland's new Progressive Democrats, Northern Ireland's Alliance Party, and Britain's Liberals and Social Democrats. At the forthcoming European Elections our objective should be to present every voter in these islands with a commonly agreed prospectus.

There is simply no point saying gloomily that consensus does not currently exist. We must build it. It is not good enough to say that partnership does not exist; we must create it. It is not good enough to say that the community is divided; we must unite it. While Northern Ireland festers we will never be able to ask 'What kind of country?' and truthfully be able to answer, 'a good one.'

Chapter Seventeen

AIDS: FREE TO CHOOSE?

'Controlling the spread of infection must be regarded as an issue of prime importance to the future of the nation' – Sir Donald Acheson, Chief Medical Officer, Department of Health and Social Security.

A man who recently died of Aids had admitted to friends that even after he had been diagnosed as HIV anti-bodies positive, he had many sexual relationships. He had not told his partners that he had Aids because he maintained, 'It's my body and I am free to do what I choose with it.' Free to choose maybe but free to take someone else's life?

John Stuart Mill's definition of liberty – and the parameters he places on personal freedom – explicitly reject the spurious and dangerous idea of unfettered liberty. He says that freedom ends and oppression begins when the exercise of our liberty interferes with the rights of another. That is why I would trenchantly argue the rights of the powerless unborn baby. Equally I would argue against the notion that we need show no sense of responsibility towards our partners. What right does someone have to knowingly put another's life in danger? What right does a person have to practice a cruel and systematic deception on another? This is to confuse liberty with license. Each of us has powerful sexual drives and many feel different sexual urges and passions. Orientation is not something which comes to order and society must uphold the rights of minorities. Scapegoating can easily occur – as it did in Hitler's Third Reich, when homosexuals joined Jews, gypsies and mental defectives – on the lonely road to the gas chambers. The rights of gay men and women should be enshrined in a Bill of Rights. Those who choose a Christian lifestyle will aspire to the chastity which the Church requires; those who opt for a secular life are entitled under the law to live in our pluralist society in relationships of their choosing. Personally, I loathe the categorisation and labelling of people as homosexual or lesbian, this or that. If people choose to describe themselves in a particular way that is essentially a matter for them. But one thing we all face – whatever our sexual orientation – is the challenge of Aids. This disease is no respecter of labels. It requires all of us to seek a new understanding of the balance which must always apply between claimed rights and personal responsibility.

Bishop David Sheppard made the following comments about Aids at the Merseyside and Region Churches' Ecumenical Assembly on Saturday 24th January, 1987. He was speaking on behalf of his two fellow presidents – Archbishop Derek Worlock and Merseyside Free Church Moderator, Rev. John Williamson. The Bishop said:

I want to make three points about Aids. First Aids is bound to raise matters of sexual morality. There is a clear piece of Christian witness to be made in this context; that is of our commitment to chastity, faithfulness to one partner and preparation and support for marriage. That must be done first and foremost through teaching at appropriate moments and in appropriate ways. It is worth commenting that Aids is certainly rife in parts of the world where the Church has regularly and fiercely condemned homosexual practices.

Side by side with that there is a pastoral calling. My second point is simply put, but is very important in our approach to an Aids sufferer. If someone is suffering from Aids that of itself does not imply moral guilt.

Thirdly as Gospel people, who believe in the acceptance, forgiveness and new beginnings which Jesus Christ brings, we have a pastoral concern for all people in need, whether they have some personal responsibility for being in need or not. Pastoral concern means meeting people where they are, rather than where we might like to be. Many of us will find ourselves in the position of ministering to Aids sufferers – It is very important that we should have thought out clearly our own attitudes.

Even if the most lurid and scaremongering headlines are ignored, the only certainty about Aids is that it is potentially the greatest threat to health worldwide this century. Dr Halfdon Mahler, Director General of the World Health Organisation, says: 'We stand nakedly in front of a pandemic as mortal as any pandemic has ever been.' The statistics are frightening. Aids is the biggest single killer of men in their 30s in New York; in parts of Africa whole communities are infected with the Aids virus; and countries like Zambia may be economically and socially destroyed. In Britain, the figures for those with fullblown Aids are still low, but the Department of Health and Social Security expects 4,000 deaths by the end of 1989.

The first question when considering the government response to Aids is to ask how swiftly they have reacted to the crisis. While the government has achieved much which has been constructive and deserves the praise and support of all the political parties, I believe that by failing to take the initiative back in 1983–4 it stored up problems for itself and has moved disastrously slowly on several important measures. In examining these achievements, the background to them, and the pressures that have constrained the government it is worth commenting on what could have been done and what must still be done.

The response to Aids, whether in or out of Parliament,

has been influenced by ignorance, caused partly – and naturally – by the nature of the disease. It was not until 1983 that the causative virus was identified and while a vast amount has been learnt in a very short time, a great deal has still to be discovered, not least a cure or vaccine. This lack of knowledge was exacerbated by our western view of the world, which led to the African situation going largely unnoticed. Aids, as a result, became associated with homosexuality as the first cases appeared in American homosexuals.

The 'gay plague' label which followed has had several serious consequences, internationally and domestically. A number of countries, which do not recognise the existence of homosexuality, also refused to recognise the existence of Aids, thus losing valuable time and research experience for themselves and the rest of the world. In Britain, intolerance of minorities has been compounded by fear of Aids and has led to additional stress and suffering for those already afraid that they might be at risk. Most serious of all, the government has had to try and correct the indifference among many heterosexuals. If the government had acted back in 1983, the extent of Aids in the homosexual population would have been less and it would have spread slower in the heterosexual population. Much suffering might have been spared.

The government finally launched its advertising campaign in late 1985, but only after a year of pressure from medical experts. It was notable that the campaign was aimed first, both in the newspapers and subsequently on television, at explaining that Aids could affect anyone. The government slogan was 'Don't die of ignorance', but the disease's long incubation period – up to five years or more – ensured that for a number of both homosexuals and heterosexuals the slogan was simply too late. Even so, the message still needs to be accepted not least in Parliament itself that Aids is not caused or spread simply through a person's sexuality. Certain sexual acts and lifestyles are a factor, and some heterosexuals are at much greater risk than many homosexuals. Hence the need for the advertising campaign to be blunt and explicit to ensure that the facts are understood.

I appreciate that getting the facts across in the necessary blunt manner poses great problems for the government. Questions of sex bring with them questions of morality, not least for a government that would pride itself on supporting family values. Many Conservatives, in Parliament and outside, would rather wash their hands of the situation and reject effective measures either because they believe that people with Aids are being punished for a lifestyle which offends God or because measures to control the spread of Aids also offend against religious teaching. The then Scottish health minister, John McKay, asserted that Aids was a totally self-inflicted disease and, effectively, that victims should blame themselves. Another Tory MP complained that the advertising campaign, at first nothing like as strong as medical advisers wished, was brutal.

No political party can or should ignore the views of the many people who for religious or other reasons advocate a moral approach to life, and who believe in chastity inside marriage and monogamy within. The Churches, while remembering the value of Christian compassion, clearly have an important view to put. However, it is up to each and every one of us, guided by our Church or convictions, to choose our manner of behaviour. No government can forget that it acts for all the people and that in our multicultural society a government imposed morality is both impractical and wrong. However, if another's rights or life is at risk the government cannot stand idly by. Clearly the government must ensure that it acts in the best interests of the whole community even if this means offending parts of it. It must also ensure that individuals are fully aware of the consequences of their actions both for themselves and for the community. I believe, for these reasons, that the balanced message of stressing the need for one partner while promoting safer sex if this is impossible is the right one.

In a debate on Gavin Strang's Bill to Control the Spread of Aids, a Tory MP asked why all the effort on a largely self-inflicted disease, when there were many suffering from other diseases who needed support. His view was in a minority even if everyone also wished that more were done for health generally. We must not judgementally simply blame the victim. The nature of Aids increases the pressure on the government. People with Aids need acute care, sometimes in hospital, at other times in the community. Yet the number of acute hospital beds has been consistently cut over the past few years and, even if prejudice can be overcome, community care is still a concept rather than a reality. Too often it is a case of dumping, rather than caring, in the community.

The health service simply does not have the beds, facilities or staff to cope with the numbers of Aids patients. The Department of Health and Social Security disclosed to my colleague, Archy Kirkwood MP, that the cost of treating an Aids patient was between £10,000 and £20,000. Despite encouraging news on recent Aids research, a cure or vaccine must be at least five years away.

The Government took a number of early measures which were sensible and uncontroversial. An expert advisory committee was set up, complemented in 1986 by a special Cabinet committee chaired by Lord Whitelaw to coordinate measures across departments. Since 1982, Aids cases have been voluntarily reported to the Communicable Disease Surveillance Centre, as have figures on HIV-positive tests. Warnings to blood donors not to donate blood if they came from a high risk group were issued, and the very low and static numbers of positive results among blood donors show that this measure is working. Since the end of 1984, heat-treated Factor VIII has been available for heamophiliacs – although the country will not be fully self-sufficient in Factor VIII until mid–1987. Guidelines have been issued to health service staff, although they are not always followed, and to employers.

Other issues are more controversial and the government's record less praiseworthy. Many of the services designed to care and treat people with Aids demand expansion and greater resources. Urgently needed are greater hospital provision, especially in the four Thames regions; community care facilities and trained staff to enable patients to remain in their homes; hospice accommodation; sufficient provision for sexually transmitted disease clinics to meet the demand for testing and provide counsellors. Yet up to the end of 1985, when there were already 108 cases of Aids, only £2 million had been allocated for these areas and for research.

The figures for 1987–1988 are more impressive: £7 million for patients care, £12.5 million for health education, and £14.5 million for research for the next three years. Yet these funds remain inadequate. The answers to questions I tabled in Parliament recently revealed that the Public Health Laboratory Service on Merseyside, which does all the local testing for HIV, tested 1,735 people in the first three months of this year compared with 249 in the first quarter of 1986. Staff and funding, however, remained constant and I was shocked to see the cramped room in which the work is undertaken when I visited the unit.

Doctors predict that £20 million will have to be diverted from other budgets to cope this year alone, and Department of Health and Social Security figures show that in 1988 the cost of caring for Aids patients will be between £20 and £30 million. The South East Thames Regional Health Authority asked for £4 million for this year. They received £700,000, yet £850,000 is needed to pay for heat-treated Factor VIII for heamophiliacs alone. Government staffing guidelines for hospitals ensure that medical staff at all levels are working under great pressure, and the bulk of the work is being done by academic rather than health service staff. The implications for the amount of time left for teaching and reserve are serious. Health authorities outside London are to receive no extra funding, yet they need resources now to enable them to plan for the future. In 1986 the independent College of Health estimated that at least £60 million per year was needed.

Norman Fowler came back from his visit to San Francisco and Amsterdam advocating the importance of caring for Aids patients within the community. Pope John Paul after his recent visit said that every Aids victim is entitled to love and care and he reminded his San Francisco audience that all of us are equal in the eyes of a loving and forgiving God and who will easily forget the Pope's embrace and kiss for a four year old boy infected with Aids? – The Pope said: 'God loves you all, without distinction, without limit. That love and respect for life must be backed up by the needed resources.

The importance of continuing preventative measures must not be underestimated. The advertising campaign will be long-running, which is very welcome. The television companies deserve our congratulations for their imaginative contributions to raising the public awareness of Aids, which has partly made up for the sensationalist, unpleasant and often inaccurate coverage in the popular newspapers. More work is still needed, even if, we have seen, the government must treat warily. The dilemmas are sharp. Cardinal Hume has said, 'We are dealing with an intrinsically moral question and not simply one of public health. . . . The Church wants to tackle promiscuity as the principal cause of infection'. Yes, but, the Churches and government must also look at the public health questions such as the provision of free condoms, and the sanctioning of needle exchange systems for drug abusers in the major cities. On both issues the government message is double-edged: don't inject or sleep around, but take precautions if you must. I believe this is right. Aids means that many need to re-evaluate their lifestyles.

Yet the government does not have time to bring about

changes in lifestyle, even if it were possible. The Minister of Health, Tony Newton, has said: 'I disagree with the view that a moral crusade would be a sufficient answer to this problem.' I believe it is therefore right to advocate that condoms should be made more widely and freely available – not to encourage sex, certainly not to attack religious values, but because it may save lives in the future and may protect those who might otherwise not be in a position to protect themselves. The government must encourage people to make the right decisions for themselves.

But if condoms are a delicate question and a dilemma so to is the question of providing free syringes. This is at least as delicate as no-one wishes to encourage drug addiction. The alternative cannot be contemplated. In Edinburgh there are believed to be 3,000 HIV carriers linked to drug abuse and the problem is rapidly spreading to other cities. The problem is also rife on the Continent. One of the reasons for the rapid spread of HIV in Edinburgh appears to be that the police confiscated syringes, forcing addicts to share equipment. The low level of HIV in the drug community in Amsterdam shows the importance of special schemes to combat Aids. A similar scheme to provide help to addicts has been operating in Liverpool where excellent relationships between addicts and police have been built, and so the number of Aids victims is mercifully small. Methadone substitution and sympathetic counselling should be integral parts of any scheme. The delay in implementing such programmes in Britain is to be deeply regretted, but now that the government is finally tackling the problem, they deserve support. The government's approach to research is deserving of rather less support. Research in all areas is admittedly paltry, but one might expect that the potential rewards to be derived from a cure or vaccine would justify the investment. Until this year, less than £.5 million was allocated for research. This has now been increased to £14.5 million over three years, although the principle researchers have repeatedly made requests for £10 million for the first year of spending. The method of allocation needs to be examined to ensure that funds reach the necessary recipients, who may not have time to comply with the present allocation rules.

Testing or screening for Aids poses a number of problems, not least the delay between infection and antibodies appearing in the blood, the lack of accuracy in the test itself, and the worrying fact that the virus appears to be mutating in, possibly, several forms. The government must plan ahead, and needs to be able to accurately estimate the possible number of cases. Voluntary testing, backed up by counselling, should be encouraged and back-up facilities must be provided on a scale commensurate with the problem.

Anonymous testing of blood samples routinely taken in hospital and screened for rubella and other diseases is another possibility. The government has rejected this at the moment because permission would not be sought for such testing and those found to be HIV-infected would not be informed. However, I believe that this is the least dangerous method of collecting general data and should be looked at again. The government has rejected, and must go on rejecting, compulsory mass screening, both for visitors to the country and the general population, and they have also rejected the possibility of isolating people with Aids. As they have said, both would be medically useless and socially deeply damaging.

The government has achieved much in many of the important areas, but increased resources have to be given now to enable health and local authorities to plan ahead and ensure that people with Aids are cared for in the best manner; for research for a cure and a vaccine; and to prevent the virus spreading any further. A national long term strategy is the best way to achieve this and should be strengthened by cross party talks to achieve a consensus and to give the government support to take the necessary measures.

I was saddened to see the Health Minister, Edwina Currie, say that 'good Christians do not die of Aids.' Haemophiliacs, people accidently infected, and many others who contract the disease are not necessarily bad people and it is unworthy of a Minister of the Crown to generalise in this way. Our Lord forgave the adulterous woman and it was her accusers – the powerful of the earth – who had to shrink away having been invited to stone her if they could themselves claim to be without sin.

Diseases are not judgemental; although suffering, pain and the response which such a condition evokes in others can tell us a lot about them, ourselves, and our relationship with God. Jesus told us not to judge and he had special words of comfort for the sinner and sufferers alike. In St Matthew's gospel, Chapter 10, he puts a premium on hospitality and compassion. Anyone, he says, who turns his followers away will receive a fate worse than the citizens of Sodom and Gomorrah. That puts things into the right perspective and serves to remind us of how a Christian society – or a Country that dares to call itself civilised should respond to the challenge which Aids provides.

Chapter Eighteen

ABORTION . . .
WHOSE CHOICE ANYWAY?

'To me, the nations with legalised abortions are the poorest nations.
The great destroyer of peace today is the crime against the innocent
unborn child. . . . In destroying the child, we are destroying love,
destroying the image of God in the world.'

—Mother Teresa of Calcutta.
Nobel Peace Prize Winner 1979

Aids has been one factor in making the 1980s a time of
radical reassessment of values and attitudes forged in the
1960s. It is important that we do not so over-react to the
bitter legacy of the 1960s that we destroy the good that
also came out of those years. An openness and tolerance
and a willingness to re-examine the accepted orthodoxy led
to far reaching changes. Legislation to protect minorities
to prevent discrimination, to further equal opportunities
and to allow greater uncensored free speech all helped
liberalise areas of the law that needed reform. The death
penalty was outlawed as people realised that institutionalised violence by the state would never prevent a psychopath
or a fanatic or a terrorist from committing murder; that
violence only begets more violence.

Yet whenever a pendulum swings, it is apt to bring its
own excesses. Which of us who lived through the sixties
and its aftermath was not affected by the all-pervading

spirit of those times? In particular the materialism of the
'you've never had it so good' years has eaten away at our
spiritual values, producing a country where possessions
and position are the only things regarded as worth having.
The clock cannot be put back – and in many areas it would
be undesirable to even try. Yet twenty years later we should
be undertaking a critical reassessment, a stock-taking of
the values and ideals, of our country and ourselves and we
must radically question some of the assumptions that have
produced the secular humanism and the greedy materialism of the 1980s.

In particular, twenty years after the passage of the
Abortion Act, I am utterly convinced that the low value
we place on the sanctity of life is symptomatic of what has
gone wrong with Britain.

For centuries medical practice and medical ethics were
dominated by the Hippocratic oath and by the Christian
understanding that humanity is special and is made in the
image of God. These high ideals find their place in the
1948 World Medical Organization's declaration that 'I will
maintain the utmost respect for human life from the time
of conception. Even under threat I will not use my medical
knowledge contrary to the laws of humanity.'

This year in Britain 600 abortions take place every day.
Each year 170,000 abortions occur – the equivalent in
population of towns the size of Swansea, Dundee or
Preston. Since 1967, 3 million abortions have been undertaken. The numbers are moving inexorably upwards.

Britain is not alone. In America 1.5 million abortions,
and in China about 5 million abortions are undertaken
annually.

In 1967 the pro-abortionists – they describe themselves
as pro choice – argued that easy abortions would decrease
illegitimacy. In 1987 it is 15% and rising. In 1967 they
said there would be less child abuse because every child
would be 'wanted'. In 1987 hardly a day passes without
the reporting of a sexual or physical assault on a child. In

1967 we were told abortion would help women and give them new rights. In 1987 there are millions of women and men, who are emotionally and psychologically scarred and the demand for post-abortion counselling is growing. As the author of 'Whatever Happened to the Human Race', Francis Schaeffer said: 'Abortion does not end all the problems, often it just exchanges one set for another'.

At the beginning of Luke's account of the life of Christ he describes the encounter between the aging Elizabeth and her cousin Mary. Far from being a 'clump of tissue' the gospel writer records how, moved by the Spirit, the baby John leapt in his mother's womb as Elizabeth greeted her cousin. The moment anyone accepts that a child can be imbued with the Spirit before birth they must surely accept the authenticity of that new individual's claim to the protection which accompanies life.

Even feminists like Kathleen McDonnell, in her book, 'Not an Easy Choice: A Feminist Re-examines Abortion', seem to conceed this. She quotes approvingly a young abortion counsellor who says 'Yes this is killing, there is no way around it. But I am willing to accept that'. McDonnell says 'There is no escaping the fact that we have with full consciousness, terminated life. This is most emphatically not the same as blaming ourselves or burdening ourselves with an unnecessary load of guilt.'

For the Christian – or surely anyone who holds dear the high ideal of the worth and dignity of humanity – such contortions are quite unacceptable. All of us sin; all of us fail and all of us have guilt. That is why forgiveness is central to the improvement of people and the world around us. Yet forgiveness is only possible when we truly strive to change. How can it be possible to say 'with full consciousness' that, yes, it was life but, no, I will never feel any sense of guilt for what I have done. That is simply not how people tick.

The poet John Donne well understood our interdependence, one for another. He wrote:

The greatest gift of God
I would think,
is the gift of life.

The greatest gift of humans,
it would seem,
would be to return that gift
ungratefully and unopened . . .

No man is an island
Any man's death diminishes me,
because I am involved in mankind;
And therefore never send to know for whom the bells toll
It tolls for thee.

The biggest problem with the abortion debate is that one disputant starts from a powerful conviction about the primacy of the mother's right to choose; while the opposing view begins from the humanity of the child and its right to life. The arguments run on tram lines that never converge. There are no shared premises or ground rules and invariably the debate degenerates. If you read the Hansard accounts of the many House of Commons' debates they are undoubtedly the nastiest that take place on any subject.

Politically the abortion issue is a bed of nails: so why should a Member of Parliament go anywhere near such a contentious issue? Since 1967 there have been 14 attempts to amend the abortion legislation. Maybe in another 20 years from now, a Wilberforce will emerge who will end abortion by the State, although a return to the back street from the shop window would hardly be progress. Whether it is legal or illegal, abortion destroys. What is really required is a change of heart and attitude. That can only happen by constantly re-opening the debate and challenging the belief that the taking of life carries no consequences.

It is not only the woman and child who are affected by

an abortion. For the medical staff abortions can also carry grave consequences. It is an especially cruel paradox that in different units of the same hospital doctors and nurses are expected to abort babies as late as seven months while babies born prematurely at 23 weeks are fighting for life. This is deeply repugnant for medical personnel and is physically and psychologically damaging to many women.

Nor do many people seem to understand what a late abortion involves. In private clinics medical staff dilate the woman's cervix, insert a pliers-like instrument up into the uterus, seize a leg or other part of the body, and with a twisting motion, tear it from the baby's body. No anaesthetic for the baby is used. This motion is repeated again and again. The spine must be snapped, and the skull crushed to remove them. The baby may be about a foot long and these procedures are needed to facilitate the baby's extrication from the womb. An attendant nurse then has the duty of re-assembling the body to ensure that nothing has been left behind that might cause infection. It is an extraordinary dilemma for doctors and nurses expected to be both destroyer and saver of life. Some have told me of the nightmares which they have suffered for years afterwards. The value we place on the baby's life was wryly summed up in a cartoon which arrived at my House of Commons office. It depicted a baby seal holding a placard demanding that we protect the unborn child.

If doctors and nurses refuse to take part they are moved sideways or passed over for promotion. The National Abortion Campaign voted to include in its aims the singularly sinister objective that all pro-life doctors 'holding positions in which they can directly or indirectly obstruct a woman seeking an abortion be removed from such posts'.

Men must, of course, come to this debate with humility and sensitivity. We rarely have to suffer the practical day to day experience of an unwanted child; and women frequently have abortions because they cannot afford to do otherwise. Very often a stigma is also attached to one-parent families. Abortion must be seen against that backdrop and in the context of badly funded National Health Service facilities, counselling and care.

Women are right to demand of men an understanding of the effect on them of male violence towards women in and outside marriage; and an acceptance by men of their responsibilities. Too often women are left in the lurch while many men use their sexuality without love, purely to prove their virility and machismo.

I am staggered that it causes such a vehement response when men and women dare to assert the rights of the powerless, the weak and the most vulnerable. That is at the heart of this matter. Post-conception a child has begun its development as a unique new individual and this over-riding right to life must always take precedence before any other claimed rights. The woman and her child are equally precious because both are human beings. Two people go to the abortionist but only one returns home.

Even if people do not accept this human rights argument I hope they will at least objectively examine the position of late abortions.

In no other Western European country are abortions available until as late as 28 weeks. Twelve to 14 weeks is the norm elsewhere and in France 10 weeks is the limit. This is one of the reasons why 42 per cent of the abortions undertaken between 19 and 20 weeks and 56 per cent of those undertaken between 21 and 24 weeks are for foreign women prevented from obtaining abortions in their own country. Eighty-eight per cent of all abortions performed after 18 weeks are in private clinics, mainly in London, where the later the abortions the more expensive they become. This a multi-million pound business and the private clinics are a powerful lobby with massive vested interests. Eleven doctors and the clinics in which they work carry out over half the 8,000 late abortions receiving £2 million for their efforts. This is a sleazy end of the market in a very sleazy business.

Let us be clear precisely what it is we allow the State to do on

our behalf. By 18 weeks a child has sentience, and it is no different
except in size and weight from the child at 28 weeks. By 20 weeks,
the baby weighs about a pound, its heart is pumping 50 pints of
blood daily; it has all its organs functioning; it has a complete
skeleton, reflexes. It can feel pain. It reacts to sound and to light.

Late abortions are also notoriously more dangerous to
the woman involved. Far too little work has been done on
the traumatic psychological implications and subsequent
anxiety and guilt felt by many women encouraged to have
abortions. It is vital that we spur the state into a more
positive response to pregnant women and not see abortion
as an everybody event. We must challenge the assumption
that abortion is of itself a prudent or desirable operation.

Abortion is not about planning a family; or a form of
contraception; nor is it about the exercise of powerful
sexual instincts in or outside marriage. By allowing abortion we are deliberately allowing a destructive and violent
act to be undertaken with the state's approval. People tell
me it is the lesser of two evils. That is mere utility and
defeatism.

One other issue needs to be met head-on. There is an
increasingly popular view that it is somehow legitimate to
abort a baby that might be disabled.

For six years, before entering Parliament, I taught handicapped and disabled children. Some were terminally ill. It
would be a brave man or woman who so self-assuredly
pronounced them better dead. The unsaid reality is that
many would simply prefer that humankind was not
burdened with deformity or handicap. We believe in a
society with no discrimination on grounds of colour, sex or
disability. We abort openly on grounds of disability. There
would be an outcry if we aborted on grounds of sex or
colour, yet in Britain today we allow without demur the
imposition of a quality control on life.

Just after I was elected one little boy I had taught died
of cystic fibrosis. Ian was 12 and had a little sister with
the same disease. He had another healthy and unaffected

sister. Ian taught me more than I ever gave him. He knew how to face life and death and the love that he generated was a source of joy and strength, not sorrow. The child with disability is so often feared by parents but will often bring more love and cohesion to a family than any other gift from man or God. After announcing my decision to challenge the eugenicists I received nearly 5,000 letters of support – many from disabled people and from their families. At meetings in Belfast, Cardiff, Leeds, Liverpool, London – and in other British cities and towns – it has been disabled people who have captivated huge audiences as they assert their right to live. What does it say about a society that snuffs out a life that is not deemed to have worth because of disease or disability. Ask the next disabled person you meet whether they are glad to be alive.

Many disabled people have written to me telling me their own stories. One young woman, Ellen Wilkie, wrote to say that 'No one can ever predict what an unborn baby will be capable of'. She should know. She was born with muscular dystrophy and was not expected to live beyond her teens. She is now 29 and has a classics degree and has now been a professional actress and poet for seven years. She asked 'Who is to play God and judge what the norm is?' Indeed who is? God forbid that we ever allow to go unchallenged the notion that imperfections should determine the right to live. That child is entitled, while dependent, to the love, care, support and guidance they need. To muddle the argument by provoking images of children who will in any event be born dead is simply a travesty.

Some paediatricians have a false conception of parental rights over children, and on that basis justify compliance with parental wishes which are contrary to the child's rights. There are limits to parental autonomy and legitimate interests to be maintained by the civil authority.

The handicapped child, like every other child, possesses the dignity proper to human beings. It is incompatible with recognition of that dignity to kill a child on the grounds that in someone else's view they have not got a worthwhile life or will have a poor 'quality of life'. The value of a human life is not to be assessed in this way. There is no room for ambivalence on this issue.

Last year more people wrote to a disabled people's adoption service wanting to adopt disabled children, than there were children available for adoption. It is true that sending your child for adoption can be painful, but surely if the alternative is abortion this must be the correct thing to do.

I refuse to believe that the overwhelming majority of people in Britain believe that abortion is of itself desirable. Many are searching for radical alternatives to utility; alternatives which find their bedrock in authentic human values. This is not some piece of Christian idiosyncrasy. It is surely central to any society which dares to call itself civilised or free.

For me this is a human rights issue. I do not come to the question from a moralistic or censorious position. I have made the same mistakes and have the same regrets about my own life as the next. But if statements like the 1948 United Nations Universal Declarations of Human Rights, which insists that 'Everyone has the right to life', are not to be so much cant then Liberals and others who hold so dearly to the rights of the individual must not be cowed into silence when it comes to the unborn child.

Beyond the slogans, the invective, the endless pickets and the personal abuse lies a weak and vulnerable baby; if those who on so many other issues spurn the powerful and cherish the powerless are not prepared to speak out on their behalf, who will?

With 4 out of 5 Women on his Side

As a sequel to my remarks about abortion, a Gallup poll has shown that 4 out of 5 women now back my Bill to stop late abortions. 27th October 1987 was the 20th anniversary of the 1967 Act. It was the day before my own Bill was first presented to Parliament. At a meeting held in Westminster's Methodist Central Hall hundreds of people heard Paula Conor, of 'Feminists opposed to Eugenic Practices', say why so many women reject the utilitarianism and brutality of abortion. At meetings up and down the land thousands of people – many of them young – have been asking why a laboratory animal used in scientific tests has more rights than an unborn child.

This is what Paula Connor said:-

I am here to represent Feminists Opposed to Eugenic Practices – a pro-life feminist organisation which was founded in August 1985. As an organisation we are committed to the emancipation of women *and* are opposed to *all* forms of killing.

Women have not and we cannot kill our way to liberation. The very notion is anathema to justice. Feminists Opposed to Eugenics are not alone in our commitment to the Rights of Women *and* the rights of pre-born infants. There is a growing movement of pro-life radicals who will take the pro-life fight into its second stage. In this country we have Women For Life, Women Exploited by Abortion, The Labour Life Group, Liberals for Life and Pro-lifers for Peace. People who defy the definitions propagandists have sought to hang us with.

It has been recognised in the pro-life movement for years that women who have an abortion get a rough deal, are damaged medically, are denied the chance to give informed consent and have been used as pawns in the state's battle to gain control of women's sexuality for eugenic purposes.

Front street abortion has made the social rights of women contingent upon the aims of our patriarchial establishment. In spite of the propaganda which legislated abortion in the name of women's freedom, nothing has changed. Women are, in 1987, the largest class of old, underpaid, poor, abandoned, medically neglected and sexually abused people in our society and yet we are expected to believe that there is a renaissance in women's lives and opportunities as a result of legal abortion. This is not the case. 51% of women in this country support David Alton's Bill. I am part of this majority because the social position of women will never change until we begin to challenge this state which promotes the killing of our children and calls it 'choice.' Abortion, whether free market or back street has usurped justice and become the establishment's answer to every form of oppression women face.

If a woman is poor and pregnant the state does not seek to provide her with economic emancipation – instead its agents encourage her to have an abortion.

If a pre-born infant is disabled the mother is deemed anti-social if she will not destroy her child.

When we are violated by male violence the state does not seek long prison sentences for rapists, has *NOT* amended sexual offences legislation to make marital rape a crime; the state does not put a curfew on male aggressers, but rather says that the *only* destructive consequence of rape or incest is pregnancy. It is not.

Abortion cannot solve the problem of violence against women because it is part of the problem of violence against women. If men ditch us when we are pregnant we are offered the escape route of killing and expected to be grateful to avoid abandonment.

Abortion legislation has *NOT* taken our bodies, ourselves outside of state control, it has simply placed our bodies and our children's lives at the disposal of a eugenic medical profession and defined the social rights of women according to male power.

Abortion is a medical disaster area for the simple reason that it involves invasive surgery on healthy women. One of the most scandalous factors about the abortion business is that women are not told that they may die, may suffer sepsis, haemorrhage, perforation of the uterus and bowel, iatrogenically induced infertility. Women are not told that they may suffer cervical incompetence or subsequent miscarriage, psychological trauma or mental illness.

The evidence now on the physical and psychological damage to women after abortion is being suppressed because it is taboo to question this most fashionable form of killing. The fact is abortion is destructive to the health of women – yet they are not told of the risks they face. Neither are they told that they may be experiments in a medic's apprenticeship in the abortion industry, or as one abortionist states: 'At this point having done somewhere around 12,000 procedures, I'm beginning to think I'm reasonably competent.' My contention about abortion is that it is a violent, destructive procedure which harms women and always aims to kill the pre-born.

For this reason I am compelled to support David Alton's Bill to restrict legal abortion to 18 weeks gestation because it is the most effective challenge to the status quo that any parliamentarian has offered.

I am opposed to all abortions but realise that we live in a pluralistic society which places pragmatism before justice – and as every piece of humanitarian social reform has been won piecemeal – this is a beginning. It will enable us to save the lives of thousands of children and help women to avoid the traumas the state pretends do not exist.

In particular I support Alton because his Bill is the first to challenge the Eugenicists – those people who do not want disabled human being to live. The eugenic clause of the Abortion Act is supposed to be a benevolent rationale for destroying people because they are different from the western model of perfect humanity. We have reached the stage when we use primitive Lombrosian ideas about defenceless children, destroy them and call it scientific progress.

David Alton will succeed in challenging the superstitious fear this society has of infants who need care and medical help more than any other and will give parents of disabled children the confidence to fight the new genetics – coercion to abort. I would oppose any eugenic exception clause to the Bill because the law itself is an exception to the principles of justice – and if we are to begin dismantling it we must start by recognising the humanity of *all* pre-born infants at the same stage.

The Bill will also stop this country being the back-street abortionist of Europe. Alton's opponents pretend that he will bring a return to backstreet methods – if they really were opposed to backstreet abortion they would support him. We are Europe's back-street abor-tionists because we abort thousands of non-resident women at a stage in pregnancy when abortion is illegal in their own countries – for very good reason, these women are offered no pre-abortion or post abortion counselling. They arrive here, are aborted, pay for the damage and are dismissed. What happens to them? The so-called 'service' private clinics offer begins and ends with abortion and accepting the cash.

Everyone whose true aim is dignity and justice for all should support David Alton. He is seeking parity with Europe, he is seeking legal recognition of the rights of disabled people. He is *not* seeking absolutism but consensus.

Democracy cannot ignore the fight.

This world of ours has killed and robbed and militar-ised and raped and murdered its way through the twentieth century. Abortion is part of this pattern and as a feminist challenge its acceptability.

I do not have any faith in mythical liberation – I adhere to that much abused philosophical idea of justice: absolute: Unconditional: Anti-Utilitarian: Justice for all. Justice which not only speaks with the voice of inalien-able human rights but gives special protection to the vulnerable.

Until justice is the foundation of our society women will not be free.

I believe David Alton's Bill will take us one step further on the road to freedom.

Part Three

WHAT KIND OF WORLD?

Chapter Nineteen

THE SEEDS OF A NEW WORLD

The first meeting of the United Nations General Assembly was held in 1946 at London's Methodist Central Hall amidst the rubble of Europe's pulverised cities and broken streets. Just as every war is supposed to end all wars both the League of Nations, founded in the wake of World War One, and the United Nations aimed to secure world wide co-operation amongst nations and to seek and guarantee peace. In 1919 Clemenceau, the French leader, rightly said that the task for victors and vanquished alike was to go as aggresively to the peace as they had gone to the war.

Yet our attempts at breaking down narrow nationalism have so far met with little success. Amongst the great nations real war had simply given way to cold war and to surrogate war.

The world in which I want to live is not one where we wrap ourselves in the Union Jack but poke fun at the European Community insignia; not one where the integrity and strengthening of the Commonwealth counts for less than the interests of Consolidated Gold Fields; not one where our common heritage, our forests and our peoples are obliterated by the endless pursuit of more; not one where the Third World becomes no world for countries submerged in debt, disease and famine; not one where the brinkmanship of the super power arms race will one day bring the four horsemen of the apocalypse galloping over the horizon.

But what other kind of world is on offer? Bluntly, there is no point arguing for less nationalism and more co-operation via Europe, the Commonwealth and the United Nations if we are less than whole hearted members of those organisations. We cannot bid the gelding be fruitful having castrated it. Every supranational organisation is cobbled by its national owners then derided because it cannot run.

It cannot be beyond the wit and ingenuity of man to recognise that all human beings are dependent on one another, that they have to share this planet and that they should plan accordingly. In the 1960's the Liverpool folk group The Spinners called it The Family of Man: 'A name every man should be proud he owns.' In the 1970's that idealism captured the commitment of millions of Britons who voted to press on with our membership of the European Family, the EEC. In the 1980's our growing internationalism has manifested itself again in Live Aid and Walk for the World, through support for Christian Aid, CAFOD and Tear Fund. As the world has shrunk and young people travel to Europe and Asia much as their parents took a day trip to Southend, the climate for greater co-operation is there. Pigmy leaders are all that stand in the way. While young people impatiently break down nationalistic barriers, (what better example than Live Aid's 'global jukebox'), xenophobic leaders look to their own country's narrow little interests.

At the end of World War Two Dean Acherson the American Secretary of State said that the problem for Britain was that she had lost an empire but was still to find a role. Today our role is more well defined but in the years that have intervened Britain has ceded sovereignty not to a United States of Europe but to the United States of America. Often we behave with all the confidence of a fifty first state. In countries where Britain still enjoys enormous respect our voice is muted. Instead of a special relationship based on mutual trust and common interest we act as hosts for American cruise missiles, we give our permission to act as a launching pad for US air strikes on Libya and send minesweepers to back up the US presence in the Gulf. Ever since the disaster of Suez on all the major international issues Britain has contented itself to feebly mouth the words 'me too' whenever the American eagle flaps its wings.

The special relationship now resembles that of the vassal and his feudal lord. Such bondage holds little appeal.

The wave of anti Americanism that has swept Europe has been born out of frustration with these policies. The policy of 'Glasnost' as pursued by Mikhail Gorbachev has been far more subtle and successful. The naive conclude that the new face of Soviet Russia (as evidenced by the well publicised release of a few well known dissidents and the out-manouvering of a clumsy President Reagan at Geneva and Rekyjavik) will offer international peace. Once already in this century Europe has learned the price of such naivety.

Yes we can and should have a special relationship with the United States: an ally, albeit a late one in the last two World Wars. The Soviet Union, also our ally in those conflicts, may one day enjoy a similar relationship too. The precondition is to assert our rights as Europeans. This will enable us to deal on an equal footing with both the USA and the USSR; to forge a sometimes role as honest-broker and to develop foreign and defence policies which will not always coincide with those of the super powers.

Chapter Twenty

BRITAIN IN EUROPE

When the European Community was formed Britain loftily declined to enter. To its credit the British Liberal Party alone championed the case for membership. After a humiliating rejection of our subsequent application, at the hands of President de Gaulle, Britain finally became the seventh member state in 1973, joining at the same time as Ireland and Denmark. Edward Heath's vision was not shared by Labour who were reluctant Europeans and subsequently campaigned for Britain to pull out. To accommodate the anti-marketeers in his own Cabinet Harold Wilson called a referendum and by a two thirds majority Britain voted to stay in Europe.

The Labour Party remained reluctant Europeans. Their attitude to Europe summed up by Labour MP, Eric Heffer: 'There is no doubt,' he said, 'that some of our socialist comrades in Europe are confused because of our decision at conference to come out of the Common Market. The point being that under the Treaty of Rome some of their people gain in certain respects whereas we are net losers.' Note the term 'their people', a term usually reserved for the class enemies but here it refers to other socialists. So much for fraternity. More to the point it reduces membership to the value of the market place in much the same way as Mrs Thatcher's attitudes do.

In the 1980's many Labour MP's still want to quit the

Community. Their lack of enthusiasm for the European ideal is often shared by the Thatcherites and by the right of the Conservative Party. Mrs Thatcher has always thought of the Community as a fast-food convenience shop. The shrill sound of the cornered fish wife haggling over what we pay and brawling for Britain on every conceivable occasion characterises the current approach to Community affairs. Her right wingers deplore the loss of sovereignty and hanker for the return of the idyllic island state. Reluctant Europeans all.

In my time in Parliament the voices raised for the European ideal have been among liberal minded Conservatives, among Social Democrats, like Roy Jenkins and Liberals like Sir Russell Johnston, surely the most passionate advocate of European Union in Westminster.

The debates usually centre on the Common Agricultural Policy – which over produces and leads to butter mountains, wine lakes and the rest. Whilst the case for reform is overwhelming the pettiness and churlishness – which rarely admits that these are problems created by success – drives me to distraction. Post-war Europe suffered famine and rationing. The Community was partially founded to ensure that our continent's not inconsiderable resources might be put at the disposal of all Europeans.

The contrasting response to the two parts of Europe to the starving of Ethiopa's marxist Menguistu regime illustrates this point most eloquently. The Community, through prudence and good husbandry, had grain to give and generously opened its silos; Eastern Europe gave nothing – its centrally planned agriculture unable to even support its own people, let alone others. Yet, we must not be complacent.

So abundant has been the produce of its agricultural system that 1.3 million tonnes of food were destroyed in Europe in the year before the Ethiopian famine. That is simply insanity and bad practice – Europe can and should cut its production levels and seek a new price support system geared to the quantities of food which the Community actually needs – that must spur us on to reform; the 750 million people who will lie hungry in their beds tonight should give us added impetus.

But Europe is about more than the CAP. Our shared experiences – especially the two world wars fought on our soil – must surely drive us inexorably to the conclusion that only by rejecting the exclusive claims of nationalism and by binding our nation states more closely can we face the seemingly intractable problems of mass unemployment, economic uncertainty and arms control. We share common histories and values just as we face the same problems of the post industrial society. To achieve the peaceful co-existence of nations will require more intellectual commitment than that required for bad tempered arguments about the stocking of the larder.

On January 1st 1981 Greece joined the Community and five years later in 1986 Spain and Portugal also acceded. Each country had to put fascism and military dictatorship behind them. Next it may be the turn of Turkey – still, in democratic terms Europe's sick man. A top priority should be to encourage the Scandanavian countries to join too. By a narrow vote Norway, in 1972, decided not to become a part of the Community although it had agreed terms and signed a preliminary treaty. It is a member of NATO however. Iceland has never taken a vote but it also is a member of NATO (despite the fact that it does not have an army of its own). The psychological hurdle for neutralist Sweden may be harder to climb; and harder still for Finland who must always look anxiously towards its Soviet neighbour.

The great challenge – probably one for the new millenium – will be to seek the reunification of the two halves of Europe.

Yugoslavia, with its mixed economy and proximity to Italy and Greece, has always shown an independence from the Soviet bloc. We should mount a formidable attempt to create favourable circumstances and terms for Yugoslavian entry to the Community. President Ceaucescu's Romanian foreign policy has also shown an independence unique amongst countries of the Warsaw Pact. This is in sharp contrast to domestic policies which are ruthless and repressive. Internal reforms and sanitisation of Eastern Europe's communist regimes would need to be a prerequisite for membership. But interim preferential trade agreements and other assistance could be given to those countries making progress towards achieving a pluralist society and a mixed economy.

In the short term Europeans in the West must take their destiny into their own hands. Those countries able to must provide greater resources for the Community Social Fund which should be used, as was the American Marshall Plan in the aftermath of World War Two, as a dynamo for reconstruction. All over the Continent the opportunities exist to build for peace and for prosperity. Decaying cities are in need of revitalisation; remote regions need improved communications and greater assistance in fostering new enterprises; the arts, music and education, the noble pursuits in which Europe can excel, require nourishment. It really is no idle fancy to see in the diversity which European Union will bring an undreamed of quality in our lives.

Europe must also take in hand its own defence arrangements. Collective security will require policies which initially build the European pillar of NATO and later accept full responsibility for our own defence and disarmament policies. Alongside a strengthened United Nations organisation a democratic United States of Europe would wish to play its full part in defending the rights of peoples to self-determination; of upholding international law; of co-operating with others who shared our democratic ideals.

Defending and Disarming

Not long after my election to Parliament in 1979 Monsignor Bruce Kent, the then General Secretary of the Campaign for Nuclear Disarmament, invited me to speak at a CND rally against Britain's intended purchase of Trident. At some length I replied to his letter and said that I would happily participate. However, I was careful to enter one caveat. I explained that as I did not share CND's commitment to unilateral nuclear disarmament or to the immediate abandonment of NATO they might like to ask a Liberal more sympathetic to their view. Bruce Kent understood my position and I subsequently spoke against Trident at the Trafalgar Square demonstration and throughout the early 1980's I spoke against the deployment of Cruise and Pershing missiles in Europe and in favour of an immediate freeze.

In Parliament between 1979 and 1983, along with my colleague Richard Wainwright, a Methodist pacifist who had bravely spent the second war at the front line in the highly exposed ambulance corps, I opposed Cruise – and at times found myself alone and against my party colleagues in the 'No Lobby' as I voted against the defence estimates presented to Parliament in May 1981.

At Llandudno in 1981, where the Party debated its policy I reluctantly opposed the leadership. I argued that Cruise and Pershing were bound to escalate the nuclear arms race. I could not, in all conscience, square the colossal cost of arms – £18 billion a year in Britain and £500 billion throughout the world in that year – with the lost opportunities for spending on the poor and needy, here and overseas. To underline our contrasting priorities, a friend reminded me of St. James's words: 'If a brother or sister is ill clad and in lack of daily food and one of you says "Go in peace, be warmed and filled" without giving them the things needed for the body, what does it profit?'

Militarily, Cruise has always had a dubious status. In

October 1984, in an article entitled 'Real Solutions to the Nuclear Arms Race', I argued that:

> The present pattern of defence spending in the United Kingdom and in NATO has been one of increasing cost and increasing reliance upon offensive and destabilising weapons. Highly accurate nuclear missiles such as Cruise and Pershing, are only useful in an aggressive role of destroying the enemy's military facilities. It provides no defensive protection. Rather than maintaining deterrence – our ability to restrain our opponents from aggression – these weapons are designed to match our opponent's abilities at every level, allowing us to prevail in a conflict. The focus of defence strategy has thus shifted from preventing a war to one of winning a war which is seemingly inevitable. In essence the planners are attempting to win the unwinnable.

My opposition to deployment centred around the belief that Cruise was bound to bring with it a commensurate increase in the Soviet arsenal and inevitably SS20's and SS21's were soon pitted against Western Europe. If either side were now rash enough to use them it would not be like rebuilding Coventry Cathedral or blitzed London. In a world where rare survivors might have been happier dead, the words of Wilfred Owen have an application beyond the trenches of 1914:

> War broke: and now the winter of the world
> With perishing great darkness closes in.
> The foul tornado, is over all the width of Europe whirled,
> Rending the sails of progress. Rent or furled
> Are all Art's ensigns. Verse wails. Now begin
> Famines of thought and feeling. Love's wine's thin.
> The grain of human autumn rots down-hurled.
>
> 1914

Opposed as I have been to the build up of the nuclear arsenal I have watched the goal-posts move since 1983. The missiles are a grim reality and the intractability of the super-powers led to the unnerving of millions of Europeans who clearly believe that a Russian or American leader might be foolhardy enough to trigger the holocaust or, more plausibly, that catastrophe might visit us through some terrible Chernobyl-style mistake.

Europeans once again hold the key. Mrs. Thatcher's 1987 visit to Moscow was an unqualified success. It demonstrated, cynics would say just in time for the General Election, that when the megaphones are put to one side Europeans can talk to one another and, in her words, 'do business'.

Mrs. Thatcher's previous eight years in office have sadly given multilateralism a bad name. Unilateral acts of rearmament − like the £10 billion purchase of Trident, Britain's own independent nuclear weapon replacement for Polaris − are not the acts of a multilateralist. They mimic the arguments of those who would unilaterally disarm tomorrow regardless of the consequences.

If we could put the genii back into the bottle who wouldn't do it? In the real world, though, Britain does not have three magic wishes and must do more than simply wish away the world's nuclear arsenal. I will not sleep easier at night knowing that Neil Kinnock will not push the button or that Britain has opted out. That makes the world no safer. Arguably such a destabilising move would dangerously tip the balance of terror.

Until her Moscow visit, which may yet prove to be an aberration, Mrs Thatcher did nothing to secure the multilateralism in which she claims to believe. Her argument is always that we must negotiate from strength. Yes, but how much strength does the West need and for how long must we be dependent on various incumbents of the White House? It never gave me much confidence to reflect on the boast of President Nixon that he simply had to push a button in the Oval Office and within 45 minutes 300 million people could be dead. This was the man who fell from office because he couldn't operate the button of a tape recorder properly.

Europeans must take charge of their own defence and disarmament policies. We will need to accept the additional cost of replacing American troops in Germany, of increasing our day to day conventional defences and in the short term pooling our exisiting nuclear weapons in a European Defence Force. The clear long term objective must be a nuclear free Europe with weapons negotiated away on both sides. One of the opponents of the European initiative has said that the thought of a dozen European leaders all with their fingers on the button horrified him. I am not suggesting such a bizarre spectacle, although it would certainly minimise the likelihood of the weapons being used. However, if the choice lies, as I believe it does, between Europeans mutually dependent on one another and requiring common consent before allowing missiles to be fired and a disinterested President of the United States who is actually prepared to talk about 'a limited nuclear war in Europe' I know where my preferences would lie. Common agreed objectives and the shared destiny which Europeans enjoy – for life or death – should drive us to aspire to collective security so that the evil weapons of mass destruction might ultimately be consigned to their silos for good.

Chapter Twenty-One

BRITAIN IN THE COMMONWEALTH

Britain's days as policemen of the world are long since past. When the Sun finally set on the Empire a legacy of disparate dependencies and tiny isolated colonies remained. The Falkland Islands was the classic example. But there are others, like Fiji, now in the news because of the succesful coup of a racist army general. Then there are places like Belize, which has the same potential for a local eruption which escalates into a full blown war with British involvement, as the Falklands.

Say Guatemala invaded Belize tomorrow. There has been a long-running territorial dispute between these two countries which still remains unresolved despite present good neighbourliness. Britain is the guarantor of Belize's independence. If there were to be conflict all the same questions that were raised by the Argentinian invasion of the Falklands would be raised again. The inhabitants of Belize might not look like dispossessed Scottish crofters but the moral dilemma would be the same: should Britain, as the guarantor of the rights of a small and valuable territory, respect a solemn undertaking.

In the case of the Falklands a fascist dictator, General Galtieri, pursued Shakespeare's dictum of distracting from domestic problems by making foreign adventures. His armed forces invaded and then took by force the liberty and the rights of the island's 1,800 citizens. I was never in any doubt that, if necessary, force must be used to restore the rights of the islanders. The doubts that I had centred on the propriety of Britain acting alone. The moral authority which the British Task Force sought to establish through its act of liberation would have been considerably enhanced if the action had been taken collectively – by the UN or by the Commonwealth.

My doubts and fears were strengthened by the behaviour of Britain's popular press, egged on by the Prime Minister. Jingoism, arrogance and perverted patriotism ranged from the banner headlines of the Sun ('Gotcha!' it screamed as the Argentinian battle cruiser the General Belgrano was sunk with the loss of hundreds of lives) to Mrs Thatcher's admonition to the country to 'rejoice, rejoice' when British troops landed on the (previously) uninhabited island of South Georgia. The hysteria affected others too: the Social Democrat MP Eric Ogden declared that we should be prepared to use our nuclear deterrent to take out Buenos Aires.

When the British blood stopped boiling the vainglorious posturing gave way to a more sober evaluation of what was going to be a difficult and hazardous expedition in treacherous conditions 8,500 miles away from home.

British casualties came with the sinking of the Atlantic Conveyor. It was a Liverpool ship. At the Memorial Service held at Liverpool Cathedral for the seamen who died with her my thoughts were on the awesome responsibility which Parliament had taken unto itself. For the first time since Suez the Commons had been hurriedly reconvened to sit on a Saturday morning. I had left Liverpool early that day and arrived at the House in time for the traditional prayers which proceed each sitting. There was no doubt in my mind that I was participating in a decision which would send men to their certain death. Unless the diplomatic mission which was ostensibly trying to secure

UN involvement was succesful our task force would certainly go into action and men would die.

Ever since parliament took that decision the Labour MP Tam Dalyell has doggedly and assiduously pursued the Prime Minister whom he has accused of cover up and whitewash. Whether she was culpable of deliberately scuttling the attempts of Senor Perez de Cueliar, the UN Secretary General, and whether the Commons were told a pack of lies about the sinking of the Belgrano I know not.

The absence of American style investigative Select Committees backed up by Freedom of Information legislation, and the Government's reticence to establish a Public Inquiry to examine the areas of public concern, mean that thirty years will pass before the truth will out.

Just as Britain must forge its destiny in Europe with our Continental neighbours, when it comes to international disputes Britain must not go it alone, hiding behind the fig leaf of UN impotence. In the Commonwealth Britain is a leading member of an organisation which must act collectively to combat aggressors.

In a speech in Parliament in November, 1983 I said:

Britain's heritage and its traditions are bound up in the Commonwealth. It is a unique organisation, a collection of heterogeneous states, membership of which enables us to reach but of Europe into the wider world. In 1971 at Singapore, the heads of Government said that 'International co-operation is essential to remove the causes of war, promote tolerance, combat injustice and secure development among the peoples of the world'. In 1988 the need for positive commitment from Her Majesty's Government to achieve these objectives has in no way been abated. Briefcases bulging with platitudes will not be enough to break the circle of poverty or to achieve the international co-operation to which Her Majesty's Government say they subscribe.

This remains true today.

A Common Education

In addition to the arrangements which the Commonwealth might make for the collective security of its member states, the Commonwealth can act as a catalyst for change; as a guardian of the democratic ideal as a channel of peace. The Commonwealth should, for instance, establish a Remedyesque Peace Corps based on the principles of the Voluntary Services Overseas. The Corps should be multinational and give young people the chance of work on environmental and agrarian projects in other member states. I have often been impressed by the impact that the provision of a well – sunk by volunteers in a previously arid area – can make on the life of a remote village. Citrus fruits, grass bushes and even forests, can bloom where before only patched earth cracked in the heat of the sun. The sense of achievement: the companionship and camaraderie: the lifting of taboos and ignorance based on the fear of the unknown; all this could create for the young people of the Commonwealth a bond which unites for life. And what an investment for future peace on the earth which mankind shares.

During summer vacations during my own student days I lived with African and Asian students in Liverpool's World Friendship House and spent the days teaching English to immigrant children. Friendships were established which I have to this day. Just as importantly it was the best possible preparation for life in a multi-racial society and a multi-cultural world.

Some caution is required in advancing the cause of overseas students. As Jonathan Fryer, a member of the Liberal Foreign Affairs Panel and consultant to the World Health Organisation and World Council of Churches, pointed out in his pamphlet 'Whose Better Future?' having acquired their wisdom many overseas students never return home – having been seduced by the affluent standard of living in the Northern hemisphere. They can also become schizo-

phrenic unduly influenced by our culture and patterns of
life. Clearly the longer term objective must be to help
poorer countries to develop universities and colleges of their
own. In 1986 I visited the new university in Muscat, and
was pleasantly surprised to find a local building firm from
my own constituency supervising the specialist work being
undertaken by mainly Indian labour. But until Nirvanah
arrives Britain should recognise that if we turn away overseas students they will end up receiving an education in
Moscow or an American university which will be even less
helpful than that which they will receive here.

Furthermore, does democracy place such little value on
its own ideals that it is prepared to surrender to a Marxist
totalitarian regime the licensing rights for education? In
1980 Palestinian fighters in the Chatilla camp in Beiruit
told me of their education in the Soviet Union. I was left
in little doubt that the remit of the educationalists extended
beyond what we might call a liberal education. As we
hamper the work of the British Council, limit the broad-
casts of the respected BBC overseas services, and chop our
subsidies to overseas students we are being penny wise and
pound foolish.

The Council for Education in the Commonwealth is an
excellent organisation and I marvel at its achievement
given its Cinderella status. It should be given a substantial
budget and a remit to develop schools, universities and
opportunities for students. But it must be a two way
process. Julius Nyerere said that we can most help the poor
by educating ourselves about their problems.

When the Conservatives came to power in 1979 they
abolished the overseas Aid and Development Ministry and
then cut funds for development education from half a
million to £150,000 p.a. only an outcry and parliamentary
pressure saved even this paltry sum. I remain convinced
that if British children are to grow up into the kind of
world I want to see we will have to massively expand
development education. I recently approached my Local

Authority to seek nine months leave of absence for a teacher who when not teaching English to immigrant children, visits local schools to talk about life and customs in the subcontinent. He had not been back to India for many years and felt the need to steep himself once more in the country's ways. Money simply wasn't available for him to go.

Within the Commonwealth we must finance both the secondment of teachers and the twinning of villages and communities in the North and South – in this way we can share more adequately our knowledge and learn about one another.

South Africa

My frustration about Britain's niggardly attitude towards Commonwealth involvement in education turns to anger and despair when I survey our record on South Africa. Without the steadying influence of Her Majesty the Queen, the arrogant and high-handed response that the British Government made to the Commonwealth's Eminent Person's Report on South Africa could easily have wrecked the Commonwealth. The Report called for somewhat limited but nonetheless symbolically important sanction against South Africa. It said 'Apartheid is awesome in its cruelty. It is achieved and sustained only through force, creating human misery and deprivation and blighting the lives of millions.' Yet Mrs Thatcher preferred to give encouragement to an international pariah rather than to show solidarity with the moral stand taken by the rest of the Commonwealth. Britain alone refused to endorse it. Mrs Thatcher came away from the crucial Commonwealth meeting crowing that she had been wonderfully resistant and had only given way on insignificant matters.

And in 1987, in Vancouver, Mrs Thatcher once again threatened the future of the Commonwealth with her intransigence on this issue. No wonder she is reviled throughout Africa and Asia but lauded as a patriot and heroine in South Africa. By sharp contrast the 1961 decision supported by the then Conservative Government to eject white South Africa from the same Commonwealth showed Britain in a more appealing light. That act of cleansing expressed a Commonwealth commitment to shared values and high ideals. Those were values of countries who could not live comfortably alongside a racist regime which had passed beyond the bounds of human decency.

In 1970, in my first public speech, I urged my student union to back the 'Stop the Seventy Tour Campaign' and later, in 1973, persuaded the Liberal-run Liverpool City Council to disinvest our South African holdings and to instruct the Authority's Central Purchasing Unit not to buy from South Africa. On becoming Chief Whip in 1985, I immediately issued instructions to remove the Liberal Central Association accounts from Barclays – who have only recently severed their considerable South African links. Many times I have stood in protest outside South Africa House. None of these gestures will end apartheid but all of us who care about the tyrannical system must find a small way of making our individual stands for human decency.

In 1986 the Archbishops of Durban, Pretoria, Bloemfontein and Cape Town wrote a joint letter to British people. They asked us to think again about our investments in their trouble torn country. They also appealed to us to remember South Africa in our prayers. They said that, 'Apartheid is an evil and sinful system which flouts God's will. We are all, black and white, the sons and daughters of the same loving God and we cannot acquiesce in a system which sets brother against brother and sister against sister as apartheid does. The violence in our land will only end when the rightful aspirations of South Africa's black people to share in the political and economic life of the nation have been met.' Commenting on the measures introduced by the South African government they said: 'the so-called reforms are a sham whose purpose is to entrench the essentials of apartheid.'

For its opposition the Churches have been the target of the Botha regime. 'Our Church,' say the Bishops, 'has suffered the imprisonment of many of its members, including clergy, religious seminarians and lay workers. Its organisations have been persecuted, its publications censored. Emergency laws and restrictions undermine our role as preachers of the truth. But our cross is made easier to bear by the heroic courage of so many of our people.'

Such agony calls to mind another poem of Wilfred Owen:

'My soul looked down from a vague height with Death
As unremembering him I rose
And saw a sad land, weak with sweats of death.'

The Show

The Commonwealth is uniquely well placed to ease the agony and to lift the sadness. In a speech to the West Midlands Regional Liberal Conference at Shrewsbury in 1986, I suggested ways in which Britain and the Commonwealth might proceed.

'The idea of using sanctions against South Africa dates back to 1962. Some politicians, usually those who support President Botha, say that we must not impose sanctions because they will harm blacks. The sudden concern for the welfare of South Africa's blacks is touching; but it is wholly inconsistent with the wishes of the overwhelming majority of black South African leaders. It is they – and not the Siren voices – who should be listened to.

I believe that Britain must think again; and that sanctions should be imposed on South Africa until they do three things.

First, in return for a ceasefire, South Africa must legalise the African National Congress.

Second, Nelson Mandela and other political prisoners must be freed.

And third, President Botha's Government must agree to get around the table and try to negotiate a new constitution which will enfranchise blacks.

Those are clear objectives; and if sanctions are to work our objectives must be stated clearly in advance.

It is not sanctions that will destroy South Africa – but the persistence of apartheid and the Government's failure to engage in fundamental political reform. The issues will not simply go away; nor can they be bombed out of existence. Obduracy and intransigence will not work.

But if South Africa must address fundamental questions then so must we. On such a clear moral issue – if we refuse to take action what does it say about us? What will it say to the blacks in our own inner city ghettos?

Britain and the Commonwealth could condemn the continued illegal occupation of Namibia and demand the full implementation of UN Resolution 435, including free and independent elections under UN supervision and the recognition of SWAPO. We must continue to apply the international financial pressure which has already led to meetings between South Africa business leaders and the ANC. The only hope of peaceful progress for all the people of South Africa lies in direct negotiations between government and black, coloured and Asian leaders who command the confidence of the majority.

I am strongly committed to:

1. The immediate imposition of an oil embargo and comprehensive economic sanctions on South Africa, including:

(a) adherence to the UN mandatory arms embargo and the imposition of a UN ban on all nuclear collaboration with South Africa; and

(b) the denial of all funds for trade missions to South Africa and the cessation of export credits for sales to South Africa;

2. The termination of the no-visa agreement with South Africa;

3. The placing of continuing public pressure on the South African Government to adhere to the UN Declaration of Human Rights and to free as well as Nelson Mandela all political prisoners unconditionally.

4. A European Community Ban on landings and overflights by South African Airways.

5. The accountability of South Africa to the international Court of Justice for their Homelands policies; and

6. The more effective implementation of the Gleneagles Agreement of sporting contacts with South Africa, and its extension in ways proposed by Donald Woods which I refer to on Page 27.

White South Africa is a predator feeding off its black population. Dean Inge succinctly explains what happens when predators feel threatened.

'The enemies of freedom do not argue; they shout and they shout.' The cornered predator may be dangerous but compared with the conflagration that is coming, it is better to face him in his lair now.

Hong Kong

The third example of where concerted Commonwealth action might be taken is in Hong Kong.

Britain has failed Hong Kong in several key respects. When I first stayed there, in 1981, I was shocked to discover that no directly elected institutions had been established; that according to fairly disinterested laid-back British colonial officials: 'the Chinese are only interested in making money,' and that 'there is simply no demand.'

During subsequent visits in late 1985 and early 1986 the situation had altered radically. A legislative Council had been established and a free, robust, at times aggressive Free Press exists. All the talk was then about the importance of putting the structures of self government in place before the British Governor leaves and Peking takes over in 1997. Britain's earlier failure to establish a Hong Kong Assembly means that any structures put in place subsequent to the signing of the Anglo Sino Agreement have little time to establish themselves and run the risk of being set to one side post 1997.

Britain and Hong Kong's business community – are relying purely on the assumption that China will not wish to touch anything that has contributed to Hong Kong's commercial success, which China desperately needs. 'Killing the goose that lays the golden egg' is how the argument goes. British lethargy in failing to establish democratic structures earlier means that Peking has made little connection between Hong Kong's wealth and the spirit created by the freedom guaranteed by a benevolent colonial authority. Peking would be quite happy to simply leave it to the businessmen to exchange one governor for another.

A second British failure has been the refusal to provide a resettlement or safety net should the worst fears of Hong Kong's pessimists be realised. Now I am not arguing that 5 million Hong Kongers should be allowed – or would even want – to come to the UK. Though heaven knows that the industrious Chinese of Liverpool quietly and assiduously create wealth and jobs through incomparable hard work; and when trades unions leaders and others talk disparagingly of the 'dangers' of private enterprise creating a 'Hong Kong on Merseyside' I can only express the view that just a little of Hong Kong's enterprise relocated in Liverpool might transform its fortunes. Already one company has, through the initiative of Littlewoods brought a third of their operation and 600 new local textile jobs to Liverpool.

If only others would disinvest a portion of their holdings into our designated free ports which have, after all, some of the economic advantages of the Hong Kong entrepot.

Some disinvestment along these lines has already occurred with people and money being welcomed into the United States of America, Canada and Australia. The significance of partial disinvestment will not be lost on the Chinese Government who will fear a total collapse. If this was backed up with rights of resettlement throughout the Commonwealth it would strongly underpin our commitment to Hong Kong and our determination to guarantee its people's rights and Britain alone cannot guarantee these rights. Is this not therefore an issue requiring concerted action and which should be placed before the next meeting of the Commonwealth Heads of Government?

Harold McMillan in 1960 – talked of the winds of change which were blowing across the British Colonies. Not even he could have envisaged a British Government compliantly handing over a colony to a Communist Government. Whilst I recognise that concessions have been extracted on behalf of Hong Kong people, I believe that they fall short of the mark. They are not sufficient to provide the undergirding of the Anglo-Sino Agreement.

This is evidenced in a third important way in which the British have further failed Hong Kong.

Even after the Revolution in 1947 China allowed religious worship in parts of the Country: although many Christian families fled to Hong Kong and Taiwan. Up until the Maoist Cultural Revolution of the 50's the City of Shanghai boasted over 500 churches. That in a city where the Chinese Communist Party was born and from where 3 of the Gang of Four originated. Today, despite the now retired President Deng's liberalisation, a very relative word in a country which has experienced 4,000 years of brutality and oppression, just 22 Catholic and 22 Protestant churches are officially open to believers: officially open and officially regulated by Shanghai's Religious Affairs Bureau.

Many of the other 450 churches are locked up or used as offices or homes. One I visited, Holy Trinity Church in Jiu-Jang Lu, is a builders yard. Were he alive today, Sir Giles Gilbert-Scott, the Catholic architect who created Liverpool's Anglican Cathedral, would grieve to see his Shanghai Church building desecrated and despoiled.

Christian leaders from Catholic and Protestant traditions have fared little better than the buildings. Leaders of the unofficial house church movement risk jail, so do Catholics who refuse to join the State sponsored 'Three-self Patriotic Churches.' In 1986, in an interview with the director of Shanghai's Religious Affairs Bureau he confirmed that four elderly Catholic priests are still in Shanghai's prison. Chen Cai Jun is over 60, Zhu Hong Seng, Chen Yun Tang, and Shen Bai Sun are all over 70 – arrested in 1981 for 'anti-revolutionary' activity and jailed for periods of up to 15 years.

In 1985 – after confinement in Chinese jails for most of the previous 30 years – Shanghai's Catholic Bishop, Gong Pinmei, was finally released. However, my request to meet him were firmly if politely refused, with the explanation that he had a cold.

The word 'Shanghai' entered our vocabulary as a description of what happened to sailors who were drugged and smuggled aboard ship. Looking northward Hong Kong's Christians wonder if in 1997 the same fate awaits them.

Once again Britain has settled for weasel words in an Agreement which offer cold comfort to the City's Christian communities fearful that considerable restrictions will be imposed on the right of religious worship and activity. For instance, the recent involvement of the Hong Kong Christian council, in organising opposition to the Construction of the Daya Bay nuclear power station just a few miles from Hong Kong's border – would certainly be prohibited.

Here once more is a role for the Commonwealth in asserting its determination to offer ultimate resettlement to anyone denied religious freedom.

In two other important respects Britain and the Commonwealth must facilitate Hong Kong's development. A small pocket handkerchief of territory, the notorious no-go Walled City, was excluded from the original Treaty which acceded Hong Kong to Britain. Never, therefore under effective British or Chinese rule, the Walled City became the centre of the opium trade.

I have seen some pretty wretched living conditions – slums in Calcutta, people living in Cairo's graves, hovels in Nepal, makeshift shanty towns in Thailand, temporary Palestinian refugee camps in Beirut (which are now in their fortieth year) and ugly dehumanising and faceless concrete blocks created for our own urban poor in Chicago, Leningrad and Liverpool; but rarely have I seen more squalor, cut my way through such a stench, or had to tread more warily carefully trying to side step comatosed drug addicts. The maze of narrow enclosed alleyways all house people. It is no wonder the authorities try to stop people going there. Britain and China have now belatedly agreed to raise the Walled City and to redevelop it as a recreation area. The residents will be rehoused – a project which will be undertaken by Hong Kong's forward looking and dynamic housing corporation. Rehousing alone will not be enough. Drug addiction, organised crime, Triad racketeering, protectionism and gangsterism will simply shift it's centre of gravity elsewhere unless this deep-rooted evil is not urgently tackled.

In her book 'Chasing the Dragon' Jackie Pullinger describes life in the Walled City. The night I saw her in action made me thankful that young British people are doing for love what colonialists and government agencies have never been prepared to do for money.

And finally, where the Hong Kong Government has been laggardly in tackling the corruption of the Walled City, it has an exemplory record in handling the many thousands of Vietnamese refugees who have arrived there.

I had visited the Aberdeen Refugee Camps on my first visit to Hong Kong in 1981. It was a depressing visit. Happily, by 1986, when I returned, many lessons had been learnt. The schools, work-shops, communal facilities and the preparation for a new life were far more impressive. The sadness was that the initial enthusiasm of the West – maybe born out of post Vietnam guilt – had now turned to compassion fatigue. It is hard to tell a little boy, clinging to your hand and who has known nothing other than life behind the camp's high fences, that no, you haven't come to take his family home.

My faith in a concerted response to the intricate problems of Hong Kong does not centre entirely on the Commonwealth: though as I have explained it wouldn't be a bad starting point. As I shall explain in a later chapter, I believe that a bold new initiative in South East Asia is urgently needed – that alone will stop the inexorable influx of the dispossessed on every turn of the tide.

Chapter Twenty-Two

ONE WORLD, ONE DAY

My lack of enthusiasm for the narrow chauvinism of the nation state leads me to the inevitable conclusion that the clear objective must be one world, one day.

The federal relationship of the nations within the United Kingdom which I seek, the federal links of a Europe United and the strong bonding of our Commonwealth of nations must be building blocks for a mutually dependent world – where countries recognise the truth that: 'No man is an island, No man stands alone.'

It was Mao Tse Tung who coined the phrase, 'Third World' as shorthand for Africa, Asia, Latin America, the Carribbean and the Pacific. The second world were the rich countries of Europe, Australasia, Canada and Japan, and the super powers were the First World.

Clearly there are enormous differences amongst countries crudely lumped together as the Third World. But if that is a misleading expression so is the Brandt Report's shorthand of a rich north and a poor south.

Poor Australia or New Zealand? And the people living in the inner cities and the deindustrialised waste lands of Northern Europe hardly constitute the rich. Yet if I have to choose, for me the 'North-South' shorthand of the Brandt Commission conveys more eloquently the gross imbalances of a sharply divided world than Mao's 'Third World'. Three quarters of the world live in Brandt's 'South' and although we who are fortunate enough to live in the comfort of the 'North' would be foolish to develop a guilt complex about our good fortune we owe it to our less favoured brothers and sisters to use our privileges our wealth and our ingenuity to ensure that our divided world becomes one world. We are all inter-dependent and our disparate communities need each other to function and survive. I firmly believe that global solutions to the complex problems of development, refugees, inter continental pollution and the destruction of world resources will require more, not less, internationalism; no less than a world wide community of nations.

If, for Britain, our leadership and contribution is to find its focus in the European Community and in the Commonwealth, there exists for other countries, in other parts of the world embryonic international umbrella organisations like the organisation for African Unity, and economic groupings like OPEC (Organisation of Petrol Exporting Countries) and defence arrangements, like NATO (North Atlantic Treaty Organisation), the Warsaw Pact and ANZUS (Australia, New Zealand and the United States). At present some of these are as much an obstacle to world development as stimulants.

I haven't yet mentioned the obvious organisation – the United Nations. I have been reluctant to do so because with the exception of agencies like UNICEF, the WHO and FAO, which deal with children, health and agriculture, many of the UN's agencies and its ineffectual General Assembly are held in a fair amount of odium. Britain became so upset with the bizarre goings on at UNESCO, the educational, scientific and cultural organ of the UN, that we walked out in a fit of pique. My colleague, Alan Beith, argued forcefully against this, believing as I do that our voice and energies would be better inside, working for reform.

In its founding statement, UNESCO sought to create a new order. It was seeking the establishment of a new world order at the end of the war, in which the dissemination of knowledge and education would militate against the prejudices that had given rise to the horrors of Nazi Germany, which unleashed the great war.

These founder members could not have conceived that at this stage we would be seeking to take Britain out of UNESCO. The organisation's problem is simply that it has grown. It is not the organisation that those men established. It has many more countries in its membership, its administration is enormously larger as a result, and that immediately poses problems, as in any large international organisation. Membership has widened. It included Governments who do not share or practise the values of the founders. They practise those values even less than we do. Who is to say that we, in every respect and action of government, abide faithfully by what the founders set out?

What should be our response to the fact that many of UNESCO's members do not share the values that the founder sought to propagate? It must be to fight on to ensure that the values are embodied in the work of the organisation. We should not say that the principal vehicle by which those values can be spread should be abandoned by the nation that was instrumental in establishing it.

Now that the reign of the long-serving Secretary General of UNESCO, Mr M'Bow has come to an end, we have an ideal opportunity to re-enter the organisation and help bring infuse a new spirit into it's work.

Whilst Britain and America believes UNESCO to be full of Marxists, the Communist countries reserve their ire for the ILO, the labour organisation, which they revile as an anti-socialist front.

Instead of trying to make the agencies work – the WHO for instance could eradicate malaria tomorrow if we just gave them the money – we heap obloquy and scorn on much of their work. Instead of responding to the UN's rational proposal to dot around the world sizeable regional grain stores as a fail safe against famine – the wisdom of which Joseph well understood in Pharaoh's Egypt, the world just walks by on the other side. Instead of giving UNIFIL (The Lebanon Peace Keeping Force) the power to operate effectively, we condemn it to the impotence of eunuchs at the emperor's court; and then we have the neck to complain about their lack of virility.

The UN, its enfeebled General Assembly – that has less clout than some parish councils – and its much maligned agencies need to have new life breathed into them. A more muscular UN might be emboldened to take on the issues with which I now want to deal – refugees, development, human rights, conflict and the world ecology.

Refugees

Among the United Nations agencies most hamstrung by lack of resources and by insufficient political will is UNRA, the refugee agency.

Refugees have been with us since time immemorial: the Jewish refugees of the Old Testament, aliens in another land. And Christ's life began as a refugee with his family's flight to Egypt, escaping Herod's infanticide. The movement of individual families – and whole peoples – is usually the consequence of tyranny, war, persecution, pogroms, famine or fear. Wave after wave of men and women have uprooted themselves to be translated into strange lands and climates. Reactions from the host community vary from the heroic to the barbarous. Men like Raoul Wallenberg went to extraordinary lengths to help Jews escape from Nazi persecution in Hungary (and as Danny Smith explains in *The Lost Hero* this led to Wallenberg's own disappearance and captivity by Soviet forces during the 'liberation' of Hungary). Catholic priests in Northern Italy organised the 'Assisi Underground', filling their convents and monasteries with Jews fleeing from the Nazi terror in Italy, disguised as nuns and monks.

A lady of my acquaintance, my local Constituency

Association President, Mrs Mintose Bibby, filled her home with Jewish emigrees escaping from Germany and Russia – including the pianist Vladimir Ashkenazy and his family. For her pains she and her husband ultimately appeared before Liverpool Magistrates Court charged with operating an illegal immigration ring. In our peculiar British way they were both found guilty but congratulated by the magistrates and fined one penny.

Not all reactions demonstrate such a hospitable disposition. We have all heard the horror stories of 'Pakki bashing' – when a new Asian family receives a less than hospitable welcome.

Our capacity to assimilate might usefully be compared with that of Calcutta – probably the world's poorest city – which has had to cope with an additional million refugees from East Pakistan since 1947.

The most serious refugee problem in the world today exists in South East Asia. A hiatus has been created by political inertia and ideological intransigence which trips its way through South East Asia like a danse macabre. In 1986, I visited Thailand, met officials of the Jesuit refugee service and questioned British officials at our Embassy about our own response to Thailand's tide of human misery.

Initially, world-wide compassion for a people fleeing their country in tiny boats led to one of the biggest re-settlement programmes since World War Two.

The world stretched out a welcoming hand but by the mid 80s, with new disasters in the Horn of Africa, it has begun to suffer from compassion fatigue. 35,000 boat people are still languishing in transit camps all over South East Asia and some 10,000 of those have been in camps for three years or more.

During that time the Hong Kong Government has pursued a thoroughly compassionate and humanitarian policy and their resettlement programme, co-ordinated by

Ken Woodhouse and a dedicated team have successfully found new homes in third countries for 112,000 people.

The Hong Kong approach contrasts markedly with the policies of Malaysia, Singapore and Indonesia – with relief workers telling me horror stories of refugees who have been shot, others whose boats have been hauled back out to sea, and others who have had temporarily constructed shelters burnt to the ground.

Again, unlike other governments within the region, Hong Kong has financed much of the programme itself – forking out over £55 million since 1979. The rest of the world is failing to match Hong Kong's liberal policies.

Despite its initial response Britain had cut its intake of Vietnamese refugees to a total of 44 in 1985. Following the publication of a critical Home Affairs Select Committee report the Government responded in September 1986 with a promise they would allow refugees with family already in the UK to be reunited.

This led to 474 refugees coming to Britain. But the Home Office then imposed a moratorium restricting the number of 200 refugees. Cruelly, refugees had their hopes raised by officially announced government policy – and have now been told they cannot come.

At Hong Kong's Hei Ling Chau closed camp I talked to a handful of the 1,500 boat people who have been in camps in this British colony for over 7 years.

Refugees – some of them there for seven years – are not allowed to leave. 1,800 people sleep in ten long dormitories – almost 180 per dormitory. They sleep in triple bunks. A few meagre possessions are piled on and around the bunks. This is home.

The closed camp provides some training in basic skills. Language is taught by a team of mainly volunteers. There are problems with this. One volunteer told me it is not ideal to have a Ugandan with broken English trying to teach English to Vietnamese.

Elsewhere in the camp there is a communal eating area

and a clinic. It is not a place that allows for much human dignity – yet after the traumas of the arduous journey from Vietnam it is at least safe.

As of September 1987, Hong Kong had a total of 9057 boat people in its camps.

Many refugees will have been attacked by marauding pirates en-route and will have seen relatives murdered, assaulted or raped. The camps should be a temporary sanctuary where people can recover from these terrible ordeals. They were never intended to be a permanent place of residence and so British criticisms of the closed camps would be better placed if the criticisms were backed up by a more determined effort to resettle the inhabitants.

Britain is not alone in forgetting the boat people. The score sheet for other European countries does not make impressive reading.

In 1986 the following countries took no Vietnamese refugees from Hong Kong: Austria, Belgium, Greece, Ireland, Italy and Spain.

In comparison with Hong Kong's refugee problem the situation in Thailand is completely out of control. The sequel of the harrowing film 'The Killing Fields' might simply be called 'Thailand'.

For it is over the border that 54,000 Cambodians escaped from the pursuing Vietnamese. They are not alone.

10,000 Vietnamese, 17,000 Karens from Burma, and a staggering 89,000 Laotians give Thailand an estimated 386,000 displaced persons and refugees.

The potential for destabilisation is obvious; conditions in the camps are an international disgrace; and in the absence of any political initiative these camps have all the makings of the 'temporary' refugee camps in which Palestinians still live in Beirut 40 years later. The ingredients for another South East Asian tragedy are all there.

The situation is far from simple. The Cambodian refugees alone comprise three uneasy but temporarily united factions: the Khmer Rouge (who ruthlessly ruled Kampuchea under Pol Pot), the Khmer People's National Liberation Front (KPLNF) and Prince Sihanouk's nationalists. This uneasy coalition is recognised by the United Nations as Kampuchea's legally constituted government.

In consolidating their position the Vietnamese have placed mines along the entire Kampuchean-Thai border often resulting in tragic deaths and loss of limbs by Cambodians trying desperately to escape the brutality of their communist masters.

To the north 89,000 Laotians have fled the Pathet Lao communists of Laos. Some of the refugees from the hill tribes were forced to flee when chemical warfare was used against them by their own government. To the west there are 17,000 Karens. They looked to Britain in 1946 and sought the establishment of a separate state from Burma. They looked in vain and following years of hostilities many have been forced to leave.

At the bottom of the pile are yet more Vietnamese refugees – about 10,000 in all. Some arrived overland, others by boat. The Jesuit Refugee Service, based in Bangkok, tell harrowing stories of the ordeals which have been endured by some of the refugees on their journeys.

The problems usually begin when the boats have been at sea for a few days. They often lose their direction in the Gulf of Siam, run low on food and water, and encounter mechanical problems.

They become sitting ducks for the pirates who infest these waters. The refugees are robbed of their valuables. The women are abducted and often raped in front of the men. The men may even be thrown overboard.

In one incident in 1985, 40 men were pushed into the sea and died from drowning. In another incident a man was axed on the back of his neck while trying to prevent his young niece from being abducted.

The boat itself will usually be rammed and badly damaged before the pirates set it free. The effects of such barbarity, humiliation and hurt can hardly be contemplated.

The searing psychological effects of these vicious attacks will remain bottled up inside the victims for the rest of their lives.

After the tragedy of all they have left behind it is hard to imagine the mentality of the robbers who stoop so low as to deprive vulnerable, defenceless refugees even of their poverty.

Once they reach the camps the destitute have some chance of survival. One refugee, called Sophal, told me: 'I was lucky; I survived because at times people have looked into my eyes and found me human. We each have our own face on which, if you care to look, you can read our story – the grief, the loss and hope that cast light on the kindly face of God.'

In her Bangkok office a young woman, Ratana Kulsiri-patana, tries desperately to keep some hope in the lives of refugees like Sophal.

The Jesuit Refugee Service, whom she works for, is just one of several voluntary organisations who are working against impossible odds. Ratana, nicknamed Lek, says that three things must happen if things are to improve.

First, there must be a political initiative. Second, the refugees should be made less dependent on aid. There is little motivation to do anything; the refugees should be encouraged to help themselves. And, thirdly, there is an urgent need to improve the security and protection within the camps.

The search for durable solutions of the Cambodian border in particular depends on political answers. At the present moment none of the super-powers have any vested interest in trying to find such a solution.

Ceasefire and resettlement will only happen when the Vietnamese withdraw their troops from Kampuchea. Sad to say for the refugees in the border country the chances of that happening are negligible.

The absence of this or an other political initiative seems certain to condemn hundreds of thousands of people to many more years of misery in one of the world's forgotten back waters.

In response to a parliamentary question I asked last summer, Ministers confirmed that political factors would not determine our attitudes and levels of help to these refugees. Yet, quite clearly our initial reluctance to assist in Ethiopia and the way in which we place resources for humanitarian assistance is only too often determined by the colour of the regime; although happily to a far lesser extent than America whose selective aid and funding seems to be largely the product of the compliance shown with American foreign policy by the recipients.

Regrettably the refugee problem in South East Asia will ultimately depend on political initiatives.

This may not happen quickly – and the bitterness will increase as time passes. The initial enthusiasm of Pakistan in receiving Afghan refugees from Mohajeddin opposing the Soviet invasion has paled with time. Over 1 million Afghan tribesmen now live on Pakistan soil – at an enormous financial cost – to say nothing of the human anguish and the distress caused to both refugee and the displaced host community. The same thing will happen in Thailand and the danger of substantial numbers of refugees in temporary, insanitary and largely unsuitable accommodation is that it leads to a 'state within a state' and to political destabilisation. Festering refugee camps are the ideal breeding grounds for this. Recognition of these realities by Western Governments would at least be a start.

Chapter Twenty-Three

RICH MAN, POOR MAN

Calcutta was once the second city of the British Empire, today it is the back side of hell: indescribable destitution, and unspeakable human misery ouse out of every orifice.

Winston Churchill once quipped to his mother that 'I shall always have been glad to have seen it – for the same reason Papa gave to have seen Lisbon namely, that it will be unnecessary for me ever to see it again!' Looking today on the face of a City named for the goddess Kali, who is believed by Hindus to represent fear and evil, it is easy to see why Churchill had no desire to return. For the estimated 12 million people living alongside the Hooghly River such choices do not exist.

In 1986, accompanied by my friend and doctor, Shiv Pande, and by the Conservative MP David Atkinson, we visited Mother Teresa's centre in Calcutta's Lower Circular Road. In room after room her missionaries of Charity care for orphaned children. Elsewhere, at Nirmal Hriday (in the shadow of Kali's temple) the Nuns run a hospice. They dress sores, clear up pools of incontinence, and delouse the dying. A mechanised conveyor belt could not produce more rapidly or efficiently to the replacements that Calcutta produces for Mother Teresa's sisters. In turn she gives them a little time of dignity before their death.

Mother Teresa's nuns are virtually the only people scuttling around and doing anything for the dying destitutes.

Nor is there much interest in Calcutta's 40,000 lepers other than that which she shows. Predictably, on a later visit to Khatmandu, it was Mother Teresa's sisters who were once more swilling out the corrugated huts and the make-shift wards where lepers and the nearly lifeless were ebbing away.

It says something that Mother Teresa has sent some of her sisters to Liverpool to care for our homeless. Her Seal Street Centre became the scene of a notorious battle with the local authority when Labour Councillors tried to close it down, telling her, when she flew in, that there was nothing she could do for the homeless people that they were not already doing. This must have reminded her of her early battles with Calcutta's Marxist Administration before she won them around. When she set up her centre to care for New York's discarded and ostracised Aids victims she said that the poverty of Calcutta was in many ways preferable to the poverty of the West. On one of the inevitable TV chat-shows she got to the heart of what is wrong with our lust for bigger and better, faster and more. When she commented on a commercial advertisement for a new slimming diet which had interrupted the programme, she said that she found it strange that in the west we spend so much time and money on trying to find ways of losing weight, when she has to spend her life caring for people dying of malnutrition in Calcutta's hostels and on its streets.

This and Eileen Egan's book, 'Such A Vision of the Street' had given me a glimpse of what commitment and humanity I might expect to see – but nothing could adequately prepare anyone for the quality of that love and its unstinting nature. In the West we talk a lot about brotherly love, and even give a little money from time to time. We pontificate and prescribe remedies ranging from increases in aid to outright revolution. Nor is this new. Seventy years ago Lenin was predicting in a remark often attributed to him that 'the road to world revolution lies through Peking, Shanghai and Calcutta.' The gradualist, meanwhile, will dust off their copy of the Brandt Report and murmur 'if only'. The cynics will impugn her motives and the scoffers will say 'not enough' but give me any day the revolution of love which Mother Theresa and her cadres are working in Calcutta's ghastly streets.

She confronts, as Jesus did before her, those pious pharisees, saducees, and scribes, who used God as an alibi for doing nothing – never seeking justice. She knows that it is not a choice of creating the kingdom on earth or in heaven; it is about both, Mother Teresa's ministry reaches out to give a helping hand to the sick and dying, and to the poor and down-trodden and to the outcasts like the lepers, just as Christ did. Her own motives are recalled in 'A Gift For God' where she says that: 'The trouble is that rich people, well-to-do people, very often don't really know who the poor are; and that is why we can forgive them, for knowledge can only lead to love, and love to service. And so, if they are not touched by the poor; it is because they do not know them.

'I try to give to the poor people for love what the rich could get for money. No, I wouldn't touch a leper for a thousand pounds; yet I willingly cure him for the love of God.'

The sisters care for 10,000 lepers in Calcutta alone – scattered around eight colonies. One, Entally, is beyond the abbatoir and close to the swampy marshes. The Dhapa Colony is close to the rubbish tip. The nuns try to ameliorate the worst ravages of this disease – more medicine and more trained personnel could halt it in its tracks – for if early enough action is taken leprosy can be countered.

And there is the rub for the West. Do we learn, as India's own prophet, Mahatma Gandhi, once counselled; that we must learn to live more simply so that others might simply live; or do we leave the poor with only one other way out – epitomised by the Maoist slogan 'Political power grows out from the barrel of the gun' daubed menacingly on the walls of many of Calcutta's slums.

In the West we are like Lazarus, the poor man who came to the table of Dives the rich man. The rich man would not even give him the crumbs from his table. Condemned to Hades the rich man asks Abraham to send Lazarus to cool his burning body. No comfort is forthcoming and the rich man is rebuked, reminded that in his life good things came his way – just as bad things come the way of Lazarus. For those in the West who say they are Christian looms the challenge of a saviour who chooses to reveal himself in the Eucharistic bread – how characteristic that concern for soul was matched by concern for body; that the cure for spiritual and bodily starvation march hand in hand. It was Gandhi, again, who said Christ could not have come to a hungry man in any other form than bread.

During our lifetimes we will eat fifty times more food than an Indian; we will earn an average of seven times more each year; and in our industrialised nations we will pollute and poison our common atmosphere fifty times more than our Indian counter-parts. Unless we urgently confront these disparities we will be polled from our thrones. The hungry will be filled with good things while the rich are sent empty away.

The Magnificat, from where those words are drawn, is undoubtedly far more revolutionary than 'Das Kapital' or the Internationale; and the story of Lazarus – with its terrible warning of an eternity in hell, far more sobering than the time expired miseries and excesses of Stalin, Hoxha and Ho.

Calcutta, India's biggest city with its horrific poverty and mind boggling decay contains isolated islands of a few fading enchantments which stand in an ocean of indescribable destitution. Its grossness and excesses confound any Westerner concerned about development. It is, however, a window on what Mao called the Third World, and what

Brandt called 'South'. Confront Calcutta and you confront the dilemma of development. If Calcutta, harbouring virtually every problem and every disease known to mankind, can be helped off its knees, it will give the lie to those who assert that justice will only come out of the barrel of a gun; it will demonstrate that values other than self advancement and personal greed flourish in the affluent and developed parts of the world.

My chief contention is that aid alone is not enough; that there must be greater co-ordination of development programmes – clearly a role for the UN; and that unless the International Monetary Fund (IMF) urgently tackles the debt crisis we will simply go on collecting back larger repayment in usurous interest charges than we will give in aid.

The problems of the Third World and the questions of aid provision are issues about which we should be deeply concerned. The theme of generosity to those in need is one that recurs time and time again in the New Testament. The rich stranger is told to sell all he has, not as an act of asceticism, but so as to give to the poor (Mark 10.21). Zacchaeus gives half his goods to those in need, and Jesus declares that salvation has come to his house (Luke 16.19–21). 'How hard it will be for the wealthy to enter the Kingdom of God!' (Mark 10.23). 'Woe to the rich!' (Luke 6.24).

Yet Christians who show concern for the under-privileged of other nations are sometimes castigated for 'being too concerned with the Third World and not enough with the next world.' I have always found this an absurd proposition. Are we supposed to pursue salvation in the next world at the cost of ignoring suffering and hardship in this? Surely this is not what Our Lord could ever have had in mind.

The problems faced by that section of the globe known as the Third World may be cruelly summarised as a growing food shortage, an overhanging burden of debt and the real possibility of a financial collapse, and an ever-increasing population. It was in 1980 that Robert McNarmara said:

> "Up to a billion of the world's people live lives of poverty which are so limited by malnutrition, illiteracy, disease, high infant mortality and low life expectancy as to be beneath any rational definition of human decency."

The reasons for the existence of these appalling conditions vary from country to country. The very poor economies – typified by the small African state – simply lack all the elements needed to meet the basic need of their people. They have low incomes and infrastructure and administrative facilities are almost totally lacking. Different sectors of the economy are closely linked. For instance, curative health services tend to be rendered ineffective by poor health, hygiene and sanitation. What is needed is a simultaneous advance on all fronts – but this is prevented by lack of finance, administration and skills.

Economies such as some of the larger countries in East Asia and Latin America, in contrast, have exhibited rapid economic growth, without, however, substantial reduction in poverty. The growth process has been too capital-intensive (usually due to mistaken attempts to emulate the Western industrialised nations) and the wealth created from it has stayed in the hands of the urban upper classes, failing to benefit the rural poor. Similarly, the level of public services is low and its distribution inegalitarian, favouring urban areas and the middle classes.

The typical Third World country, or Less Developed Country (LDC), has tended to fare a little better than either of these 'worst cases'. They have experienced moderate growth and a moderate impact on poverty. Growth in incomes has again tended to concentrate in the urban manufacturing sector, and poverty and malnutrition are concentrated in the rural areas. Public expenditure on basic services may be at quite a reasonable level, though it usually tends to be low in education.

You can see right away, that the problems faced by well-meaning Westerners are extremely complex. It is not just a question of throwing money at the problem and hoping it will go away. Indeed, in some cases, misdirected monetary aid can harm, rather than help, the country's economy. There are political problems within the less developed countries themselves – usually concerned with distribution of incomes; there are administrative barriers – even when aid is provided in sufficient quantities, and of the right type, it may be practically impossible for a poor nation to utilise it effectively; and there are problems with the economic and trading system of the world economy.

But, of course, there are cases where the most urgent need is for the immediate provision of money, materials and food. Everyone here will surely be aware of the tragedy of Ethiopia. Ethiopia was the catalyst which lifted the scales from so many people's eyes. The rains failed – not once, but again and again – and the drought destroyed crops and farms all over the northern part of the country. People wandered out of their villages to die by the roadside, in front of Western television cameras.

It was the TV that brought this tragedy into our living rooms, and prompted the generous response of our people. But where were the television cameras in the years before the drought? In a normal year, up to one million people are expected to die in Ethiopia from some kind of malnutrition. Food production in Africa has been declining for at least fifteen years, due to an insidious process of desertification and deforestation that is undercutting Africa's agricultural base. As if that were not enough, Africa's population is continuing to grow. The entire aid world had been screaming from the rooftops for the previous 18 months that a calamity was expected to occur – yet it was only when we saw it in colour on our TV sets that we and the Government acted.

When the crops fail, people move in search of food. The exodus of refugees from Eritrea and Tigre has caused a new crisis in the Sudan. One of the relief centres, Wad Kowli, is now the third largest city in the country. Earlier in the year, the Minister for Overseas Aid assured us food would be properly distributed in the Sudan because they had 'a strong private enterprise trucking agency.' What he didn't say was, because of its debt problem of between $8 and 9 billion, Sudan has not been able to buy the fuel needed to ensure that these lorries can be used for food distribution. Hundreds of thousands of tons of food have piled up in ports in Ethiopia and Sudan because of the lack of transport, and because of the civil war in Ethiopia. Sudan has repeatedly asked for fuel, and for finance for railway projects, but the West's response was lamentable.

Why, then, should we help the developing countries of the world at cost to ourselves? It can, and has been, argued that we have enough problems at home in Britain to bother about the problems of foreigners. I reject that argument unequivocally. However, harrowing our plight here, it is as nothing to the miseries that afflict the Third World.

UNICEF estimated that in 1978 alone more than 12 million children under the age of five died of starvation. Many millions more died of disease, violence and neglect. The World Bank hazards the view that 800 million people – 15 people for every citizen of this country – are in an absolute state of starvation and despair. According to the UN, there are still 34 countries where over 80 percent of the population are illiterate. Such frightening figures almost pass beyond the limits of our comprehension. If we were to witness personally a fraction of the suffering and degradation that lie behind these statistics the horror of what is happening would strike deep into our souls.

Behind the huge challenge of world poverty and global inequality looms the growing threat of nuclear conflict and a capacity for self-destruction of quite staggering proportions. The link between a hungry and divided world and peace and security should be obvious. As the 1981 Commonwealth Conference in Melbourne declared:

> "The gross inequality of wealth and opportunity currently existing in the world, and the unbroken circle of poverty in which the lives of millions in developing countries are confined, are fundamental sources of tension and instability in the world . . ."

Self-interest alone should drive the rich, industrialised nations of the North to realise that the cries of distress that they hear from hundreds of millions wracked by starvation and disease are a chilling warning of what might be the ultimate political explosion.

Self-interest is not an argument I am particularly fond of stressing, yet it can sometimes be a useful one to deploy. Investment in Third World aid is not only investment in peace and stability, but investment in our own economy. The transfer of resources from the North to the South would put money into the hands of the poor who would then buy our goods. This in turn would create employment in the North and prosperity in the South. The Marshall Aid programme transformed our Western economy after the Second World War and a similar stimulation could once again set the wheels of Western industry turning.

Britain itself has a special responsibility for the development of the Third World. Our past connections with developing countries and our position as part of the world's largest trading bloc, the European Community equip us uniquely to play a leading role in establishing a co-ordinated response to the needs of the Third World.

I hope I have shown that there are many reasons why we in Britain should take action to relieve the distress of the millions in the developing countries. But is this not the Government's responsibility? What are they doing about it?

Since the publication of the Brandt report in 1980, the

plight of developing countries has been debated in national Assemblies and Parliaments, and has brought together Heads of Government at Ottowa, Cancun and Melbourne. But, if anything, since 1980, the gulf between North and South, the affluent and the deprived, the haves and the have-nots, seems to have become greater.

In October 1970, the United Nations passed resolution 2626 calling for 0.7 percent of our gross national product to be set aside in development aid. We in Britain live in what is still one of the top 25 richest countries in the world, yet our total contribution is less than half of even that very modest target. The £1130 million that the UK set aside in aid in 1985–6 represents less than 0.33 percent of GNP. This is the lowest figure ever in Britain's history of aid provision, and represents a cut of about 20 percent since 1979, the year the Conservatives came into office.

This cut in Britain's aid came at a time when the aid programme faced unprecedented demands to meet the famine in Africa. The Government's contribution towards famine aid came solely from switching funds within the existing aid budget. No new money came from the Government's central contingency funds.

The British public responded extraordinarily generously to the Ethiopian crisis, giving over £60 million – more than is usually given in total to the aid charities in a year. In its report 'Famine in Africa,' the House of Commons Foreign Affairs Select Committee commented that 'the generosity of the British people has not been matched by the British Government.'

It may help to put some of these figures into perspective. The 0.33 percent of our GNP devoted to aid compares with 0.49 percent from West Germany, 0.76 percent from France, 0.91 percent from the Netherlands, or 1.06 percent from Norway. This year the United States of America will spend more on potted plants and flowers than on overseas aid and development. Last year, the British public spent more than six times as much on tobacco as we did on aid.

The contradictions become even more clear when we consider military expenditure. The world's governments spend more in a day on arms than 2000 million of their poorest citizens earn in a year. Redirecting seven hours' worth of world military expenditure could eradicate malaria from the face of the Earth forever. In the Third World, there is now one doctor for every 1290 people, but one soldier for every 250. The cost of a single modern tank would provide classrooms for 30,000 children. The cost of a modern jet fighter would provide one and a half million people with safe, clean, water. Nearer home, our Government is spending nearly ten times more on our independent nuclear weapon, Trident, than on Third World aid.

What, then, should be done, by our Government and our nation? There are several possible areas in which action can be taken, but the first which springs to everyone's mind is: Aid.

Britain was a pioneer in establishing a Ministry responsible for assisting in the development of the LDCs, separate from the ministries responsible for foreign affairs, trade and finance. But the Ministry of Overseas Development was abolished by Mrs Thatcher in 1979, and reduced to the Overseas Development Administration (ODA) within the Foreign Office. The ODA has become a backwater, without independent status or senior leadership, and making little mark either at home or overseas.

I believe this is a situation which must be rectified. We should aim to recreate the separate Ministry, with a Minister in the Cabinet. It should be fully integrated into the Whitehall machine with its officials accepted as being as valuable a part of British government as any others. It is also essential to bring in scientific and technical experts of top calibre, in a wide range of disciplines and at all levels. Room should be found for people of passionate motivation and a track record of effective work in the field, who have no previous experience of administration.

Having created our new Ministry, what should it do?

Economic growth by itself does not inevitably lead to the wholesale alleviation of poverty. Although it is often the case that a proportion of the benefits from aid will eventually permeate through the economy, it is not generally effective merely to throw money at the developing countries. Instead, aid, needs to be directed to those sectors where it will do most good. In 1981, however, only just over a quarter of ODA capital aid was devoted to projects aimed specifically at poor communities; this figure moreover, was the lowest for eight years.

The ODA was originally designed for initiating major capital-intensive industrial projects, such as steel works. However, these not only consume large sums of money, but mainly benefit the urban dweller, a minority of the population of most LDCs. Indeed, implementation of such projects may have the unfortunate effect of promoting migration to the towns, with accompanying loss of food production and increasing pressures on inadequate urban infrastructure – housing, water supplies, and so on.

Instead, the ODA ought to be trying to carry out projects aimed at alleviating poverty directly – for instance, rural water supplies, provision of improved seed, simple facilities for crop storage, development of fisheries and village woodlots, primary health care, territorially-based livestock grazing projects, minor irrigation using intermediate technology, and so on. Rural development projects are difficult to administer from a distance, and almost defy financial control. This implies a need for substantial reform in ODAs priorities, including a decentralised administration with more staff based overseas, greater administrative and financial flexibility, and an injection of expertise gained in the field into the centres of decision making.

Allocation between conflicting priorities within the aid budget is at least as crucial a question as consideration of the overall size of the budget itself. One of the major questions is how should the aid be given – bilaterally (government to government) or multilaterally (through the UN or EEC), or agencies such as Oxfam?

Multilateral aid tends to be of rather uneven quality. While aid administered through the World Bank and certain UN agencies is mostly very effective, some other agencies have a poor name. Among these, sad to say is the EEC's European Development Fund. Much Community aid is politically and commercially motivated; the staff complement is inadequate, and there are few valid procedures for project monitoring. As a first priority, the European Parliament – our elected representatives – should be given a far greater say over the EDF's administration. In more general terms, we should increase the funding of voluntary agencies such as Oxfam, War on Want, Save the Children and Christian Aid, all of which have an excellent reputation.

Bilateral aid is of course much easier to control, and allows us to discriminate with more care – for instance, to compensate for the US' refusal to provide aid to Nicaragua. In recent years, this has borne the brunt of the cuts, however and the most urgent need is simply to increase the amount of money available. A sensible balance between bilateral and multilateral aid can be achieved without too much difficulty.

The next thorny problem concerns aid allocation by country. I fully endorse the Brandt contention that 'More aid should be directed to the poorest countries and to programmes attacking the roots of poverty.' It is primarily for historical reasons that Britain currently gives aid to as many as 123 countries under the bilateral programme – though many of those programmes are very small. We should concentrate the aid programme on fewer countries, thereby increasing our effectiveness, and incidentally saving money on administrative overheads. The criteria for selecting these countries should be: relative degree of poverty, the existence of traditional ties (such as with commonwealth nations) and the country's capacity and political will to implement poverty-focused projects. Concentration on fewer countries should be associated with the establishment of permanent overseas aid missions for the purpose of identifying, appraising and servicing aid programmes for all major recipients of British aid – eg, Sudan, India, Bangladesh. Benefits would stem from a decentralised administration, drawing it closer to the people to whom the aid is directed, while providing UK aid administrators with the opportunity of gaining long-term overseas experience at first hand.

The central question, of course, is, on what should the resources devoted to aid be spent? ODA has to be much firmer in guiding overall priorities in aid allocation and its most urgent priority must be for Third World agriculture.

Every day, there are an extra 174,000 new faces at the world's breakfast table. Just to keep pace, an additional 30 million tons of grain are needed each year. If every one is to be fed properly, it will be necessary to quadruple farming productivity in the course of a single generation. This requires a degree of commitment to agricultural development (and also to policies of population control) far higher than has so far been achieved.

The International Fund for Agricultural Development (IFAD) was created after the 1974 World Food Conference (called to discuss the food crisis of the early '70's), and focuses on helping small landholders and landless farm labourers to increase food production. In the period up to early 1985, IFAD had financed projects designed to increase food production by 20 million tons of grain annually, equal to about a fifth of the Third World's total cereal imports. IFAD has been able to design projects for small farmers and the poor in rural areas with an average investment cost of little more than $200 per ton of food produced, and this extra production will continue every year. This compares with the total cost of getting just one ton of food to famine-stricken populations of between $200 and $400.

Because of the particularly urgent situation in Africa, the IFAD agreed to establish the Special Fund for Africa.

And what has been the response of the British Government to the need of IFAD, one of the most successful of all agencies operating in the Third World? They have contributed about £18 million to IFAD's funds (percent of the total) and nothing at all to the Special Fund for Africa. IFAD's proven record on helping the poor to grow more food means that contributing to IFAD's Special Fund for sub-Saharan Africa would be one of the most effective ways by which the British Government could help prevent future famines in Africa.

Priority should also be given to infrastructural improvements related to agricultural development – village water supplies, irrigation, road maintenance, crop marketing and storage, and so on.

One of the most controversial of all questions in the area of aid is that of food aid. Food aid is increasing in value at a time when all other aid programmes are being cut back. The bulk of the food aid programme arises from our membership of the European Community, and, regrettable, seems principally aimed at relieving Europe of its immense food surpluses rather than improving conditions in the Third World in the long term.

The necessity for food aid is obvious in such catastrophes as have afflicted Ethiopia. Neverthless, for all its apparent humanitarian intents, there must be grave doubts about the wisdom of providing such aid other than as a short term palliative in the case of crisis. Compared with cash aid, food is by and large an inferior form of aid, being tied, expensive, and difficult to store and transport. Most seriously of all, long term programmes of food provision can have a marked depressive effect on local food prices and the food distribution system, such that all incentives for food production are undermined, local farm production and investment decline, and food shortages are the ironic

– and tragic – consequence. Indiscriminate provision of food aid is not, therefore, the answer.

Going on from the provision of agricultural and food aid, we come to the question of whether, in other sectors, aid should principally be channelled into specific projects or into generalised material support, such as balance of payments support. It is my belief, that, if we are to maintain our aim of directing aid as far as possible towards the world's poor, it is essential that the bulk of the programme should be comprised of specific project aid. These projects must be carefully considered however – for instance, it is no good providing funds for road development if the recipient country has no facilities for maintaining the roads once they are completed. Voluntary agencies – Oxfam and its colleagues – are particularly good at identifying such projects and directing aid to the poorest, and, as I said before, the ODA should increase the funding of such bodies.

The transfer of British 'know-how' is particularly important to long term development of Third World countries. This transfer of expertise, usually in the form of British experts working overseas or training provided for local people (whether inside or outside their own country) is a highly cost-effective means of assisting the poorest people in the poorest countries, and it will be a long time indeed before professional capacity in LDCs in such fields as tropical agriculture will prove sufficient. Nevertheless, the number of funded technical co-operation officers have declined from 11,220 in 1976 to 6,512 in 1981. The ODA is thus threatening the technical and specialist skills upon which the provision and utilisation of effective aid is so dependent. This trend must be reversed, as must be the general decline in the funding of ODA's research and development departments.

Lastly, there has been a deliberate decision that a part of the aid programme should be determined by 'political, industrial and commercial' considerations, and an increasing proportion of that programme is being used to subsidise British exports. This is the so-called Aid-Trade Provision which currently accounts for over 80% of net bilateral aid. As examples of this in operation, consider the high level of political prompting from ODA that led to the provision of ships to India worth £40 million: this would be better regarded as aid to Scotland rather than the developing world. As another example, aid to Bangladesh in the form of UK railway wagons cost two to three times more than if the equivalent wagons had been imported from India.

Projects thus financed represent a diversion of aid funds from poor people overseas to firms in this country; as such, these subsidies, if really considered desirable, should not be taken from the aid budget, but from the export promotion budget of the Department of Trade. Tied aid – aid tied to the purchase of the products of the donor country – can lead to serious resource misallocation in LDCs, thereby appreciably diminishing the value of the aid provided. No less than 63% of UK programme aid was tied in 1980, and a further small amount was partially tied.

By comparison, most OECD countries record a figure of 20 – 30%. The British performance in this respect is worse than that of any other country.

To sum up, Britain, with our long history of contacts with the developing world – contacts which were by no means all imperialistic or malign – and her myriad international associations and trade interests, must play a more positive role in world development and be geared up administratively so to do. At present the world cries out for leadership, but we have allowed the opportunities to pass us by; even the limited achievements of yesteryear are now in the process of being dismantled and destroyed in the face of narrow nationalistic aspirations. A reinvigorated and powerful Ministry of Overseas Development would instead provide a new focus for harnessing the dedication and experience necessary to the cause of fighting world poverty.

In Washington in April, Nigel Lawson told the IMF meeting that the world economic conditions were the best they'd been for six years. In contrast, just weeks earlier, Tom Clausen, head of the World Bank, warned that the future would bring 'more Ethiopias with ever-increasing frequency' unless action was taken now. He described Africa's plight as 'the worst economic crisis any region has faced since World War Two.' That economic crisis is contributing to the hunger crisis.

The African countries south of the Sahara have debts of $80 billion, these are small compared to the total Third World debt – about $900 billion – but they are crippling to countries which are already desperately poor. Most of the debts of the least developed countries are official debts – to governments or to the World Bank. Britain has had a good record, for once it means writing off our bilateral loans just as our High Street banks have done, to these countries. In all but five cases past loans to the poorest countries have been converted to grants. The Government should now encourage other nations to write off their loans, and call for the wiping out of official debt via the World Bank. I cannot underestimate the importance of this problem. Even in the last year, Ethiopia has had to pay back to the West more in debt repayments than she has received in aid.

The International Monetary Fund (IMF) is an important source of funds for LDC's. However, the conditions that the IMF impose on their debtors tend to place burdens disproportionately on the poor. Measures of financial austerity such as cutting already minimal health and welfare services, food subsidies, minimum wages, boosting exports, often at the expense of local food production, and so on, simply worsen the hunger problems of the poor. In Jamaica, for example, debt service consumes 40% of all export earnings and contributes to the spiralling child malnutrition rate as food prices soar and wages fall.

In Zambia UNICEF have drawn strong correlations between austerity measures and the infant death rate. Julius Nyerere complained bitterly of the IMF. 'They asked me to make a choice between paying the debts of Tanzania and feeding the people of Tanzania,' he said, 'for me that is no moral choice, it is not even a practical choice.' The British Government should call for a review of IMF policies, and in particular argue that all rescheduling packages should be subject to a scrutiny of the likely effect of the measures intended on low income groups.

The debt crisis is a time bomb waiting to explode. Unless we take action now, it could not only cause immense suffering for the poor of the Third World, but cause possible chaos in our own financial institutions.

Trade is the one major factor emphasising the severity of the debt crisis. For the past 30 years, the prices of the developing countries' raw materials have been falling steadily in comparison with the price of the manufactured goods needed by those countries. This fall in prices has been particularly steep since 1980 when times have been hardest. Take, for example, the case of Ghana, a country which depends on its cocoa trade. In 1980 it earned £1,500 a ton. By mid 1982, this had dropped to £900 a ton. The price of cotton fell by 30% over the same period; that of coffee, by almost 50% in just two years, developing countries saw a fall in their overseas earnings of over $21 billion – just as the debt crisis was beginning to bite.

The other side of the trade coin is the need for fledgling industries in the Third World to gain admission for their products to the mass markets of the developed countries, including the UK. Yet what has been to response of the developed countries? To raise trade barriers of every kind against imports from the Third World. After the 'Kennedy round' of tariff reductions in 1967, the average tariff on total imports was 6%; that on imports from LDCs, 12%. Non-tariff barriers, such as quota restrictions have similarly been used to keep out LDCs' manufactured products.

They have attempted to restrict the economies of LDCs to dependence on a few primary products.

The reason behind this is given as the need to protect the developing countries' own domestic industries from foreign competition. This argument does not bear close examination. The amount of money that must be expended on buying the products of the less efficient domestic industries is often greater than the amount that would need to be spent on retraining and starting up alternative sources of employment if we allowed free entry to Third World products. The UK cotton textile industry is a good example, having suffered a steady decline since 1951 in the face of competition from Hong Kong, India and Pakistan, which, being Commonwealth countries, did not suffer from export restriction. Although the cotton manufacturers asked for protection, successive British governments preferred to compensate firms and workers who left the industry – the transfer of resources out of the cotton textile industry then proceeded quite smoothly. For instance, three quarters of the cotton mills which closed from 1951–64 were soon reoccupied for other purposes.

This type of solution makes sound economic sense, not only for the Third World, but also for ourselves. It does, however, require a firm commitment on the part of our Government to industrial regeneration and retraining, a commitment which has not yet been much in evidence from Mrs Thatcher's Conservatives.

The area of trade is one where the developing countries can do much to help themselves. Often the products they export are more appropriate to other Third World countries than to the developed nations, and we should encourage them to form trade associations amongst themselves. We should similarly encourage the formation of trade cartels to give them more leverage, one word that springs to most people's minds when OPEC is mentioned is that of rising petrol prices, the other side of that coin is rising income for the oil markets. OPEC is such a cartel, and although the first image that springs to most people's mind is that of rising petrol prices, the other side of that coin is rising income for the oil producers.

Again, the response of the developed nations to Third World attempts at solidarity in world trade has been reprehensible. A colleague of mine, Paddy Ashdown, the Liberal MP for Yeovil, used to be a diplomat with the Foreign Office. He recounted to me how, at the fourth UN Conference on Trade and Development in Nairobi in 1974, he, on the instructions of the then Labour minister Frank Judd, had to go round breaking up such merging associations. No wonder Willy Brandt said in 1974, 'I am unable to detect any justice in the present system of economic and social relations'.

We need a whole new look at the world economic system. In January of 1983, the Secretary General of the Commonwealth, Sir Sonny Ramphal, asked:

"Was it not inevitable that sooner or later – for a long time it seemed later – we should have to begin again the rigorous intellectual journey that led in 1944 to Bretton Woods and must now lead us to the threshold of a new era of international economic arrangements and relationships?"

He went on to say:

"Bretton Woods was about money and finance and about trade; it was esoteric and to many barely intelligible, but it was, in the end, about people. Indeed, to a greater degree than was attainable at Bretton Woods in the twilight world of those early post-war years, the world's trading and financial system of the '80s and beyond must be responsive to the needs of all the world's people."

There will be 750 million people, maybe more, hungry

when they try to sleep tonight; 30 million in Africa are on the brink of starvation; Calcutta festers. Four years after the 1984 Ethiopian famine relief agencies are once again battling to bring sufficient food to 5.2 million Ethiopians facing starvation. More than 1.2 million tonnes of food are needed. Abba Kidane-Mariam Ghebray, secretary general of the Ethiopian Catholic Secretariat, explains that 'food is so sacred in Ethiopia that if you drop a piece of bread on the ground, you kiss it before eating it.' Despite the continuing challenge of poverty and famine Britain's aid programme is 17% less in real terms than 6 years ago. The IMF allows the debts to mount: Petty differences, jealousy and national pride combine to stymie a co-ordinated international response. And yet we call ourselves civilised.

There is a story told about the two Raphaelite artists, Rossetti and Morris. Confronted with a beggar, Rossetti would empty his pockets and forget about the man. Morris never gave a penny to a beggar, but devoted his life to working for a world in which there would be no beggars. Rossetti was all heart, Morris all head. Today, we need both – heart and head.

In his Christmas Eve broadcast shortly before he was killed, Martin Luther King outlined his vision for humanity. I hope you will forgive me for altering just two words to bring it more closely into context:

"I still have a dream this morning that one day every Negro in this country, every coloured person in the world, will be judged on the basis of the content of his character rather than the colour of his skin, and every man will respect the dignity and worth of human personality. I still have a dream today that one day the idle industries of the West be revitalised and the empty stomachs of the Third World will be filled, and brotherhood will be more than a few words at the end of a prayer, but rather the first item on every legislative agenda. I still have a dream today that one day justice will roll down like water, and righteousness like a mighty stream. I still have a dream today that in all of our state houses and city halls men will be elected to go there who will do justly, and love mercy and walk humbly with their God. I still have a dream today that one day war will come to an end, that men will beat their swords into ploughshares and their spears into pruning hooks, that nations will no longer rise up against nations, neither will they study war any more. . . . I still have a dream that with this faith we shall be able to bring a new light into the dark chambers of pessimism. With this faith we will be able to speed up the day when there will be peace on earth and goodwill toward men. It will be a glorious day, the morning stars will sing together, and the sons of God will shout for joy."

Chapter Twenty-Four

PROCLAIM A YEAR OF JUBILEE – PRESSURE AND PRAYER

It is all too easy for each of us to pay an annual subscription to Amnesty International and then assume we've done our bit for human rights. Amnesty is at the forefront of the battle to highlight human rights abuses but they would be the first to concede that their effectiveness is limited.

As we approach the last decade of the millenium, it is estimated that 1,500 official executions still occur world-wide each year. Furthermore, thousands of lives are taken deliberately, but covertly, by the repressive activities of the state. Precise figures are never known because of official government denials of actions taken on their behalf. Victims may be deliberate political killings, or unarmed civilians massacred by the police or army; in some countries the authorities sanction the activities of 'death squads'. Torture is still common-place and in many places prisoners are simply allowed to die through ill-treatment and neglect. In nearly half the countries of the world, Amnesty International have documented cases of prisoners of conscience who are held in state prisons.

These acts of barbarism, often sanctioned by the state, are an indictment of our 'civilised world'. Too much toler-ance is still shown towards the worst of the offending countries. From my own experience I can see little evidence that Government to Government representations for particular individuals or situations, are pursued with much vigour. This is despite the important work of organisations like Amnesty International, and the 1973 Helsinki Conference on Security and Co-operation in Europe. The Helsinki Final Act (1975) included a section on 'The Respect of Human Rights and Fundamental Freedoms'. Only in the case of Soviet dissidents and refusniks has there been a concentrated western attempt to demand that the terms of the Helsinki Accords are honoured.

At Easter in 1986, I met with Vladimir Slepak and his wife, Masha, at their home in Moscow. This brave couple were, with Anatoly Shcharansky, the founding members of the Helsinki Monitoring Group. They had banded together to work towards the implementation of the Helsinki Agreement, to which the Soviet Union had been a signatory. For seventeen years the Slepaks have been waiting for an exit visa; Gorbachev's 'glasnost' has failed to make the difference for them. They were refused permission to leave because their 'departure was not in the interest of the Government'. In that time they have suffered repeated forced entry to their home by the KGB, and their furniture smashed. Books, personal letters and photographs were confiscated. Vladimir spent five years in internal exile in Siberia. In winter the temperature in the place he was staying fell to below 55 degrees below freezing. There was no snow but constant icy winds. In the brief summer there was a plague of mosquitoes.

Despite these traumatic experiences I found the Slepaks in good spirits. They remain determined not to be ground down by the pestle which is so powerfully wielded by the State. They joked and laughed with me and showed little sign of the deep emotional pain which all these years of suffering and waiting must have left in their hearts and souls.

For many years the 35 Group – organised by Jewish

women – has ensured that the West has not forgotten the plight of men and women like the Slepaks. Although known officially as the 'Women's Campaign for Soviet Jewry', they had earned their better known name in 1971, when they were first founded. At that time relatively few people were aware of the plight of the Soviet Jews, and the severe difficulties they faced in seeking exit visas. The Jews who had been refused an exit were to become known as 'refusniks'.

The Campaign started by organising a protest by thirty-five 35 year olds who waged a hungerstrike on behalf of a 35–year-old Soviet Jewess called Raiza Palatnik. There-after the Press named them the 35's. The group grew steadily as an activist movement, raising individual cases of prisoners of conscience, and of refusniks. They staged protests to keep the position of Soviet Jewry in the public's minds. In response to the demotion of a scientist to sweeping laboratory floors, elegantly dressed women took to sweeping the Bayswater Road in London. Every news-paper carried the picture and the story of the scientist, who received a visa six days later! They organised for women dressed as lawyers to stand outside the Law Courts, and for two pantomime elephants dressed as Jumbo Jets to 'lobby' Aeroflot, the Soviet State airline.

It is only more recently that a Christian counter-part has been set up to groups like the Women's Campaign for Soviet Jewry. The Jubilee Campaign was established in London out of a growing concern amongst Christians for the Suffering Church. The primary mover is Danny Smith – who organised the successful campaign to secure the release of the seven Siberian Christians who locked them-selves into the basement of Moscow's American Embassy. More recently he – along with Michael and Lorna Bordeaux and Mike Rowe of Keston College (who monitor Christian human rights abuses in Eastern Europe) campaigned to end the imprisonment of Valeri Barinov.

The main purpose of my 1986 visit to Russia, in which

I was accompanied by David Campanale (a Social Democrat) and Bill Hampson, of the Jubilee Campaign, was to meet Barinov's wife, Tanya, in Leningrad.

Valeri is a Christian musician who was accused to trying to leave the USSR. Though he was arrested while returning home to Leningrad, he was sentenced to three years in jail. The real crime was that his group, The Trumpet Call, had made underground recordings of rock music which have a Christian theme. These tapes have been widely circulated among young Christians, making Valeri too popular for the liking of the authorities. We were sickened to learn of the conditions which Barinov was enduring in his captivity. He was confined to a subterranean cell with water pouring down its walls; day and night the light were kept on. He was kept on a diet of bread and water and suffered a major breakdown in health.

Following the campaign undertaken for his freedom by his friends in the West, Valeri was finally released to rejoin his family. Like many released prisoners in Russia, Valeri's troubles did not end there. His unwillingness to conform made emigration the only road to freedom for Valeri and his family.

On November 27th, 1987, I was privileged to greet the Barinov's as they arrived at Heathrow – free at last. In her book *The Trumpet Call*, Lorna Bordeaux graphically describes Barinov's ordeal. She and Danny Smith of the jubilee campaign were both present in the Jubilee Room in Parliament to hear Barinov thank all those who worked through pressure and prayer to secure his release.

In Moscow, we also met with Inna Begun whose husband, Josef, was in Chistopol prison – several days travel away. The authorities had even refused Begun a copy of the Hebrew Bible. She told us of the privations her husband had experienced. The stark brutality of the regime was underlined by the presence of KGB men in a car outside her apartment. Having listened in on our phone-call to Inna, they were now watching our arrival.

Through the British Embassy in Moscow we arranged to visit the Kremlin's Religious Affairs Bureau. It's Director, Mr Volodin, took a careful note of all we said and it came as some satisfaction that each of those on whose behalf we made representations were subsequently released. Ours may have been the role of the boy in Greek mythology who played the lute to make the sun come up. It is arguable that it might have come up anyway. However, in the era of 'glasnost', it is imperative to maintain pressure on the Soviet Union. A slightly more humane human rights policy must not be used as window dressing. The prison camp regime is still as harsh, and refusniks still face the same problems in seeking to leave the Soviet Union. At the present rate of emigration it would take 60 years for those waiting, to receive permission to go. Anyone doubting the harshness of Soviet prison conditions should read Amnesty International's report on the conditions in the Mordovian corrective labour colony, where the Christian poetess, Irina Ratushinskaya was held. In 1982 she was charged with 'anti-Soviet agitation and propaganda' and finally sentenced in March 1983 to seven years' hard labour and five years of internal exile. In 1986 she was allowed to come to the West – after parliamentary pressure.

Her exit visa was granted by the authorities to permit medical treatment for kidney and heart infection contracted during her time in prison camps. Since her arrival in the West she has compiled a collection of 260 poems, of which 150 were recalled from their original inscription in jail on bars of soap.

In one of her poems Irina Ratushinskaya ponders on who her executioners might be:

I was in a concrete basement
From which the dawn was not visible
And then one of my classmates appeared. . . .

Full of excuses, the friend has a nice flat, a mother to worry about, and his wife wants a washing machine. He doesn't want those jeopardised: 'It'll all be the same to you. . . . at dawn If they hadn't sent me, it'd have been another.'

And of course, this is what every repressive regime relies upon.

Elsewhere in the Eastern bloc we should not be deceived by countries like Romania – who practise a relatively liberal foreign policy – into believing that they deal similarly with domestic issues. Romania is probably the most repressive of all the Eastern European countries. President Ceaucescu rules with a vice-like grip – with one in four of the population estimated to be in the state's employ as spies.

In 1984 I represented the British Liberal Party at the 40th anniversary celebrations commemorating the liberation of the country from fascism. One veteran British diplomat who was present at the Bucharest march past said he had seen nothing like it since Nuremburg. Certainly it was hard to see precisely what Romania had been liberated from.

While I was there I made representations on behalf of the Romanian orthodox dissident priest, Father Gheorghe Calciu, who had been in and out of jail for over 21 years. They had even broken his hands to prevent him from making the sign of the cross. Father Calciu was down to just over six stone in weight. In one instance a cockroach saved his sanity. The Communist authorities had imprisoned him in solitary confinement, and only permitted his wife to see him once a year, and just for 20 minutes. Solitude for long periods had caused him literally to lose his ability to speak. To make sure it wouldn't happen again he forced himself to chat to the insect every day.

In a country where the 'Department of Cults' keeps a firm control on believers, it is also common place for churches to be demolished to make way for 'urban renewal' programmes. Despite the difficulty of access of Christians to copies of the Bible, the government also notoriously pulped 10,000 editions of the Bible in Hungarian into toilet paper. These had been destined for the large Hungarian minority that lives in Transylvania, and which suffers acutely at the hands of the Romanian authorities.

Thanks to the help of Dr Nicko Bujor, the former chargé d'affaires at the Romanian Embassy in London, I was able to return to London with word for David Steel – whose letter about Father Calciu I delivered to President Ceaucescu – the news was that Fr. Calciu had been released. He and his wife were ultimately allowed to leave the country and travel to America.

Cases like those of Fr. Calciu, Valeri Barinov, Irina Ratushinkaya and Josef Begun illustrate the problems which dissenters face in Eastern Europe. They also provide an illustration of what might be done to assist them. Inna Begun – in answer to a question I put to her about whether outside intervention might make matters worse – told me that would be a near impossibility; the bigger risk is that the West may forget or turn a blind eye as it anxiously seeks progress on arms control. That, she said, was a far greater danger.

Elsewhere in the world there are violations every bit as brutal as in the Soviet Union. Nepal is one example. Talk of this country and images are conjured up of an inaccessible mountain Kingdom; spectacular beauty and the grandeur of the Himalaya Mountains, of soaring Everest, of fertile valleys and plains. But the country which fired every school boy's imagination with tales of Sherpa Tenzing, or Sir Edmund Hilary and the brave but ferocious Gurkha regiments is again, by contrast, a country of appalling brutality and intolerance.

Nepal is the world's only Hindu country (India is a secular state). The law stipulates that no citizen of Nepal may change their religion or try to influence other citizens to change theirs. This rigid code is a cover for acts of humiliation, torture and misery which are inflicted on the Kingdom's tiny Christian minority.

To the extent that a country might wish to protect it's culture and individual identity the attitude of the Nepalese Government might seem understandable. Memories of the Hippy influence embodied in Khatmandhu's Freak Street and the current surge in misuse of hard drugs by the country's young people, have all created a hostility to Western influences which borders on paranoia. Memories also persist of 'rice Christianity' – the blatant bribery of impoverished people by missionaries over-identified with colonialists and Western imperialists.

But none of these arguments justify what is happening in Nepal today, nor do they reflect the nature of the brave and distinctly Nepalese Christian churches. In a fact finding visit to Nepal, and over a course of five days our delegation travelled over 1,000 miles within the country and took evidence from more than three dozen individuals who have been subjected to inhuman and barbaric treatment. We saw groups of people who despite constant harassment and brutality have built small churches and meeting places and whose pastors and priests have nurtured the growth of Christianity in this mountain kingdom.

In 1975 the Protestant churches had just 2,500 members and that has grown to an estimated 35,000 members today, while the Catholic presence in Nepal dates back 200 years. One leading Christian evangelist in Nepal is the Reverend Charles Mendies, who, for proclaiming the Gospel, faces six years imprisonment. In 1986 more than 80 other Christians were charged with 'preaching Christianity and causing a disturbance to Hinduism.' Driving with Charles Mendies for over 12 hours one night we arrived in East Nepal in the town of Dahran. There we took evidence from Christians who had been beaten and tortured. Among those we heard about was a three year old girl who was arrested for clapping her hands and singing a Christian hymn.

Evidence we took at a village called Lamagara, near

Gurkha in the Western region of Nepal, was more encouraging. Local officials in that region seemed sympathetic to the plight of their Christian minority, though the pastor, Kali Bahadur Tamang, has often been interrogated by the local police. Even while we were there in the small village church – reached after an hour's trek across open countryside, a river and paddy fields – the police arrived to find out what was going on. The village itself was established by Christians from throughout the region who were escaping persecution.

It is a gentle, quiet oasis: one family now boasts three generations of Christians. The man who founded the village told me: 'I am just a simple, illiterate man. I had been ill and someone told me to pray to get better. I did. Then I prayed to get to heaven.'

One dilemma which he and other Christians have faced is that when they apply for citizenship they are forced to declare their religion. Citizens admitting their Christianity face refusal and reprisals. Up until the recent past the Catholics in Nepal have tried to get on quietly with their lives, abiding by the stipulation that they must not try to convert people. One priest even refused to baptise people lest it upset the authorities. Yet Catholics, too, are facing punitive retaliation, including the brutal harassment and public humiliation of two nuns.

At the heart of the problem is the unjust law forbidding Nepal's citizens to change their religion. This is in total contradiction to article 18 of the United Nations Declaration on Human Rights which Nepal says it supports. In Nepal that right is being denied to Christians each day of the week.

After having heard of every kind of primeval barbary and torture – from the stocks to the assault of women – we presented the evidence to the Nepalese Foreign Minister.

Along with the Conservative MP, David Atkinson, I have subsequently raised these issues in a special adjournment debate and meetings with both Sir Geoffrey Howe and the Nepalese Ambassador in London, yet the abuses and arrests continue unabated. As recently as November 1987 Amnesty International published their own damning indictment of Nepalese human rights abuses.

One of the great advantages of our democracy is that the British public have channels to pursue cases of human rights abuse. They are backed up by campaign groups like the 35's whose example has shown that persistent campaigning produces results. In 1986, in order to galvanise further parliamentary support for individuals suffering for their beliefs, I helped establish the Jubilee Campaign at Westminster. Over 70 MPs have now sponsored named prisoners in many parts of the world and have committed themselves to campaign on behalf of that individual.

The right of people to think for themselves, to hold their beliefs, to practise their faith, to say what they think; these are all things which we in the western democracies take for granted. We are sometimes too cavalier in so lightly viewing privileges which millions of others will never attain. Whether it is by raising individual cases with MPs or by writing to Government Ministers, Foreign Ambassadors or Governments we can all play some part in demonstrating our concern to uphold each other's human rights; and in doing so we underline the interdependence we each have for one another.

Chapter Twenty-Five

COPING WITH CONFLICT – CENTRAL AMERICA AND THE GULF

Conflict represents the breakdown of consent within, or between countries. Sometimes conflict arises out of the tensions of an unjust political system; other times it is caused by religious or political fanaticism; sometimes it arises out of territorial jealousies or long standing grievances rooted deep in history.

Human nature is such that conflict is never likely to completely disappear. Therefore the question for the world is how best does it manage and respond to conflict. Once more I place longer term trust in confederal arrangements between nations – with the establishment of effective United Nations peace keeping forces; a Commonwealth rapid deployment force; and European defence arrangements. I have argued for each of these elsewhere.

It would be whistling in the wind to imagine that such an objective is going to be achieved rapidly – since many of the principal players are still fomenting their own narrowly perceived national interests. Those interests may still cause the United States to lob a bomb or two on Tripoli; or cause them to thwart the Arias Peace Plan in Central America – but they are reluctant to mount full scale invasions or to act independently (note the enthusiastic encouragement to

Britain to send warships to the Gulf). This suggests an America much chastened by the humiliation of Vietnam which brought considerable troop losses and disillusionment; similarly, after Afghanistan, the Soviet Union is showing a reticence to openly engage in foreign adventures. Of course, both super powers will continue to resort to subtle methods of de-stabilisation – ranging from assassination attempts of national leaders to to overt intereference in a nation's internal elections (for example, President Reagan's endorsement of Mrs Thatcher and his assertion that Labour's defence policy was incompatible with membership of NATO).

If the Super Powers must learn to resist the temptation to reach for the nearest gun, they must also learn that it can be a positive virtue to be above the storm. Impetuous decisions based on imperialism can destabilise whole regions – while spatchcocked solutions arrived at in Washington or Moscow will be resented by the very people they were designed to help.

Our efforts should go into strengthening international policy and co-operation. In those regions where internationalism has no writ, we must act to contain the conflict, not to influence it. We must learn again the art of patience as others learn the lessons which even Europe has only come to partially understand, despite two cataclysmic world wars. Some humility is required before lecturing others on the better management of their affairs.

The conflict in Central America is a classic example of where locally arrived at solutions might be made to stick, while outside interference can only exacerbate the conflict. It is also a region where early international peace keeping might have avoided the destructive cyclone of violence which has swept through Nicaragua, El Salvador and Guatemala.

Fighting the Last Battle in the Wrong Ditch

On 24th March 1980 Oscar Romero, Archbishop of El Salvador, was murdered at the altar of his Cathedral church in San Salvador. Gustavo Gutierrez, the 'father' of Liberation Theology has described his martyrdom as dividing Latin American history into 'before' and 'after'. Romero was the first episcopal martyr of the new movement for justice, although 800 priests and religious had already been killed. Romero was murdered because he had defended the poor and the oppressed of his country against the government. His was the voice of the powerless, the voice of those no one else would speak for. For those in power it was an inconvenient, prophetic voice silenced through murder like those of Oliver Plunkett and Thomas a Becket, two turbulent priests before him.

Before his elevation to the Archbishopric, Romero had been a conservative cleric, on one occasion even objecting to the local seminarians wearing shorts instead of long trousers for football. Many saw his appointment as a 'safe bet' designed to uphold the innate conservatism of the Church and its institutions. Gradually he saw that to be an effective pastor to the oppressed he had to become their defender and champion, he had to embody their hopes, aspirations and ideals.

He recognised the necessity to understand and accommodate the struggle of people wrestling with economic servitude and the oppressive hegemony of the landowner. He once said:

> In my country it is very difficult to speak of anti-communism because anti-communism is what the Right preaches, not out of love for Christian sentiments, but out of a selfish concern to promote its own interests.

The killing of Romero by the Right has its echoes elsewhere in Latin America. In May 1986 a hired assassin shot

Fr. Josimo Tavares in the back. The murderer justified his crime on the grounds that the priest's support for land reform proved he was a communist.

It is totally to misunderstand Romero to suggest that he was pleading for Marxism. It is impossible to plead the Marxist analysis and detach it from its prescriptions. What Romero saw was that you do not need to be a Marxist to believe in justice. He clearly perceived that totalitarianism can come as easily from the Right as from the Left. Hence the undesirability of responding in an identical and universal way to communism. The communist aggressor in Poland and Eastern Europe gives the lie to Marxist claims and demonstrates the fallacy of making sweeping global statements. Even within Romero's Central American region there are diverse and diverging interests: a civil war in El Salvador, a military dictatorship in Guatemala and a left wing regime replacing a hated dictatorship in Nicaragua.

The danger for the upholder of Liberal democratic values is that the Marxist and readers of Herbert Marcuse come to identify our democracies as crippled with institutional arthritis. This failure to respond gives them a monopoly of anger and concern, and the young European or American will often embrace Marxism out of a sense of transferred guilt. It is a simple way for atoning for their wealth, liberty and for our collective failure to identify with the needs of the exploited majority.

The liberation theologians of Latin America argue that not only are global caricatures irrelevant but so are global remedies. One of the most outspoken voices – that of the Franciscan Leonardo Boff – says that European style 'formal democracy' – merely voting so often – is inadequate. 'Social' democracy bringing justice, liberty and fraternity must be the goal. Gustavo Gutierrez, a Peruvian Indian, the father of Liberation Theology, defines it as the release of people from the injustices that stem from human egoism. Significantly, he has opposed 'liberation move-

ments' like the Maoist Sendero Luminoso in Peru, casti-
gating totalitarianism as the 'negation of human liberty'.

These church leaders who have taken the side of the
poor are vilified by President Reagan's administration in
Washington. For Reagan life is entirely a Manichean
struggle between the forces of good and evil, or in 'B' movie
terms the 'goodies and the baddies'. Communist countries
are all part of an evil empire which a Ramboesque Reagan
will singlehandedly destroy. In the simplistic but neat 'evil
versus good' argument the Presidents' men are unerringly
on the side of good. Yet life is rarely so simple.

In Nicaragua for instance President Daniel Ortega's
Sandinista government has sustained itself in the face of
virtually open-ended support for the insurgent Contras by
President Reagan's Administration. This in itself is a testi-
mony to the existence of broad popular support for
Ortega's government gained in fair elections as opposed to
the fear of the Contras many of whom learnt their trade of
oppression under the brutal regime of Somoza.

The insatiable American appetite to destroy Ortega's
Nicaragua led it into the foolish Irangate scandal – where
receipts from the sale of arms to Iran were illicitly transferred to provide funds to the Contras after the American
Congress had put a stop to direct aid. This foolhardy policy
badly backfired. Reagan forfeited his integrity and Ortega
survived. American covert actions from Laos to Cuba have
rarely brought anything but discredit on those making
hypocritical claims to be upholders of high morality, liberty
and the democratic ideal.

In El Salvador roles are reversed. Here President Jose
Duarte's right wing government is supported by Washington but on past evidence is incapable of either destroying the left wing guerrilla movement or controlling the
murderous fanatics of its own. At present there exists a
deadly stalemate characterised by the 'disappearance' of
opposition politicians and supporters at the hands of the
death squads and endemic civil strife.

Each of the Central American countries has watched with alarm as the conflict of the region has escalated. Guatemala with its appalling human rights record can expect the violence of civil war to take deep root there too. Since General Rios Montt created Military Tribunals empowered to impose the death penalty for political 'crimes' following a secret trial the catalogue of deaths and torture has continued. Trade Unionists and opposition politicians remain the favourite targets and like El Salvador, recent years have been marked by the increasing activity of the death squads.

The first tentative steps out of the Central American conflict came in August 1987 when President Oscar Arias Sanchez of Costa Rica secured the acceptance of a peace plan by the five Central American countries. This requires the Sandinistas to open their political system, while simultaneously requiring an end to the American aid which supports the Contras. The United States has always maintained that it could not and would not talk to the Ortega government until it secured agreement with its Central American neighbours. Central America's leaders have now done this. Washington will need new excuses and to date their negative response will have done nothing to enhance American prestige. It has become all too clear that merely softening rather than ending Sandinista rule is not enough for the Reaganites. Paradoxically this will strengthen the arm of those in Central America whom President Reagan finds most distasteful. America's willingness to back corrupt regimes with no popular base has thrust more people into the arms of communism than the ballot box.

The Arias plan, regional consensus, co-operation among neighbouring states, are all welcome developments in Central America. The United States, its Central American policy in tatters, by responding negatively to these developments will end up reviled. It must learn that it is not a loner but team player among the nations; until then its policies will regularly end up in a shambles.

In Europe we must learn what Latin American liberation theologians have understood: that our mode of Western organisation and closely defined relationships between state and people are not necessarily a paradigm for the rest of the world; and that, rather than fighting the last battle vin the wrong ditch we must get ourselves on the side of the people we claim to care for.

Islam's Sword – fundamentalism

The revolution which is underway in Iran is another point of conflict which will require a measured and patient response. Revolutions, and a fundamentalist Islamic revolution especially cannot be willed away or overturned by outsiders, and as acts of brutal terrorism in Paris and the abduction of the Anglican Envoy, Terry Waite – illustrate that these are ruthless and fanatical men bent on nothing less than world wide Islamic revolution.

The best the West can hope for is containment. A hope shared by the Sunni Muslim countries of the Gulf, and most Arab leaders from Riyadh to Tangiers.

In 1918 the Western powers, joined by Japan, tried to stop the Russian revolution. They were derailed; the revolution was not. The Iran-Iraq war began not long after I entered Parliament, in 1980. Since then Iran has sustained more casualties than the United States lost in World War Two, Korea and Vietnam combined. If a good proportion of the 50 million Iranians did not believe in the revolution, such massive human sacrifice could not have been sustained. With such unity in a country where 45 percent of the citizens are now under 16 years of age and thus more likely to be both malleable and impressionable – we should not assume that the revolution will simply burn itself out with the passing of Ayatollah Ruhollah Khomeini. The Iranian revolution and the Gulf War will probably simply burn on.

Secondly, it would be absurd for the West to believe that

post Khomeini it might grandly impose a successor from outside. In 1953 the United States helped bring back the Shah by orchestrating a coup that overthrew the militantly nationalist prime minister, Mohammed Mossadeh. Deep and bitter resentment about outside interference in its internal affairs helped bring us to the present vale of tears.

Within Iran, and in European exile, there undoubtedly exists a realistic alternative to religious fanaticism. Since the early 1980's I have acted as a London sponsor for the People's Mohajeddin, the supporters of Mr Rajavi. In 1983 and 1986 at our Harrogate and Eastbourne Assemblies I helped organise, and spoke at, meetings on their behalf.

They tell a harrowing tale of brutal repression of democratic ideas and they claim considerable support amongst anti-Khomeini factions and the crushing of dissidents. The Ayatollah's death will be a signal to the dissidents. Their attack will be combined with fresh turmoil as Kurdish insurgents continue to demand their independence, along with like-minded insurgents in Baluchistan. Post Khomeini Iran is going to be seething with disorder.

That disorder may not be enough to create a counter revolution. Iranian fundamentalism has to be defeated by a combination of action and ideas – and Muslims themselves must wage that struggle. If they fail to provide an intellectually credible and popular alternative to medieval theocracy it will not only be Iran that sinks into the fundamentalist sands. Not one of the Governments that rule the 140 million Arabs can claim to be a full democracy and it would be difficult to take the side of Iraq against Iran on the basis that the regime was very much more progressive. Without the legitimacy which the high democratic ideal can alone confer, the danger of fundamentalist revolution will endure. This will mean more revolutions like one which occurred in Iran in 1979. Through the Muslim world the tensions between Shi'ites and Sunnis will also remain. Although the 700 million Sunnis substantially outnumber the 90 million Shi'ites, who rule Iran and have majorities in the Lebanon, Bahrain and Iraq – the often bloody feud between Islam's two branches has the potential for further eruption at any time. One fascinating caveat is the position of Iraq's Shi'ites, who make up 60 percent of the population and have chosen to be Iraqi first and Shi'ite second. This gives a clue to how best we might counter Khomeini's objective of using his network of Shi'ite radicals and terrorists to activate his world revolution.

Significantly also, the Soviet Union has to tread with great delicacy before adding to the West's discomfort. Khomeini's fiery appeals to the Muslim communities in the Soviet Union make them unlikely to court a fundamentalist regime that threatens them too.

In the last eight years Iran has lost millions of people in the conflicts which have gripped it. Entire towns have been erased from the map of Khuzistan. Tehran has been blitzed by Iraqi missiles, chemical weapons have been used, and wave after wave more of young Iranians have sought a martyr's crown in this Holy War. In dispensing with the illusion that some easy way exists to bring this conflict to a speedy conclusion we must temper our judgement with patience and wisdom. Patience in letting this cyclone blow itself out. Wisdom in encouraging Muslims to seek more rational ways of living. We can best limit the conflict by providing international policy on the boundaries of the war; and by reducing the carnage by stopping the flow of weapons.

Incidentally, I am glad to see that the government has finally moved against the Iranians arms procurement office that for years operated from London's Victoria Street (ironically close to the national headquarters of our own department of Trade and Industry). Both I and David Steel have campaigned for the closure of this branch of the death trade. The Government's motivation, it appears, was more to do with the embarrassment of having British Navy vessels newly arrived in the Gulf being fired on by freshly supplied British weaponry.

Internationalism is ultimately the best antidote to fundamentalism. Reaction must be countered by progress not by
revolution. Fundamentalism must be confronted by ideas
and ideals. All over the world fanatical religious figures
pervert their beliefs or distort them into shrieking and
intolerant calls to victory. It is all done in the name of
God, Jehovah, Jesus or Allah. In Nepal, I met Christian
villagers who had been beaten or put in stocks because
King Behrendra believes he is a Hindu god and in his
theocratic state no tolerance is shown towards those who
deviate. In Cairo I met President Sadat, later shot dead
by Muslim fanatics who believe in the Jihad and the rigid
imposition on others of the strictures of the Koran. In
Jerusalem I have talked to Zionist extremists who seek the
creation of a Biblical Israel – swallowing up the homes and
lands of all who stand before them.

In Belfast I have encountered the bigotry and the prejudice of men who have made a scandal of Christianity; and
in America the moral majority of Christian fundamentlism
preach the electronic gospel as a way which leaves no room
for doubt. In Alabama, Tennesee and Louisiana, it has led
to attempts to ban 'The Diary of Anne Frank' because it
recognises the worth of other religions. Such certitude, such
absolutism and such fanaticism are all incompatible with
the tolerance and respect for human rights that runs like a
rich vein through an enlightened society. Let us understand
what it is we are fighting in Iran but let us pause also to
examine the plank in our own eye.

Chapter Twenty-Six

GOOD STEWARDSHIP OF THE EARTH

If anyone ever seriously believed it is possible to turn the clock back to the days of the independent European nation state, the disaster at Chernobyl changed all that. Pollution, whether acid rain or a radioactive cloud, does not respect national boundaries. Our interdependence is glaringly obvious. Yet just as Britain shirks many other international responsibilities our track record on environmental issues is abysmal. Our failure, for instance, to join the '30% Club' of European nations committed to cutting emmisions of sulphur dioxide from power stations by 30% has earned us the title of 'dirty man of Europe'. The British were the first to pollute their country with an industrial revolution and will be the last in putting right its consequences.

Failure to act in a concerted way; failure to press for the highest of standards; and our continued insistence on putting company profits before a proper appreciation for the quality of life jeopardises forests, heritage and people alike. Grab what you can; do unto others before they do you; insist on bigger, faster, better and more. These are all the characteristics of the developed countries. Rights matter, responsibilities do not. We say it is our right to have continued increases in our standards of living; never mind that alarming depletion of our planet's natural resources. It is our right to guzzle as much petrol and oil as money can buy; never mind that all known reserves of oil are likely to be used up by the end of this century and never mind that the metals needed to make the cars will be exhausted 50 years from now. So long as we can grab what we can it doesn't much matter how much sulphur dioxide we pump into the air; how much radioactive waste we dump in the sea; how much sewage, DDT or garbage and rubbish we strew across countryside, farmland and rivers. Future generations will wonder what we could have been thinking of, as they ponder on a society which acted, not as custodian and steward of God-given resources, but squandered and frittered them away.

Just briefly, during the oil crisis of the mid 70's, the West was forced to examine its priorities, causing the then Archbishop of Canterbury to thank God 'for acting through his servant Sheik Yamani of OPEC' to tick us off for wasting his oil. Jimmy Carter then introduced conservation measures and we all turned off the lights when they were not needed. Then the crisis went and we largely returned to our former ways.

Talking about the French Revolution, Edmund Burke said that 'A state without the means of some change is without the means of its conservation.' Applying his axiom more widely we have a clear choice in the world today to change and conserve or to waste away.

Over the past few decades we have produced more waste than ever before. There has been a massive acceleration in the discharge of effluent, much of it toxic into the atmosphere, the rivers, oceans and onto land. In the western democracies this has fostered ecology groups and the green movement. I especially admire Friends of the Earth and the Council for the Preservation of Rural England. In some countries – notably Germany, Greens have even been elected to Parliament, although in the UK our electorial system makes it impossible for The Green Party to be elected here. Many environmentalists, therefore, join and work with one of the three major parties. Disappointingly despite their efforts to give Green issues a high political profile they hardly received a mention in the 1987 election.

However, the pressure of the single issue groups and greater political awareness in general has had its impact on industry with many companies beginning to take a more enlightened view.

One fallacy which has been actively encouraged by the Greens, is that the objective of economic progress and growth is incompatible with conservation and environmental sanity. If that were so it would condemn countless millions to lives of interminable and dire poverty. Mindless Luddism, smashing the machines. Simply railing against growth is not what is required. Instead, we must consider together how best we might develop, share and conserve the earth and its resources. We are stewards of our Universe not conquerors or masters.

Between 1983 and 1986 I served on the Environment Select Committee of the House of Commons. During that time we undertook several major enquiries – including an examination of acid rain, an enquiry into the disposal of nuclear waste, and the position of Britain's greenbelt, its wildlife and countryside. Our enquiries involved taking evidence and speaking to expert witnesses in the UK and abroad. The thing which struck me most throughout my time on the committee was the irresponsibility of Britain's policies relating to the production of energy and in dealing with the pollution which inevitably accompanies it.

Imagine a forest where half the trees are dead or dying; or lakes that are so badly polluted that fish can no longer survive; or great buildings that have survived pillage, sackings and war, but are now crumbling away from the effects of air pollution. Imagine all this and worse. And then ask what kind of world it is that allows such grisly fantasy to become a reality?

I have rarely felt more depressed than on a recent visit to Germany's Black Forest. Nearly every fir is diseased and officials in the State of Baden-Wurtenberg say that half of the forest's trees are beyond recall. Since the mid–1970's the silver firs have been dying in their thousands: and since 1981 there has been a dramatic escalation with spruce firs and deciduous trees also affected.

As long as 1972, at a specially convened conference in Stockholm, the impending disaster was predicted by scientists, but Governments throughout Europe have complacently stood by as the trees have died.

The phenonmenon known as Acid Rain has been sweeping across Central Europe's forests like a cyclone of death. Its effects are also beginning to be increasingly felt in these islands.

As Governments have adopted a do-nothing approach, the situation has worsened to the point where every second spruce in the Black Forest is now diseased and even nursery saplings are withering. The foresters, in the face of this man-made disaster, are virtually helpless. Time is running out for them and for their trees. The psychological impact on a country like Germany, where a third of the land is covered with woodland, is difficult for a Briton to fully appreciate.

The forests are central to German culture and heritage. But the economic and ecological considerations are mind boggling by comparison. 250,000 jobs in Baden-Wurtenburg alone are dependent upon forestry activities. The disappearance of the trees will also fundamentally alter the ecology of Western Europe.

The forests protect ground water: retain rain water; preserve the fertility of the soil; provide protection against erosion and affect climatic conditions. Wildlife is also dependent on the forest for its survival.

It is obvious to even the most casual observer that for many of the trees it is already too late. A walk in the Black Forest is like a walk in a graveyard. The skeletons of the trees leave no room for scepticism about the seriousness of the situation.

But buildings, too, as well as trees, are threatened by the dangerous levels of European pollution. At the top of Cologne Cathedral, in Liverpool's twin city, the chief stone mason described to me how 67 stone masons are employed full time in replacing corroded stone: 'some had been replaced four times in 20 years; the cathedral will soon be a replica of a replica.'

The Acropolis in Athens is another victim of this malignant cancer. Buildings all over Britain are being subjected to this insidious process.

The destruction of the forests and erosion of buildings has created a political backlash in Germany through the emergence of the Greens.

But concern for the environment and the quality of life is no longer simply confined to the Greens. The three orthodox political parties in Germany are all desperately trying to out bid one another in appearing to be the most concerned about environmental issues. Probably because, as Herr Carl Dieter Spragner, a Federal Minister of the Interior, admitted. 'The environment now ranks only after unemployment as the most important issue on the German political agenda, even before peace.'

And political sentiment is at last being matched by bipartisan legislation recently agreed by the Bundestag and backed up by the State Parliaments.

Germany has recognised what Britain will soon have to accept: the price being paid for air pollution is too high and greater controls are desperately needed.

Even though the scientists remain divided about the exact causes there is general consensus that air pollution is the principal cause of the dying forests. The actual term 'acid rain' is really a misnomer.

The expression 'acid rain' was actually first coined by the first Chief Alkali Inspector, Adam Smith, as long ago as 1872. Today the expression is used misleadingly. The atmosphere rather than the rain seems to be the killer. At the root of the problem are emissions of sulphur (S02) and nitrogen (NOx) oxides. Ironically, and significantly, with the Clean Air Programme and the introduction of smokeless fuels the level of sulphur emissions has grown with the growth of car ownership.

Some German scientists believe that as the smog has been cleared away it has made a photo chemical interaction easier. This is caused by the impact of the sun's rays, and particularly ozone, acting on nitrogen oxides. So as the sulphur dioxide is being reduced it can actually increase the dangers from other pollutants.

Britain's Central Electricity Generating Board have been trying to minimise the problem of air pollution and acid rain. Instead of doing anything positive they have been calling for more research, hoping that expensive de-sulphurisation equipment will not have to be fitted to their coal burning power station.

Faced with the same evidence the Germans have plunged into a massive programme. The Government has made available 10–15 billion Deutsch Marks for filter equipment in power stations; but some of the costs will be passed on to consumers who may face up to 30% increases in the price of fuel. A small price to pay, say the environmentalists.

The advocates of de-sulphurisation also point out that, as usual, the Japanese have stolen a march on everybody else and are the only country producing sophisticated environmental technology.

German industry is now catching up fast and by 1988 German-made desulphurisation plants will be positioned in three quarters of all German power stations – reducing emissions from 80,000 tonnes to 20,000 tonnes over the intervening four years. Preparations are now in hand for the removal of nitrogen dioxide (NOx). That work will involve planning, erection and construction – and the creation of thousands of jobs.

The Germans are also taking urgent action to introduce

lead-free petrol. Britain has simply announced its intention to travel the same road by the end of the decade. When the lead is removed a catalyst can be added to the petrol to prevent NOx emissions from vehicles. The Germans are working on the technology for this too.

Meanwhile, British scientists are still haggling and arguing about the conflicting theories. Germany has recognised that there is no smoke without fire and have acted to reduce pollution regardless of whether it is the sole cause of the forests dying.

Unilateral action by Germany in tackling air pollution is simply inadequate. Only 50% of their pollution is home grown; the rest is imported from neighbouring states.

The Black Forest receives more pollutants from external sources than from internally generated emissions: 32% from the German Federal Republic; 32% from France and the rest comes from countries such as Czechoslavakia, the Netherlands and Britain.

German scientists say that pollution of the air in Czechoslovakia has become so bad that recently children had to be evacuated from one border town to a spa town for recuperation. Britain's Department of Energy recently admitted that at least 10 other European countries receive more than one percent of our emissions of sulphur – and in Scandinavia this has led to the acidification of lakes and the death of marine life.

Certainly there should be a concerted European approach to research into pollution and its causes; but the need for research must not impede the development of abatement techniques, and an immediate commitment to reducing our sulphur dioxide emissions.

Here in the United Kingdom we have no cause for smugness or complacency. We are a massive exporter of pollution but growing evidence of acidification in Scottish lochs and streams and evidence from parts of Wales and Cumbria all point to a visitation of this plague much closer to home.

Failure to act will ensure the continued death of forests, the deterioration of cultural sites in Europe and unknown but half-guessed at damage to human health.

If Britain does re-fit its coal burning power stations via scrubbers it will radically diminish our output of sulphur dioxide. It will also enable us to meet international obligations and to create thousands of jobs in our construction industry. It will enable us to place less reliance on the development of nuclear energy.

I am not prepared to say that there will be a time when the world will not have to build new nuclear reactors. Scientists may even find ways of overcoming the waste disposal problems. If they do, and of politicians can get a grip of the civil liberties issues and sever links between civil and military uses if safety can be radically improved and if medical experts give the industry a clean bill of health, then circumstances might be created in which nuclear energy could be developed. As yet none of those criteria have been satisfactorily met. That is why I have not and will not vote for the construction for new nuclear power stations. Indeed it is worth recording that in 1977 Liberals alone – led by David Steel and David Penhaligon – voted against Tony Benn's proposal to build the £1 billion thermal oxide reprocessing plant at Sellafield.

Unhesitatingly, I regard domestic nuclear energy as infinitely more dangerous and potentially more catastrophic than the nuclear weapons stashed away in our silos. The political parties and protest movements do not see it that way yet, although post Chernobyl, many attitudes have altered.

In order to ensure unanimity for the key recommendation of our Select Committee inquiry into nuclear waste disposal – namely the ending of reprocessing at the Sellafield plant – I signed the report. However, in many key areas I believe that the report is weak and tries to hedge in bits – this was partly because of the failure of the industry and Government to be sufficiently open with us.

On the question of radiation related diseases, the report is at its most unsatisfactory. By way of amendment I thought to introduce a whole new chapter challenging the Government and industry's complacency in facing the health issue.

In America the Committee visited Hanford in the State of Washington. This is where the Manhattan Project was based (which developed the Hiroshima and Nagasaki bombs). It is situated on a former Indian reservation – which was signed over to the Federal Government by Chief Seattle. Today, the visitor will see 30 decommissioned power stations which litter the site of the reservation. They will be radioactive and dangerously contaminated for million of years. In a piece of prophetic writing Chief Seattle included this warning with the 1854 treaty.

If we sell you our land, you must remember that it is sacred and teach your children that it is sacred . . . the rivers are our brothers they quench our thirst . . . the air is precious to the red man, for all things share the same breath . . . the beast, the tree, the man, they all share the same breath. . . This we know.

The earth does not belong to man: man belongs to the earth. All things are connected like the blood which unite one family. All things are connected.

Whatever befalls the earth befalls the sons of the earth.

The white man too shall pass: perhaps sooner than all the other tribes. Continue to contaminate your beds, and you will one night suffocate in your own waste'.

Chief Seattle had a wisdom and uncanny foresight which ought to trouble the decision makers who blithely pollute and poison the earth on which we live.

I have already argued that – with the right safeguards – to eliminate acid rain – Britain can place greater emphasis on coal and less on nuclear energy. We can also do far more to conserve the energy we waste and to develop alternative sources of energy. In Liverpool, for instance, a

tidal barrage should be built on the Mersey. I have advocated this since the early 1970s and I often raise the matter
in the House of Commons.

The Mersey barrage is a perfect example of the kind
of infrastructure project that the country needs, but this
Government has neglected.

A barrage is a large sea wall or dam across a river
estuary. It contains within it turbine generators for electricity. Sluices and locks for shipping. Two tidal schemes
connected with barrages are currently in operation elsewhere in the world, near St Malo on the La Rance estuary,
and in the Soviet Union near Murmansk. Preliminary
studies carried out by the now defunct Merseyside County
Council identified three feasible sites across the Mersey.
The Mersey barrage scheme would offer several advantages. It would generate about a third of Merseyside's
electricity requirements, coming on line as early as 1997.
It would provide deep sea water facilities in the mouth of
the Mersey, linking in excellently with the nearby free port
facilities. The sheltered basin behind the barrage would in
turn create extra opportunities for navigation, amenity and
recreation – and the barrage itself would provide a third
river crossing.

Perhaps most importantly in the short term, the project
would create new jobs for Merseyside. During the first four
years or so there would be massive construction activity,
with a short-term peak of 5,000 new jobs. Longer-term
employment effects would arise from development of activities and opportunities around the basin.

Many of the 130,000 jobless on Merseyside have worked
in the construction and related industries. This scheme
would provide work for many of them. It is a crazy waste
to keep those people on the dole queues at such a high cost
to the Exchequer.

The idea of the Mersey barrage is supported by the
Merseyside Docks and Harbour Company. Feasibility
studies have been carried out by the Merseyside barrage

group of Marintech North West (formerly North Western Universities Consortium for Marine Technology). This scheme would improve the infrastructure, create work, harness a renewable source of energy, and provide a symbol of faith in the future for a part of Britain where commitment, faith and hope have been in desperately short supply.

Yet even a barrage brings some environmental problems – by disturbing the resting grounds of birds. The environmental plusses of a clean river, resource created for human recreation, the jobs, and the energy for homes and for industry far outweigh these considerations. It is a good example of responsible growth, green growth – where a great river can be harnessed through modern technology and where the benefits are shared by all.

There are other ways of creating energy too: energy needs in developing countries must be met in imaginative ways. As the Brandt Report stated 'Left to itself, private enterprise does not undertake sufficient exploration for, and production of, energy in the developing countries.' They recommended that a global energy research centre should be created under UN auspices to co-ordinate information and projection and to support research on new energy resources. To finance new initiatives an energy affiliate of the World Bank would be required. This was discussed at the Cancun Summit and vetoed by the USA – probably because of pressure from some US oil companies. If the US are not prepared to reverse their policy the other developed nations should proceed anyway.

European action to tackle energy related pollution must be matched by a greater interest in the developing countries – where the most urgent international action is required.

It is not development or growth but grinding poverty that leads to desertification in Sub-Saharan Africa, to the stripping of trees and shrubs for fuelwood in Nepal. It is not development but desperation that drives people to destroy fisheries, and wipe out whole species of animals and plants.

Disasters like that which occurred at Bhopal hit the headlines but Bhopal was simply a badly thought out and badly administered industrial development. In time, that can all be put right but what cannot be so easily remedied is the destruction of the world's ecosystem.

In 1980, the World Wild Life Fund, the United Nations Environment Programme and the International Union for the Conservation of Nature published their World Conservation Strategy. Like Chief Seattle before them, they argued that man is just a part of the ecological order, not its master; that we lack a sense of responsibility in caring for creation. In the developing countries the situation is disastrous.

* The deserts of the World are now expanding by 60,000 kilometres annually – almost the size of Ireland.
* Poor land management and deforestation lead to the annual loss of 6,000 million tonnes of top soil in India alone.
* Fuelwood is so scarce in the poorer parts of the Andean Sierra and Africa's Sahel that the cost of clothing and heating can constitute a quarter of a family's budget;
* Every minute 20 hectares of tropical rainforest are destroyed – these are the most important ecosystem on the globe. The area of productive forest will be halved during the 1980s and 1990s.
* 25,000 plant species and 1,000 species and sub species of mammals, birds, amphibians, reptiles and fish, face extinction.

The bulldozers and chainsaws hack down the forests, the aircraft spray their defoliants, the factory ships ruthlessly deplete fish stocks, and the prospectors extract minerals while destroying flora, fauna and anything else that stands in the way of a quick buck. We have the cheek to call this progress.

A World Conservation Strategy could maintain real progress without these dire consequences.

Britain and the EEC should emulate Denmark's admirable Environmental Investments Support Act by directing loans and grants into appropriate technologies. We should increase our aid programme and direct a high proportion of the extra funds at tackling environmental damage and the depletion of resources. We should improve our own skills and knowledge about the management of forestry, the assessment of resources and pest and disease control: and make the know how available to the developing world. We should take positive action against multinationals and other companies who wantonly destroy and irresponsibly pollute. Non governmental agencies should target the very poorest people and plant fast growing energy crops and digs wells – to combat soil erosion and deforestation. Taken together such a strategy would ensure the sustainable use of natural resources by us and by future generations while at the same time improving the lives of the poorest people living in the poorest countries.

It is very hard for those of us privileged to live in the rich world to fully understand the awfulness of the poor world. Mine is not an appeal to simply cast away the products of the Consumer Society. When the juggernaut slows down and our economies stagnate it is the poor who inevitable come off the worst. There are lots of things we could no doubt do without, but economic flagellation and hair shirts hold little appeal for most people.

Anyway, if we simply stew in our guilt berating our good fortune our complexes would stop us even turning on an electric light for fear of burning a fossil fuel.

In looking at these new issues this entire book is an appeal for a greater sense of responsibility in how we use our gifts. This is no unattainable or dreamy ideal. Mankind must urgently recognise that our complex world is politically and economically interconnected; that each of us is dependent on the other. We should dare to devise policies and will the way for one world one day.

Seven hundred years ago Saint Francis well understood the interdependence of people one to another and the need for justice. Political leaders have been known to use the words of Saint Francis from time to time; they would be well to heed the 'letter to the Rulers of the People' he wrote in AD 1220.

"Keep a clear eye towards life's end. Do not forget your purpose and destiny as God's creature. What you are in His sight is what you are and nothing more. Do not let wordly cares and anxieties or the pressures of office blot out the divine life within you or the voice of God's Spirit guiding in your task of leading humanity to wholeness. If you open yourself to God and His plan printed deeply in your heart, God will open Himself to you.

Remember that when you leave this earth, you can take with you nothing that you have received, fading symbols of honour, trappings of power, but only what you have given: a full heart enriched by honest service, love, sacrifice and courage.

Embrace the God of us all and His Word wherever it surfaces. Imitate his preference for the poor and powerless. Enter into His plan of liberating all peoples from everything that oppresses them and obstructs their development as human beings. Do not grow tired of working for peace among all people. Help remove unjust social structures and patterns of exploitation. Uphold the rights and dignity of the human person. Foster the creation of a society where human life is cherished and where all peoples of the planet can enjoy its gifts, which God created for all in a Spirit of love and justice and equality."

In his 'Canticle of Brother Sun', Francis talks of the quality of our lives:

"Be praised, my lord, for sister water
So necessary yet so humble, precious, and chaste
Be praised, my lord, for our sister, Mother Earth
Who nourishes and watches us
While bringing forth abundant fruits with coloured
flowers and herbs."

Perhaps one day an incoming Prime Minister will recite
this prayer of St. Francis from the steps of Downing Street;
and then act to make its sentiments a reality.